Travel phrasebooks collection
«Everything Will Be Okay!»

T&P Books Publishing

PHRASEBOOK

— POLISH —

By Andrey Taranov

THE MOST IMPORTANT PHRASES

This phrasebook contains
the most important
phrases and questions
for basic communication
Everything you need
to survive overseas

T&P BOOKS

Phrasebook + 3000-word dictionary

English-Polish phrasebook & topical vocabulary

By Andrey Taranov

The collection of "Everything Will Be Okay" travel phrasebooks published by T&P Books is designed for people traveling abroad for tourism and business. The phrasebooks contain what matters most - the essentials for basic communication. This is an indispensable set of phrases to "survive" while abroad.

This book also includes a small topical vocabulary that contains roughly 3,000 of the most frequently used words. Another section of the phrasebook provides a gastronomical dictionary that may help you order food at a restaurant or buy groceries at the store.

T&P Books Publishing
www.tpbooks.com

ISBN: 978-1-78492-454-6

This book is also available in E-book formats.
Please visit www.tpbooks.com or the major online bookstores.

FOREWORD

The collection of "Everything Will Be Okay" travel phrasebooks published by T&P Books is designed for people traveling abroad for tourism and business. The phrasebooks contain what matters most - the essentials for basic communication. This is an indispensable set of phrases to "survive" while abroad.

This phrasebook will help you in most cases where you need to ask something, get directions, find out how much something costs, etc. It can also resolve difficult communication situations where gestures just won't help.

This book contains a lot of phrases that have been grouped according to the most relevant topics. The edition also includes a small vocabulary that contains roughly 3,000 of the most frequently used words. Another section of the phrasebook provides a gastronomical dictionary that may help you order food at a restaurant or buy groceries at the store.

Take "Everything Will Be Okay" phrasebook with you on the road and you'll have an irreplaceable traveling companion who will help you find your way out of any situation and teach you to not fear speaking with foreigners.

TABLE OF CONTENTS

Pronunciation   5
List of abbreviations   7
English-Polish   9
Topical vocabulary   73
Gastronomic glossary   191

T&P Books Publishing

PRONUNCIATION

Letter	Polish example	T&P phonetic alphabet	English example

Vowels

Letter	Polish example	T&P phonetic alphabet	English example
A a	fala	[a]	shorter than in ask
Ą ą	są	[ɔ̃]	strong
E e	tekst	[ɛ]	man, bad
Ę ę	pięć	[ɛ]	fang
I i	niski	[i]	shorter than in feet
O o	strona	[ɔ]	bottle, doctor
Ó ó	ołów	[u]	book
U u	ulica	[u]	book
Y y	stalowy	[ɪ]	big, America

Consonants

Letter	Polish example	T&P phonetic alphabet	English example
B b	brew	[b]	baby, book
C c	palec	[ts]	cats, tsetse fly
Ć ć	haftować	[ʧ]	church, French
D d	modny	[d]	day, doctor
F f	perfumy	[f]	face, food
G g	zegarek	[g]	game, gold
H h	handel	[h]	huge, hat
J j	jajko	[j]	yes, New York
K k	krab	[k]	clock, kiss
L l	mleko	[l]	lace, people
Ł ł	głodny	[w]	vase, winter
M m	guma	[m]	magic, milk
N n	Indie	[n]	name, normal
Ń ń	jesień	[n]	canyon, new
P p	poczta	[p]	pencil, private
R r	portret	[r]	rice, radio
S s	studnia	[s]	city, boss
Ś ś	świat	[ɕ]	sheep, shop

Letter	Polish example	T&P phonetic alphabet	English example
T t	taniec	[t]	tune, student
W w	wieczór	[v]	very, river
Z z	zachód	[z]	zebra, please
Ź ź	żaba	[z]	gigolo
Ż ż	żagiel	[ʒ]	forge, pleasure

Combinations of letters

ch	ich, zachód	[h]	huge, humor
ci	kwiecień	[ʧ]	cheese
cz	czasami	[ʧ]	church, French
dz	dzbanek	[ʣ]	beads, kids
dzi	dziecko	[ʥ]	jeans, gene
dź	dźwig	[ʥ]	jeans, gene
dż	dżinsy	[j]	yes, New York
ni	niedziela	[ɲ]	canyon, new
rz	orzech	[ʒ]	forge, pleasure
si	osiem	[ɕ]	sheep, shop
sz	paszport	[ʃ]	machine, shark
zi	zima	[z]	gigolo

Comments

˙ Letters Qq, Vv, Xx used in foreign loanwords only

LIST OF ABBREVIATIONS

English abbreviations

ab.	-	about
adj	-	adjective
adv	-	adverb
anim.	-	animate
as adj	-	attributive noun used as adjective
e.g.	-	for example
etc.	-	et cetera
fam.	-	familiar
fem.	-	feminine
form.	-	formal
inanim.	-	inanimate
masc.	-	masculine
math	-	mathematics
mil.	-	military
n	-	noun
pl	-	plural
pron.	-	pronoun
sb	-	somebody
sing.	-	singular
sth	-	something
v aux	-	auxiliary verb
vi	-	intransitive verb
vi, vt	-	intransitive, transitive verb
vt	-	transitive verb

Polish abbreviations

ż	-	feminine noun
ż, l.mn.	-	feminine plural
l.mn.	-	plural
m	-	masculine noun
m, ż	-	masculine, feminine
m, l.mn.	-	masculine plural
n	-	neuter

POLISH PHRASEBOOK

This section contains
important phrases that may
come in handy in various
real-life situations.
The phrasebook will help
you ask for directions, clarify
a price, buy tickets, and
order food at a restaurant

T&P Books Publishing

PHRASEBOOK
CONTENTS

The bare minimum	12
Questions	15
Needs	16
Asking for directions	18
Signs	20
Transportation. General phrases	22
Buying tickets	24
Bus	26
Train	28
On the train. Dialogue (No ticket)	29
Taxi	30
Hotel	32
Restaurant	35
Shopping	37
In town	39
Money	41

Time   43
Greetings. Introductions   45
Farewells   47
Foreign language   49
Apologies   50
Agreement   51
Refusal. Expressing doubt   52
Expressing gratitude   54
Congratulations. Best wishes   56
Socializing   57
Sharing impressions. Emotions   60
Problems. Accidents   62
Health problems   65
At the pharmacy   68
The bare minimum   70

T&P Books Publishing

The bare minimum

Excuse me, ...	**Przepraszam, ...** [pʃɛ'praʃam, ...]
Hello.	**Witam.** ['vʲitam]
Thank you.	**Dziękuję.** [dʑiɛŋ'kujɛ]
Good bye.	**Do widzenia.** [dɔ vʲi'dzɛɲa]
Yes.	**Tak.** [tak]
No.	**Nie.** [ɲɛ]
I don't know.	**Nie wiem.** [ɲɛ 'vʲɛm]
Where? | Where to? | When?	**Gdzie? | Dokąd? | Kiedy?** [gdʑɛ? | 'dɔkɔnt? | 'kʲɛdɨ?]

I need ...	**Potrzebuję ...** [pɔtʃɛ'bujɛ ...]
I want ...	**Chcę ...** ['xtsɛ ...]
Do you have ...?	**Czy jest ...?** [tʃɨ 'jɛst ...?]
Is there a ... here?	**Czy jest tutaj ...?** [tʃɨ 'jɛst 'tutaj ...?]
May I ...?	**Czy mogę ...?** [tʃɨ 'mɔgɛ ...?]
..., please (polite request)	**..., poproszę** [..., pɔ'prɔʃɛ]

I'm looking for ...	**Szukam ...** ['ʃukam ...]
restroom	**toalety** [tɔa'lɛtɨ]
ATM	**bankomatu** [bankɔ'matu]
pharmacy (drugstore)	**apteki** [a'ptɛkʲi]
hospital	**szpitala** [ʃpʲi'tala]
police station	**komendy policji** [kɔ'mɛndɨ pɔ'ʎitsji]
subway	**metra** ['mɛtra]

taxi	**taksówki** [ta'ksufkʲi]
train station	**dworca kolejowego** ['dvɔrtsa kɔlɛjɔ'vɛgɔ]

My name is ...	**Mam na imię ...** [mam na 'imʲiɛ ...]
What's your name?	**Jak pan /pani/ ma na imię?** ['jak pan /'paɲi/ ma na 'imʲiɛ?]
Could you please help me?	**Czy może pan /pani/ mi pomóc?** [tʃi 'mɔʒɛ pan /'paɲi/ mʲi 'pɔmuts?]
I've got a problem.	**Mam problem.** [mam 'prɔblɛm]
I don't feel well.	**Źle się czuję.** [ʑlɛ ɕiɛ 'tʃujɛ]
Call an ambulance!	**Proszę wezwać karetkę!** ['prɔʃɛ 'vɛzvatɕ ka'rɛtkɛ!]
May I make a call?	**Czy mogę zadzwonić?** [tʃi 'mɔgɛ za'dzvɔɲitɕ?]

I'm sorry.	**Przepraszam.** [pʃɛ'praʃam]
You're welcome.	**Proszę bardzo.** ['prɔʃɛ 'bardzɔ]

I, me	**ja** ['ja]
you (inform.)	**ty** ['ti]
he	**on** [ɔn]
she	**ona** ['ɔna]
they (masc.)	**oni** ['ɔɲi]
they (fem.)	**one** ['ɔnɛ]
we	**my** ['mi]
you (pl)	**wy** ['vi]
you (sg, form.)	**pan /pani/** [pan /'paɲi/]

ENTRANCE	**WEJŚCIE** ['vɛjɕtɕɛ]
EXIT	**WYJŚCIE** ['vijɕtɕɛ]
OUT OF ORDER	**NIECZYNNY** [ɲɛ'tʃinni]
CLOSED	**ZAMKNIĘTE** [za'mkɲiɛntɛ]

OPEN	**OTWARTE** [ɔ'tfartɛ]
FOR WOMEN	**PANIE** ['paɲɛ]
FOR MEN	**PANOWIE** [pa'nɔvʲɛ]

Questions

Where?	**Gdzie?** [gdʑɛ?]
Where to?	**Dokąd?** ['dɔkɔnt?]
Where from?	**Skąd?** ['skɔnt?]
Why?	**Dlaczego?** [dla'ʧɛgɔ?]
For what reason?	**Dlaczego?** [dla'ʧɛgɔ?]
When?	**Kiedy?** ['kʲɛdʲ?]

How long?	**Jak długo?** ['jag 'dwugɔ?]
At what time?	**O której godzinie?** [ɔ 'kturɛj gɔ'dʑiɲɛ?]
How much?	**Ile kosztuje?** ['ilɛ kɔ'ʃtujɛ?]
Do you have ...?	**Czy jest ...?** [ʧɨ 'jɛst ...?]
Where is ...?	**Gdzie jest ...?** [gdʑɛ 'jɛst ...?]

What time is it?	**Która godzina?** ['ktura gɔ'dʑina?]
May I make a call?	**Czy mogę zadzwonić?** [ʧɨ 'mɔgɛ za'dzvɔɲiʨ?]
Who's there?	**Kto tam?** [ktɔ tam?]
Can I smoke here?	**Czy mogę tu zapalić?** [ʧɨ 'mɔgɛ tu za'paʎiʨ?]
May I ...?	**Czy mogę ...?** [ʧɨ 'mɔgɛ ...?]

Needs

I'd like ...	**Chciałbym /Chciałabym/ ...** ['xtɕawbim /xtɕa'wabim/ ...]
I don't want ...	**Nie chcę ...** [ɲɛ 'xtsɛ ...]
I'm thirsty.	**Jestem spragniony /spragniona/.** ['jɛstɛm spra'gɲoni /spra'gɲona/]
I want to sleep.	**Chce mi się spać.** ['xtsɛ mʲi ɕɛ 'spatɕ]

I want ...	**Chcę ...** ['xtsɛ ...]
to wash up	**umyć się** ['umitɕ ɕɛ]
to brush my teeth	**umyć zęby** ['umitɕ 'zɛmbi]
to rest a while	**trochę odpocząć** ['trɔxɛ ɔ'tpɔt͡ʃɔntɕ]
to change my clothes	**zmienić ubranie** ['zmʲɛɲitɕ u'braɲɛ]

to go back to the hotel	**wrócić do hotelu** ['vrutɕitɕ dɔ xɔ'tɛlu]
to buy ...	**kupić ...** ['kupʲitɕ ...]
to go to ...	**iść ...** ['iɕtɕ ...]
to visit ...	**odwiedzić ...** [ɔ'dvʲɛdʑitɕ ...]
to meet with ...	**spotkać się z ...** ['spɔtkatɕ ɕɛ s ...]
to make a call	**zadzwonić** [za'dzvɔɲitɕ]

I'm tired.	**Jestem zmęczony /zmęczona/.** ['jɛstɛm zmɛ'nt͡ʃɔni /zmɛ'nt͡ʃɔna/]
We are tired.	**Jesteśmy zmęczeni /zmęczone/.** [jɛs'tɛɕmi zmɛ'nt͡ʃɛɲi /zmɛ'nt͡ʃɔnɛ/]
I'm cold.	**Jest mi zimno.** ['jɛst mʲi 'ʑimnɔ]
I'm hot.	**Jest mi gorąco.** ['jɛst mʲi gɔ'rɔntsɔ]
I'm OK.	**W porządku.** [f pɔ'ʒɔntku]

I need to make a call.

Muszę zadzwonić.
['muʃɛ za'dzvɔɲitɕ]

I need to go to the restroom.

Muszę iść do toalety.
['muʃɛ 'iɕtɕ dɔ tɔa'lɛti]

I have to go.

Muszę iść.
['muʃɛ 'iɕtɕ]

I have to go now.

Muszę już iść.
['muʃɛ 'juʒ 'iɕtɕ]

Asking for directions

Excuse me, ...	**Przepraszam, ...** [pʃɛ'praʃam, ...]
Where is ...?	**Gdzie jest ...?** [gdʑɛ 'jɛst ...?]
Which way is ...?	**W którą stronę jest ...?** [f 'kturɔ̃ 'strɔnɛ 'jɛst ...?]
Could you help me, please?	**Czy może pan /pani/ mi pomóc?** [ʧi 'mɔʒɛ pan /'paɲi/ mʲi 'pɔmuts?]

I'm looking for ...	**Szukam ...** ['ʃukam ...]
I'm looking for the exit.	**Szukam wyjścia.** ['ʃukam 'vɨjɕtɕa]
I'm going to ...	**Jadę do ...** ['jadɛ dɔ ...]
Am I going the right way to ...?	**Czy idę w dobrym kierunku do ...?** [ʧi 'idɛ v 'dɔbrim kʲɛ'runku 'dɔ ...?]

Is it far?	**Czy to daleko?** [ʧi tɔ da'lɛkɔ?]
Can I get there on foot?	**Czy mogę tam dojść pieszo?** [ʧi 'mɔgɛ tam 'dɔjɕtɕ 'pʲɛʃɔ?]
Can you show me on the map?	**Czy może mi pan /pani/ pokazać na mapie?** [ʧi 'mɔʒɛ mʲi pan /'paɲi/ pɔ'kazatɕ na 'mapʲɛ?]
Show me where we are right now.	**Proszę mi pokazać gdzie teraz jesteśmy.** ['prɔʃɛ mʲi pɔ'kazatɕ gdʑɛ 'tɛras jɛ'stɛɕmi]

Here	**Tutaj** ['tutaj]
There	**Tam** [tam]
This way	**Tędy** ['tɛndi]

Turn right.	**Należy skręcić w prawo.** [na'lɛʒɨ 'skrɛntɕitɕ f 'pravɔ]
Turn left.	**Należy skręcić w lewo.** [na'lɛʒɨ 'skrɛntɕitɕ v 'lɛvɔ]
first (second, third) turn	**pierwszy (drugi, trzeci) skręt** ['pʲɛrfʃi ('drugi, 'ʧɛtɕi) 'skrɛnt]

to the right	**w prawo** [f 'pravɔ]
to the left	**w lewo** [v 'lɛvɔ]
Go straight.	**Proszę iść prosto.** ['prɔʃɛ 'içtɕ 'prɔstɔ]

Signs

WELCOME!	**WITAMY!** [vʲi'tamɨ!]
ENTRANCE	**WEJŚCIE** ['vɛjɕtɕɛ]
EXIT	**WYJŚCIE** ['vɨjɕtɕɛ]

PUSH	**PCHAĆ** ['pxatɕ]
PULL	**CIĄGNĄĆ** ['tɕiɔ̃ŋgnɔntɕ]
OPEN	**OTWARTE** [ɔ'tfartɛ]
CLOSED	**ZAMKNIĘTE** [za'mkɲiɛntɛ]

FOR WOMEN	**PANIE** ['paɲɛ]
FOR MEN	**PANOWIE** [pa'nɔvʲɛ]
MEN, GENTS	**TOALETA MĘSKA** [tɔa'lɛta 'mɛ̃ska]
WOMEN, LADIES	**TOALETA DAMSKA** [tɔa'lɛta 'damska]

DISCOUNTS	**ZNIŻKI** ['zɲiʃkʲi]
SALE	**WYPRZEDAŻ** [vʲi'pʃɛdaʒ]
FREE	**ZA DARMO** [za 'darmɔ]
NEW!	**NOWOŚĆ!** ['nɔvɔɕtɕ!]
ATTENTION!	**UWAGA!** [u'vaga!]

NO VACANCIES	**BRAK WOLNYCH MIEJSC** ['brag 'vɔlnɨx 'mʲɛjsts]
RESERVED	**REZERWACJA** [rɛzɛ'rvatsja]
ADMINISTRATION	**ADMINISTRACJA** [admʲini'stratsja]
STAFF ONLY	**TYLKO DLA PERSONELU** ['tɨlkɔ 'dla pɛrsɔ'nɛlu]

BEWARE OF THE DOG!	**UWAGA PIES** [u'vaga 'pʲɛs]
NO SMOKING!	**ZAKAZ PALENIA** ['zakas pa'lɛɲa]
DO NOT TOUCH!	**NIE DOTYKAĆ!** [ɲɛ dɔ'tɨkatɕ!]
DANGEROUS	**NIEBEZPIECZNE** [ɲɛbɛ'spʲɛtʃnɛ]
DANGER	**NIEBEZPIECZEŃSTWO** [ɲɛbɛspʲɛ'tʃɛɲstfɔ]
HIGH VOLTAGE	**WYSOKIE NAPIĘCIE** [vɨ'sɔkʲɛ na'pʲiɛntɕɛ]
NO SWIMMING!	**ZAKAZ PŁYWANIA** ['zakas pwɨ'vaɲa]

OUT OF ORDER	**NIECZYNNY** [ɲɛ'tʃɨnnɨ]
FLAMMABLE	**ŁATWOPALNY** [watfɔ'palnɨ]
FORBIDDEN	**ZABRONIONE** [zabrɔ'ɲɔnɛ]
NO TRESPASSING!	**WSTĘP WZBRONIONY!** ['fstɛmb vzbrɔ'ɲɔnɨ!]
WET PAINT	**ŚWIEŻO MALOWANE** ['ɕvʲɛʒɔ malɔ'vanɛ]

CLOSED FOR RENOVATIONS	**ZAMKNIĘTE NA CZAS REMONTU** [za'mkɲiɛntɛ na 'tʃas rɛ'mɔntu]
WORKS AHEAD	**ROBOTY DROGOWE** [rɔ'bɔtɨ drɔ'gɔvɛ]
DETOUR	**OBJAZD** ['ɔbjazt]

21

Transportation. General phrases

plane	**samolot** [sa'mɔlɔt]
train	**pociąg** ['pɔtɕiɔŋk]
bus	**autobus** [aw'tɔbus]
ferry	**prom** ['prɔm]
taxi	**taksówka** [ta'ksufka]
car	**samochód** [sa'mɔxut]

schedule	**rozkład jazdy	rozkład lotów** ['rɔskwat 'jazdi	'rɔskwat 'lɔtuf]
Where can I see the schedule?	**Gdzie znajdę rozkład jazdy?** [gdʑɛ 'znajdɛ 'rɔskwat 'jazdi?]
workdays (weekdays)	**dni robocze** ['dɲi rɔ'bɔtʃɛ]
weekends	**weekend** [vɛ'ɛkɛnt]
holidays	**święta** ['ɕviɛnta]

DEPARTURE	**WYJAZDY	PRZYLOTY** [vi'jazdi	pʃi'lɔti]
ARRIVAL	**PRZYJAZDY	ODLOTY** [pʃi'jazdi	ɔ'dlɔti]
DELAYED	**OPÓŹNIONY** [ɔpu'ʑɲɔni]
CANCELED	**ODWOŁANY** [ɔdvɔ'wani]

next (train, etc.)	**następny** [na'stɛmpni]
first	**pierwszy** ['piɛrfʃi]
last	**ostatni** [ɔ'statɲi]

When is the next ...?	**O której jest następny ...?** [ɔ 'kturɛj 'jɛst na'stɛmpni ...?]
When is the first ...?	**O której jest pierwszy ...?** [ɔ 'kturɛj 'jɛst 'piɛrfʃi ...?]

When is the last ...?

O której jest ostatni ...?
[ɔ 'kturɛj 'jɛst ɔ'statɲi ...?]

transfer (change of trains, etc.)

przesiadka
[pʃɛ'ɕatka]

to make a transfer

przesiąść się
['pʃɛɕiɔ̃ɕtɕ ɕiɛ]

Do I need to make a transfer?

Czy muszę się przesiadać?
[tʃɨ 'muʃɛ ɕiɛ pʃɛ'ɕadatɕ?]

Buying tickets

Where can I buy tickets?	**Gdzie mogę kupić bilety?** [gdʑɛ 'mɔgɛ 'kupʲitɕ bʲi'lɛti?]
ticket	**bilet** ['bʲilɛt]
to buy a ticket	**kupić bilet** ['kupʲitɕ 'bʲilɛt]
ticket price	**cena biletu** ['tsɛna bʲi'lɛtu]

Where to?	**Dokąd?** ['dɔkɔnt?]
To what station?	**Do której stacji?** [dɔ 'kturɛj 'statsji?]
I need ...	**Poproszę ...** [pɔ'prɔʃɛ ...]
one ticket	**jeden bilet** ['jɛdɛn 'bʲilɛt]
two tickets	**dwa bilety** ['dva bʲi'lɛti]
three tickets	**trzy bilety** [tʃi bʲi'lɛti]

one-way	**w jedną stronę** [f 'jɛdnɔ̃ 'strɔnɛ]
round-trip	**w obie strony** [v 'ɔbʲɛ 'strɔni]
first class	**pierwsza klasa** ['pʲɛrfʃa 'klasa]
second class	**druga klasa** ['druga 'klasa]

today	**dzisiaj** ['dʑiɕaj]
tomorrow	**jutro** ['jutrɔ]
the day after tomorrow	**pojutrze** [pɔ'jutʃɛ]
in the morning	**rano** ['ranɔ]
in the afternoon	**po południu** [pɔ pɔ'wudɲu]
in the evening	**wieczorem** [vʲɛ'tʃɔrɛm]

aisle seat

miejsce przy przejściu
['mʲɛjstsɛ pʃɨ 'pʃɛjɕtɕu]

window seat

miejsce przy oknie
['mʲɛjstsɛ pʃɨ 'ɔkɲɛ]

How much?

Ile kosztuje?
['ilɛ kɔ'ʃtujɛ?]

Can I pay by credit card?

Czy mogę zapłacić kartą?
[ʧɨ 'mɔgɛ za'pwatɕitɕ 'kartɔ̃?]

Bus

bus
autobus
[aw'tɔbus]

intercity bus
autobus międzymiastowy
[aw'tɔbus mʲiɛndzimʲa'stɔvɨ]

bus stop
przystanek autobusowy
[pʃɨ'stanɛk awtɔbu'sɔvɨ]

Where's the nearest bus stop?
Gdzie jest najbliższy przystanek autobusowy?
[gdʑɛ 'jɛst najb'ʎiʃʃɨ pʃɨ'stanɛk awtɔbu'sɔvɨ?]

number (bus ~, etc.)
numer
['numɛr]

Which bus do I take to get to ...?
Którym autobusem dojadę do ...?
['kturɨm awtɔ'busɛm dɔ'jadɛ dɔ ...?]

Does this bus go to ...?
Czy ten autobus jedzie do ...?
[tʃɨ 'tɛn aw'tɔbus 'jɛdʑɛ dɔ ...?]

How frequent are the buses?
Jak często jeżdżą autobusy?
['jak 'tʃɛ̃stɔ 'jɛʒdʒɔ̃ awtɔ'busɨ?]

every 15 minutes
co piętnaście minut
['tsɔ pʲiɛ'ntnaɕtɕɛ 'mʲinut]

every half hour
co pół godziny
['tsɔ 'puw gɔ'dʑinɨ]

every hour
co godzinę
['tsɔ gɔ'dʑinɛ]

several times a day
kilka razy dziennie
['kʲilka 'razɨ 'dʑɛnɲɛ]

... times a day
... razy dziennie
[... 'razɨ 'dʑɛnɲɛ]

schedule
rozkład jazdy
['rɔskwat 'jazdɨ]

Where can I see the schedule?
Gdzie znajdę rozkład jazdy?
[gdʑɛ 'znajdɛ 'rɔskwat 'jazdɨ?]

When is the next bus?
O której jest następny autobus?
[ɔ 'kturɛj 'jɛst na'stɛmpnɨ aw'tɔbus?]

When is the first bus?
O której jest pierwszy autobus?
[ɔ 'kturɛj 'jɛst 'pʲɛrfʃɨ aw'tɔbus?]

When is the last bus?
O której jest ostatni autobus?
[ɔ 'kturɛj 'jɛst ɔ'statɲi aw'tɔbus?]

stop
przystanek
[pʃɨ'stanɛk]

next stop

następny przystanek
[na'stɛmpnɨ pʃɨ'stanɛk]

last stop (terminus)

ostatni przystanek
[ɔ'statɲi pʃɨ'stanɛk]

Stop here, please.

Proszę się tu zatrzymać.
['prɔʃɛ ɕɛ tu za'tʃɨmatɕ]

Excuse me, this is my stop.

Przepraszam, to mój przystanek.
[pʃɛ'praʃam, tɔ muj pʃɨ'stanɛk]

Train

train	**pociąg** ['pɔtɕiɔŋk]
suburban train	**kolejka** [kɔ'lɛjka]
long-distance train	**pociąg dalekobieżny** ['pɔtɕiɔŋk dalɛkɔ'bʲɛʒnʲi]
train station	**dworzec kolejowy** ['dvɔʒɛts kɔlɛ'jɔvi]
Excuse me, where is the exit to the platform?	**Przepraszam, gdzie jest wyjście z peronu?** [pʃɛ'praʃam, gdʑɛ 'jɛsd 'vijɕtɕɛ s pɛ'rɔnu?]

Does this train go to ...?	**Czy ten pociąg jedzie do ...?** [tʃi 'tɛn 'pɔtɕiɔŋk 'jɛdʑɛ dɔ ...?]
next train	**następny pociąg** [na'stɛmpnʲi 'pɔtɕiɔŋk]
When is the next train?	**O której jest następny pociąg?** [ɔ 'kturɛj 'jɛst na'stɛmpnʲi 'pɔtɕiɔŋk?]
Where can I see the schedule?	**Gdzie znajdę rozkład jazdy?** [gdʑɛ 'znajdɛ 'rɔskwat 'jazdɨ?]
From which platform?	**Z którego peronu?** [s ktu'rɛgɔ pɛ'rɔnu?]
When does the train arrive in ...?	**O której ten pociąg dojeżdża do ...?** [ɔ 'kturɛj 'tɛn 'pɔtɕiɔŋk dɔ'jɛʒdʒa dɔ ...?]

Please help me.	**Proszę mi pomóc.** ['prɔʃɛ mʲi 'pɔmuts]
I'm looking for my seat.	**Szukam swojego miejsca.** ['ʃukam sfɔ'jɛgɔ 'mʲɛjstsa]
We're looking for our seats.	**Szukamy naszych miejsc.** [ʃu'kamɨ 'naʃix 'mʲɛjsts]
My seat is taken.	**Moje miejsce jest zajęte.** ['mɔjɛ 'mʲɛjstsɛ 'jɛsd za'jɛntɛ]
Our seats are taken.	**Nasze miejsca są zajęte.** ['naʃɛ 'mʲɛjstsa 'sɔ̃ za'jɛntɛ]

I'm sorry but this is my seat.	**Przykro mi ale to moje miejsce.** ['pʃikrɔ mʲi 'alɛ tɔ 'mɔjɛ 'mʲɛjstsɛ]
Is this seat taken?	**Czy to miejsce jest zajęte?** [tʃi tɔ 'mʲɛjstsɛ 'jɛsd za'jɛntɛ?]
May I sit here?	**Czy mogę tu usiąść?** [tʃi 'mɔgɛ tu 'uɕiɔ̃ɕtɕ?]

On the train. Dialogue (No ticket)

Ticket, please.

I don't have a ticket.

I lost my ticket.

I forgot my ticket at home.

Bilety, proszę.
[bʲi'lɛtʲi, 'prɔʃɛ]

Nie mam biletu.
[ɲɛ 'mam bʲi'lɛtu]

Zgubiłem bilet.
[zgu'bʲiwɛm 'bʲilɛt]

Zostawiłem bilet w domu.
[zɔsta'vʲiwɛm 'bʲilɛt v 'dɔmu]

You can buy a ticket from me.

You will also have to pay a fine.

Może pan /pani/ kupić bilet ode mnie.
['mɔʒɛ pan /'paɲi/ 'kupʲitɕ 'bʲilɛt 'ɔdɛ 'mɲɛ]

Będzie pan musiał /pani musiała/ również zapłacić mandat.
['bɛndʑɛ pan 'muɕaw /'paɲi mu'ɕawa/ 'ruvɲɛʒ za'pwatɕitɕ 'mandat]

Okay.

Where are you going?

I'm going to ...

Dobrze.
['dɔbʒɛ]

Dokąd pan /pani/ jedzie?
['dɔkɔnt pan /'paɲi/ 'jɛdʑɛ?]

Jadę do ...
['jadɛ dɔ ...]

How much? I don't understand.

Write it down, please.

Okay. Can I pay with a credit card?

Yes, you can.

Ile kosztuje? Nie rozumiem.
['ilɛ kɔ'ʃtujɛ? ɲɛ rɔ'zumʲɛm]

Czy może pan /pani/ to napisać?
[tʃi 'mɔʒɛ pan /'paɲi/ tɔ na'pʲisatɕ?]

Dobrze. Czy mogę zapłacić kartą?
['dɔbʒɛ. tʃi 'mɔgɛ za'pwatɕitɕ 'kartɔ̃?]

Tak, można.
[tak, 'mɔʒna]

Here's your receipt.

Sorry about the fine.

That's okay. It was my fault.

Enjoy your trip.

Oto pański /pani/ rachunek.
['ɔtɔ 'paɲskʲi /'paɲi/ ra'xunɛk]

Przykro mi z powodu mandatu.
['pʃikrɔ mʲi s pɔ'vɔdu ma'ndatu]

W porządku. To moja wina.
[f pɔ'ʒɔntku. tɔ 'mɔja 'vʲina]

Miłej podróży.
['mʲiwɛj pɔ'druʒi]

Taxi

taxi	**taksówka** [ta'ksufka]
taxi driver	**taksówkarz** [ta'ksufkaʃ]
to catch a taxi	**złapać taksówkę** ['zwapatɕ ta'ksufkɛ]
taxi stand	**postój taksówek** ['pɔstuj ta'ksuvɛk]
Where can I get a taxi?	**Gdzie mogę wziąć taksówkę?** [gdʑɛ 'mɔgɛ vʑi'ɔ̃tɕ ta'ksufkɛ?]

to call a taxi	**zadzwonić po taksówkę** [za'dzvɔɲitɕ pɔ ta'ksufkɛ]
I need a taxi.	**Potrzebuję taksówkę.** [pɔtʃɛ'bujɛ ta'ksufkɛ]
Right now.	**Jak najszybciej.** ['jak na'jʃiptɕɛj]
What is your address (location)?	**Skąd pana /panią/ odebrać?** ['skɔnt 'pana /'paɲɔ̃/ ɔ'dɛbratɕ?]
My address is ...	**Mój adres to ...** [muj 'adrɛs tɔ ...]
Your destination?	**Dokąd pan /pani/ chce jechać?** ['dɔkɔnt pa'n /paɲi/ 'xtsɛ 'jɛxatɕ?]

Excuse me, ...	**Przepraszam, ...** [pʃɛ'praʃam, ...]
Are you available?	**Czy jest pan wolny?** [tʃi 'jɛst pan 'vɔlni?]
How much is it to get to ...?	**Ile kosztuje przejazd do ...?** ['ilɛ kɔ'ʃtujɛ 'pʃɛjazd dɔ ...?]
Do you know where it is?	**Wie pan /pani/ gdzie to jest?** ['vʲɛ pan /'paɲi/ gdʑɛ tɔ 'jɛst?]
Airport, please.	**Na lotnisko, proszę.** [na lɔt'ɲiskɔ, 'prɔʃɛ]
Stop here, please.	**Proszę się tu zatrzymać.** ['prɔʃɛ ɕɛ tu za'tʃimatɕ]
It's not here.	**To nie tutaj.** [tɔ ɲɛ 'tutaj]
This is the wrong address.	**To zły adres.** [tɔ 'zwi 'adrɛs]
Turn left.	**Proszę skręcić w lewo.** ['prɔʃɛ 'skrɛntɕitɕ v 'lɛvɔ]
Turn right.	**Proszę skręcić w prawo.** ['prɔʃɛ 'skrɛntɕitɕ f 'pravɔ]

How much do I owe you?	**Ile płacę?** ['ilɛ 'pwatsɛ?]
I'd like a receipt, please.	**Poproszę rachunek.** [pɔ'prɔʃɛ ra'xunɛk]
Keep the change.	**Proszę zachować resztę.** ['prɔʃɛ za'xɔvatɕ 'rɛʃtɛ]

Would you please wait for me?	**Czy może pan /pani/ na mnie poczekać?** [ʧi 'mɔʒɛ pan /'paɲi/ na mɲɛ pɔ'ʧɛkatɕ?]
five minutes	**pięć minut** ['pʲiɛntɕ 'mʲinut]
ten minutes	**dziesięć minut** ['dʑɛɕiɛntɕ 'mʲinut]
fifteen minutes	**piętnaście minut** [pʲiɛ'ntnaɕtɕɛ 'mʲinut]
twenty minutes	**dwadzieścia minut** [dva'dʑɛɕtɕa 'mʲinut]
half an hour	**pół godziny** ['puw gɔ'dʑinɨ]

Hotel

Hello.	**Witam.** ['vʲitam]
My name is ...	**Mam na imię ...** [mam na 'imʲiɛ ...]
I have a reservation.	**Mam rezerwację.** [mam rɛzɛ'rvatsjɛ]

I need ...	**Potrzebuję ...** [pɔtʃɛ'bujɛ ...]
a single room	**pojedynczy pokój** [pɔjɛ'dɨntʃɨ 'pɔkuj]
a double room	**podwójny pokój** [pɔ'dvujnɨ 'pɔkuj]
How much is that?	**Ile to kosztuje?** ['ilɛ tɔ kɔ'ʃtujɛ?]
That's a bit expensive.	**To trochę za drogo.** [tɔ 'trɔxɛ za 'drɔgɔ]

Do you have any other options?	**Czy są inne pokoje?** [tʃɨ 'sɔ̃ 'innɛ pɔ'kɔjɛ?]
I'll take it.	**Wezmę ten.** ['vɛzmɛ 'tɛn]
I'll pay in cash.	**Zapłacę gotówką.** [za'pwatsɛ gɔ'tufkɔ̃]

I've got a problem.	**Mam problem.** [mam 'prɔblɛm]
My ... is broken.	**... jest zepsuty /zepsuta/.** [... 'jɛsd zɛ'psutɨ /zɛ'psuta/.]
My ... is out of order.	**... jest nieczynny /nieczynna/.** [... 'jɛst ɲɛ'tʃɨnnɨ /ɲɛ'tʃɨnna/.]
TV	**Mój telewizor ...** [muj tɛlɛ'vʲizɔr ...]
air conditioning	**Moja klimatyzacja ...** ['mɔja kʎimatɨ'zatsja ...]
tap	**Mój kran ...** [muj 'kran ...]

shower	**Mój prysznic ...** [muj 'prɨʃɲits ...]
sink	**Mój zlew ...** [muj 'zlɛf ...]
safe	**Mój sejf ...** [muj 'sɛjf ...]

door lock	**Mój zamek ...** [muj 'zamɛk ...]
electrical outlet	**Moje gniazdko elektryczne ...** ['mɔjɛ 'gɲaztkɔ ɛlɛ'ktritʃnɛ ...]
hairdryer	**Moja suszarka ...** ['mɔja su'ʃarka ...]

I don't have ...	**Nie mam ...** [ɲɛ 'mam ...]
water	**wody** ['vɔdɨ]
light	**światła** ['ɕvʲatwa]
electricity	**prądu** ['prɔndu]

Can you give me ...?	**Czy może mi pan /pani/ przynieść ...?** [tʃɨ 'mɔʒɛ mʲi pan /'paɲi/ 'pʃɨɲɛɕtɕ ...?]
a towel	**ręcznik** ['rɛntʃnik]
a blanket	**koc** ['kɔts]
slippers	**kapcie** ['kaptɕɛ]
a robe	**szlafrok** ['ʃlafrɔk]
shampoo	**szampon** ['ʃampɔn]
soap	**mydło** ['mɨdwɔ]

I'd like to change rooms.	**Chciałbym /chciałabym/ zmienić pokój.** ['xtɕawbɨm /xtɕa'wabɨm/ 'zmʲɛɲitɕ 'pokuj]
I can't find my key.	**Nie mogę znaleźć mojego klucza.** [ɲɛ 'mɔgɛ 'znalɛɕtɕ mɔ'jɛgɔ 'klutʃa]
Could you open my room, please?	**Czy może pani otworzyć mój pokój?** [tʃɨ 'mɔʒɛ 'paɲi ɔ'tfɔʒɨtɕ muj 'pokuj?]
Who's there?	**Kto tam?** [ktɔ tam?]
Come in!	**Proszę wejść!** ['prɔʃɛ 'vɛjɕtɕ!]
Just a minute!	**Chwileczkę!** [xvʲi'lɛtʃkɛ!]
Not right now, please.	**Nie teraz, proszę.** [ɲɛ 'tɛras, 'prɔʃɛ]

Come to my room, please.	**Proszę wejść do mojego pokoju.** ['prɔʃɛ 'vɛjɕtɕ dɔ mɔ'jɛgɔ pɔ'kɔju]
My room number is ...	**Mój numer pokoju to ...** [muj 'numɛr pɔ'kɔju tɔ ...]

I'd like to order food service.	**Chciałbym /chciałabym/ zamówić posiłek do pokoju.** ['xtɕawbɨm /xtɕa'wabɨm/ za'muvʲitɕ pɔ'ɕiwɛg dɔ pɔ'kɔju]
I'm leaving ...	**Wyjeżdżam ...** [vɨ'jɛʒdʒam ...]
We're leaving ...	**Wyjeżdżamy ...** [vɨjɛ'ʒdʒamɨ ...]
right now	**jak najszybciej** ['jak na'jʃɨptɕɛj]
this afternoon	**po południu** [pɔ pɔ'wudɲu]
tonight	**dziś wieczorem** ['dʑiɕ vʲɛ'tʃɔrɛm]
tomorrow	**jutro** ['jutrɔ]
tomorrow morning	**jutro rano** ['jutrɔ 'ranɔ]
tomorrow evening	**jutro wieczorem** ['jutrɔ vʲɛ'tʃɔrɛm]
the day after tomorrow	**pojutrze** [pɔ'jutʃɛ]
I'd like to pay.	**Chciałbym zapłacić.** ['xtɕawbɨm za'pwatɕitɕ]
Everything was wonderful.	**Wszystko było wspaniałe.** [fʃɨstkɔ 'bɨwɔ fspa'ɲawɛ]
Where can I get a taxi?	**Gdzie mogę wziąć taksówkę?** [gdʑɛ 'mɔgɛ vʑi'ɔtɕ ta'ksufkɛ?]
Would you call a taxi for me, please?	**Czy może pan /pani/ wezwać dla mnie taksówkę?** [tʃɨ 'mɔʒɛ pan /'paɲi/ 'vɛzvatɕ 'dla 'mɲɛ ta'ksufkɛ?]

Restaurant

Can I look at the menu, please? **Czy mogę prosić menu?**
[ʧi 'mɔgɛ 'prɔɕitɕ 'mɛnu?]

Table for one. **Stolik dla jednej osoby.**
['stɔʎig 'dla 'jɛdnɛj ɔ'sɔbɨ]

There are two (three, four) of us. **Jest nas dwoje (troje, czworo).**
['jɛst 'naz 'dvɔjɛ ('trɔjɛ, 'ʧvɔrɔ)]

Smoking **Dla palących.**
['dla pa'lɔntsix]

No smoking **Dla niepalących.**
['dla ɲɛpa'lɔntsix]

Excuse me! (addressing a waiter) **Przepraszam!**
[pʃɛ'praʃam!]

menu **menu**
['mɛnu]

wine list **lista win**
['ʎista 'vʲin]

The menu, please. **Poproszę menu.**
[pɔ'prɔʃɛ 'mɛnu]

Are you ready to order? **Czy są Państwo gotowi?**
[ʧi 'sɔ̃ 'paɲstfɔ gɔ'tɔvʲi?]

What will you have? **Co Państwo zamawiają?**
['tsɔ 'paɲstfɔ zama'vʲajɔ̃?]

I'll have … **Zamawiam …**
[za'mavʲam …]

I'm a vegetarian. **Jestem wegetarianinem /wegetarianką/.**
['jɛstɛm vɛgɛtaria'ɲinɛm /vɛgɛta'riankɔ̃/]

meat **mięso**
['mʲiɛ̃sɔ]

fish **ryba**
['rɨba]

vegetables **warzywa**
[va'ʒɨva]

Do you have vegetarian dishes? **Czy są dania wegetariańskie?**
[ʧi 'sɔ̃ 'daɲa vɛgɛta'riaɲskʲɛ?]

I don't eat pork. **Nie jadam wieprzowiny.**
[ɲɛ 'jadam vʲɛpʃɔ'vʲinɨ]

He /she/ doesn't eat meat. **On /Ona/ nie je mięsa.**
[ɔn /'ɔna/ ɲɛ 'jɛ 'mʲiɛ̃sa]

I am allergic to …	Jestem uczulony /uczulona/ na …
	['jɛstɛm utʃu'lɔnɨ /utʃu'lɔna/ na …]
Would you please bring me …	Czy może pan /pani/ przynieść mi …
	[tʃi 'mɔʒɛ pan /'paɲi/ 'pʃiɲɛɕtɕ mʲi …]
salt	pepper	sugar	sól	pieprz	cukier
	['suʎ	'pʲɛpʃ	'tsukʲɛr]
coffee	tea	dessert	kawa	herbata	deser
	['kava	xɛ'rbata	'dɛsɛr]
water	sparkling	plain	woda	gazowana	bez gazu
	['vɔda	gazɔ'vana	'bɛz 'gazu]
a spoon	fork	knife	łyżka	widelec	nóż
	['wiʃka	vʲi'dɛlɛts	'nuʒ]
a plate	napkin	talerz	serwetka
	['talɛʃ	sɛr'vɛtka]

Enjoy your meal!	Smacznego!
	[sma'tʃnɛgɔ!]
One more, please.	Jeszcze raz poproszę.
	['jɛʃtʃɛ 'ras pɔ'prɔʃɛ]
It was very delicious.	To było pyszne.
	[tɔ 'bɨwɔ 'pɨʃnɛ]

check	change	tip	rachunek	drobne	napiwek
	[ra'xunɛk	'drɔbnɛ	na'pʲivɛk]
Check, please.	Rachunek proszę.
(Could I have the check, please?)	[ra'xunɛk 'prɔʃɛ]
Can I pay by credit card?	Czy mogę zapłacić kartą?
	[tʃi 'mɔgɛ za'pwatɕitɕ 'kartɔ̃?]
I'm sorry, there's a mistake here.	Przykro mi, tu jest błąd.
	['pʃɨkrɔ mʲi, tu 'jɛsd 'bwɔnt]

Shopping

Can I help you?	**W czym mogę pomóc?** [f 'tʃim 'mɔgɛ 'pɔmuts?]
Do you have ...?	**Czy jest ...?** [tʃi 'jɛst ...?]
I'm looking for ...	**Szukam ...** ['ʃukam ...]
I need ...	**Potrzebuję ...** [pɔtʃɛ'bujɛ ...]

I'm just looking.	**Tylko się rozglądam.** ['tilkɔ ɕiɛ rɔ'zglɔndam]
We're just looking.	**Tylko się rozglądamy.** ['tilkɔ ɕiɛ rɔzglɔn'dami]
I'll come back later.	**Wrócę później.** ['vrutsɛ 'puʑɲɛj]
We'll come back later.	**Wrócimy później.** [vru'tɕimi 'puʑɲɛj]
discounts | sale	**zniżka | wyprzedaż** ['zɲiʃka | vi'pʃɛdaʒ]

Would you please show me ...	**Czy może mi pan /pani/ pokazać ...** [tʃi 'mɔʒɛ mʲi pan /'paɲi/ pɔ'kazatɕ ...]
Would you please give me ...	**Czy może mi pan /pani/ dać ...** [tʃi 'mɔʒɛ mʲi pan /'paɲi/ datɕ ...]
Can I try it on?	**Czy mogę przymierzyć?** [tʃi 'mɔgɛ pʃi'mʲɛʒitɕ?]
Excuse me, where's the fitting room?	**Przepraszam, gdzie jest przymierzalnia?** [pʃɛ'praʃam, gdʑɛ 'jɛst pʃimʲɛ'ʒalɲa?]
Which color would you like?	**Jaki kolor pan /pani/ sobie życzy?** ['jakʲi 'kɔlɔr pan /'paɲi/ 'sɔbʲɛ 'ʒitʃi?]
size | length	**rozmiar | długość** ['rɔzmʲar | 'dwugɔɕtɕ]
How does it fit?	**Jak to leży?** ['jak tɔ 'lɛʒi?]

How much is it?	**Ile to kosztuje?** ['ilɛ tɔ kɔ'ʃtujɛ?]
That's too expensive.	**To za drogo.** [tɔ za 'drɔgɔ]
I'll take it.	**Wezmę to.** ['vɛzmɛ 'tɔ]

Excuse me, where do I pay?

Przepraszam, gdzie mogę zapłacić?
[pʃɛ'praʃam, gdʑɛ 'mɔgɛ za'pwatɕitɕ?]

Will you pay in cash or credit card?

Czy płaci pan /pani/ gotówką czy kartą?
[ʧi 'pwatɕi pan /'paɲi/ gɔ'tufkɔ̃ ʧi 'kartɔ̃?]

In cash | with credit card

Gotówką | kartą kredytową
[gɔ'tufkɔ̃ | 'kartɔ̃ krɛdi'tɔvɔ̃]

Do you want the receipt?

Czy chce pan /pani/ rachunek?
[ʧi xtsɛ pan /'paɲi/ ra'xunɛk?]

Yes, please.

Tak, proszę.
[tak, 'prɔʃɛ]

No, it's OK.

Nie, dziękuję.
[ɲɛ, dʑiɛ'ŋkujɛ]

Thank you. Have a nice day!

Dziękuję. Miłego dnia!
[dʑiɛŋ'kujɛ. mʲi'wɛgɔ dɲa!]

In town

Excuse me, please.	**Przepraszam.** [pʃɛ'praʃam]
I'm looking for ...	**Szukam ...** ['ʃukam ...]
the subway	**metra** ['mɛtra]
my hotel	**mojego hotelu** [mɔ'jɛgɔ xɔ'tɛlu]
the movie theater	**kina** ['kʲina]
a taxi stand	**postoju taksówek** [pɔ'stɔju ta'ksuvɛk]
an ATM	**bankomatu** [bankɔ'matu]
a foreign exchange office	**kantoru wymiany walut** [ka'ntɔru vɨ'mʲanɨ va'lut]
an internet café	**kafejki internetowej** [ka'fɛjkʲi intɛrnɛ'tɔvɛj]
... street	**ulicy ...** [u'ʎitsɨ ...]
this place	**tego miejsca** ['tɛgɔ 'mʲɛjstsa]
Do you know where ... is?	**Czy wie pan /pani/ gdzie jest ...?** [tʃɨ 'vʲɛ pan /'paɲi/ gdʑɛ 'jɛst ...?]
Which street is this?	**Na jakiej to ulicy?** [na 'jakʲɛj tɔ u'ʎitsɨ?]
Show me where we are right now.	**Proszę mi pokazać gdzie teraz jesteśmy.** ['prɔʃɛ mʲi pɔ'kazatɕ gdʑɛ 'tɛras jɛ'stɛɕmɨ]
Can I get there on foot?	**Czy mogę tam dojść pieszo?** [tʃɨ 'mɔgɛ tam 'dɔjɕtɕ 'pʲɛʃɔ?]
Do you have a map of the city?	**Czy ma pan /pani/ mapę miasta?** [tʃɨ ma pan /'paɲi/ 'mapɛ 'mʲasta?]
How much is a ticket to get in?	**Ile kosztuje wejście?** ['ilɛ kɔ'ʃtujɛ 'vɛjɕtɕɛ?]
Can I take pictures here?	**Czy można tu robić zdjęcia?** [tʃɨ 'mɔʒna tu 'rɔbʲitɕ 'zdjɛntɕa?]
Are you open?	**Czy jest otwarte?** [tʃɨ 'jɛst ɔ'tfartɛ?]

When do you open?

Od której jest czynne?
[ɔt 'kturɛj 'jɛst 'tʃinnɛ?]

When do you close?

Do której jest czynne?
[dɔ 'kturɛj 'jɛst 'tʃinnɛ?]

Money

money	**pieniądze** [pʲɛ'ɲiɔndzɛ]
cash	**gotówka** [gɔ'tufka]
paper money	**pieniądze papierowe** [pʲɛ'ɲiɔndzɛ papʲɛ'rɔvɛ]
loose change	**drobne** ['drɔbnɛ]
check | change | tip	**rachunek | drobne | napiwek** [ra'xunɛk | 'drɔbnɛ | na'pʲivɛk]

credit card	**karta kredytowa** ['karta krɛdɨ'tɔva]
wallet	**portfel** ['pɔrtfɛl]
to buy	**kupować** [ku'pɔvatɕ]
to pay	**płacić** ['pwatɕitɕ]
fine	**grzywna** ['gʒɨvna]
free	**darmowy** [da'rmɔvɨ]

Where can I buy ...?	**Gdzie mogę kupić ...?** [gdʑɛ 'mɔgɛ 'kupʲitɕ ...?]
Is the bank open now?	**Czy bank jest teraz otwarty?** [ʧɨ 'bank 'jɛst 'tɛraz ɔ'tfartɨ?]
When does it open?	**Od której jest czynny?** [ɔt 'kturɛj 'jɛst 'ʧɨnnɨ?]
When does it close?	**Do której jest czynny?** [dɔ 'kturɛj 'jɛst 'ʧɨnnɨ?]

How much?	**Ile kosztuje?** ['ilɛ kɔ'ʃtujɛ?]
How much is this?	**Ile to kosztuje?** ['ilɛ tɔ kɔ'ʃtujɛ?]
That's too expensive.	**To za drogo.** [tɔ za 'drɔgɔ]

Excuse me, where do I pay?	**Przepraszam, gdzie mogę zapłacić?** [pʃɛ'praʃam, gdʑɛ 'mɔgɛ za'pwatɕitɕ?]
Check, please.	**Rachunek proszę.** [ra'xunɛk 'prɔʃɛ]

Can I pay by credit card?

Czy mogę zapłacić kartą?
[ʧi ˈmɔgɛ zaˈpwatɕiʨ ˈkartɔ̃?]

Is there an ATM here?

Czy jest tu gdzieś bankomat?
[ʧi ˈjɛst tu gdʑɛɕ bankɔˈmat?]

I'm looking for an ATM.

Szukam bankomatu.
[ˈʃukam bankɔˈmatu]

I'm looking for a foreign exchange office.

Szukam kantoru wymiany walut.
[ˈʃukam kaˈntɔru vɨˈmʲanɨ ˈvalut]

I'd like to change ...

Chciałbym /Chciałabym/ wymienić ...
[ˈxtɕawbɨm /xtɕaˈwabɨm/ vɨˈmʲɛɲiʨ ...]

What is the exchange rate?

Jaki jest kurs?
[ˈjakʲi ˈjɛst ˈkurs?]

Do you need my passport?

Czy potrzebuje pan /pani/ mój paszport?
[ʧi pɔʧɛˈbujɛ pan /ˈpaɲi/ muj ˈpaʃpɔrt?]

Time

What time is it?	**Która godzina?** ['ktura gɔ'dʑina?]
When?	**Kiedy?** ['kʲɛdi?]
At what time?	**O której godzinie?** [ɔ 'kturɛj gɔ'dʑiɲɛ?]
now | later | after ...	**teraz | później | po ...** ['tɛraz | 'puʑɲɛj | pɔ ...]

one o'clock	**godzina pierwsza** [gɔ'dʑina 'pʲɛrʃʃa]
one fifteen	**pierwsza piętnaście** ['pʲɛrʃʃa pʲiɛ'ntnaɕtɕɛ]
one thirty	**pierwsza trzydzieści** ['pʲɛrʃʃa tʃi'dʑɛɕtɕi]
one forty-five	**za piętnaście druga** [za pʲiɛ'ntnaɕtɕɛ 'druga]

one | two | three	**pierwsza | druga | trzecia** ['pʲɛrʃʃa | 'druga | 'tʃɛtɕa]
four | five | six	**czwarta | piąta | szósta** ['tʃvarta | 'pʲiɔnta | 'ʃusta]
seven | eight | nine	**siódma | ósma | dziewiąta** ['ɕudma | 'usma | dʑɛ'vʲiɔnta]
ten | eleven | twelve	**dziesiąta | jedenasta | dwunasta** [dʑɛ'ɕiɔnta | jɛdɛ'nasta | dvu'nasta]

in ...	**za ...** [za ...]
five minutes	**pięć minut** ['pʲiɛntɕ 'mʲinut]
ten minutes	**dziesięć minut** ['dʑɛɕiɛntɕ 'mʲinut]
fifteen minutes	**piętnaście minut** [pʲiɛ'ntnaɕtɕɛ 'mʲinut]
twenty minutes	**dwadzieścia minut** [dva'dʑɛɕtɕa 'mʲinut]

half an hour	**pół godziny** ['puw gɔ'dʑini]
an hour	**godzinę** [gɔ'dʑinɛ]

in the morning	**rano** ['ranɔ]
early in the morning	**wcześnie rano** ['ftʃɛɕɲɛ 'ranɔ]
this morning	**tego ranka** ['tɛgɔ 'ranka]
tomorrow morning	**jutro rano** ['jutrɔ 'ranɔ]

at noon	**w południe** [f pɔ'wudɲɛ]
in the afternoon	**po południu** [pɔ pɔ'wudɲu]
in the evening	**wieczorem** [vʲɛ'tʃɔrɛm]
tonight	**dziś wieczorem** ['dʑiɕ vʲɛ'tʃɔrɛm]

at night	**w nocy** [f 'nɔtsɨ]
yesterday	**wczoraj** ['ftʃɔraj]
today	**dzisiaj** ['dʑiɕaj]
tomorrow	**jutro** ['jutrɔ]
the day after tomorrow	**pojutrze** [pɔ'jutʃɛ]

What day is it today?	**Jaki jest dzisiaj dzień?** ['jakʲi 'jɛst 'dʑiɕaj 'dʑɛɲ?]
It's ...	**Jest ...** ['jɛst ...]
Monday	**poniedziałek** [pɔɲɛ'dʑawɛk]
Tuesday	**wtorek** ['ftɔrɛk]
Wednesday	**środa** ['ɕrɔda]

Thursday	**czwartek** ['tʃvartɛk]
Friday	**piątek** ['pʲiɔntɛk]
Saturday	**sobota** [sɔ'bɔta]
Sunday	**niedziela** [ɲɛ'dʑɛla]

Greetings. Introductions

Hello.
Witam.
['vʲitam]

Pleased to meet you.
Miło mi pana /panią/ poznać.
['mʲiwɔ mʲi 'pana /'paɲiɔ̃/ 'pɔznatɕ]

Me too.
Mi również.
[mʲi 'ruvɲɛʒ]

I'd like you to meet …
Chciałbym żeby pan poznał /pani poznała/ …
['xtɕawbɨm 'ʒɛbɨ pan 'pɔznaw /'paɲi pɔ'znawa/ …]

Nice to meet you.
Miło pana /panią/ poznać.
['mʲiwɔ 'pana /'paɲiɔ̃/ 'pɔznatɕ]

How are you?
Jak się pan /pani/ miewa?
['jak ɕɛ pan /'paɲi/ 'mʲɛva?]

My name is …
Mam na imię …
[mam na 'imʲiɛ …]

His name is …
On ma na imię …
['ɔn ma na 'imʲiɛ …]

Her name is …
Ona ma na imię …
['ɔna ma na 'imʲiɛ …]

What's your name?
Jak pan /pani/ ma na imię?
['jak pan /'paɲi/ ma na 'imʲiɛ?]

What's his name?
Jak on ma na imię?
['jak 'ɔn ma na 'imʲiɛ?]

What's her name?
Jak ona ma na imię?
['jak 'ɔna ma na 'imʲiɛ?]

What's your last name?
Jak pan /pani/ się nazywa?
['jak pan /'paɲi/ ɕɛ na'zɨva?]

You can call me …
Może się pan /pani/ do mnie zwracać …
['mɔʒɛ ɕɛ pa'n /'paɲi/ dɔ 'mɲɛ 'zvratsatɕ …]

Where are you from?
Skąd pan /pani/ jest?
['skɔnt pan /'paɲi/ 'jɛst?]

I'm from …
Pochodzę z …
[pɔ'xɔdzɛ s …]

What do you do for a living?
Czym się pan /pani/ zajmuje?
['tʃɨm ɕɛ pan /'paɲi/ zaj'mujɛ?]

Who is this?
Kto to jest?
[ktɔ tɔ 'jɛst?]

Who is he?
Kim on jest?
['kʲim 'ɔn 'jɛst?]

Who is she?	**Kim ona jest?** ['kʲim 'ɔna 'jɛst?]
Who are they?	**Kim oni są?** ['kʲim 'ɔɲi sɔ̃?]

This is ...	**To jest ...** [tɔ 'jɛst ...]
my friend (masc.)	**mój przyjaciel** [muj pʃi'jatɕɛl]
my friend (fem.)	**moja przyjaciółka** ['mɔja pʃija'tɕuwka]
my husband	**mój mąż** [muj 'mɔ̃ʒ]
my wife	**moja żona** ['mɔja 'ʒɔna]

my father	**mój ojciec** [muj 'ɔjtɕɛts]
my mother	**moja matka** ['mɔja 'matka]
my brother	**mój brat** [muj 'brat]
my sister	**moja siostra** ['mɔja 'ɕɔstra]
my son	**mój syn** [muj 'sin]
my daughter	**moja córka** ['mɔja 'tsurka]

This is our son.	**To jest nasz syn.** [tɔ 'jɛst 'naʃ 'sin]
This is our daughter.	**To jest nasza córka.** [tɔ 'jɛst 'naʃa 'tsurka]
These are my children.	**To moje dzieci.** [tɔ 'mɔjɛ 'dʑɛtɕi]
These are our children.	**To nasze dzieci.** [tɔ 'naʃɛ 'dʑɛtɕi]

Farewells

Good bye!	**Do widzenia!** [dɔ vʲi'dzɛɲa!]
Bye! (inform.)	**Cześć!** ['tʃɛɕtɕ!]
See you tomorrow.	**Do zobaczenia jutro.** [dɔ zɔba'tʃɛɲa 'jutrɔ]
See you soon.	**Na razie.** [na 'raʑɛ]
See you at seven.	**Do zobaczenia o siódmej.** [dɔ zɔba'tʃɛɲa ɔ 'ɕudmɛj]
Have fun!	**Bawcie się dobrze!** ['baftɕɛ ɕɛ 'dɔbʒɛ!]
Talk to you later.	**Do usłyszenia.** [dɔ uswɨ'ʃɛɲa]
Have a nice weekend.	**Miłego weekendu.** [mʲi'wɛgɔ vɛɛ'kɛndu]
Good night.	**Dobranoc.** [dɔ'branɔts]
It's time for me to go.	**Czas na mnie.** [tʃas na 'mɲɛ]
I have to go.	**Muszę iść.** ['muʃɛ 'iɕtɕ]
I will be right back.	**Wracam za chwilę.** ['vratsam za 'xvʲilɛ]
It's late.	**Późno już.** ['puʑnɔ 'juʒ]
I have to get up early.	**Muszę wstać wcześnie.** ['muʃɛ 'fstatɕ 'ftʃɛɕɲɛ]
I'm leaving tomorrow.	**Wyjeżdżam jutro.** [vɨ'jɛʑdʒam 'jutrɔ]
We're leaving tomorrow.	**Wyjeżdżamy jutro.** [vɨjɛʑ'dʒamɨ 'jutrɔ]
Have a nice trip!	**Miłej podróży!** ['mʲiwɛj pɔ'druʒɨ!]
It was nice meeting you.	**Miło było pana /panią/ poznać.** ['mʲiwɔ 'bɨwɔ 'pana /'paɲiɔ/ 'pɔznatɕ]
It was nice talking to you.	**Miło się rozmawiało.** ['mʲiwɔ ɕɛ rɔzma'vʲawɔ]
Thanks for everything.	**Dziękuję za wszystko.** [dʑɛɲ'kujɛ za 'fʃɨstkɔ]

I had a very good time.	**Dobrze się bawiłem /bawiłam/.** ['dɔbʒɛ ɕɛ ba'vʲiwɛm /ba'vʲiwam/]
We had a very good time.	**Dobrze się bawiliśmy.** ['dɔbʒɛ ɕɛ bavʲi'ʎiɕmʲi]
It was really great.	**Było naprawdę świetne.** ['biwɔ na'pravdɛ 'ɕvʲɛtnɛ]
I'm going to miss you.	**Będę tęsknić.** ['bɛndɛ 'tɛ̃skɲitɕ]
We're going to miss you.	**Będziemy tęsknić.** [bɛ'ndʑɛmʲi 'tɛ̃skɲitɕ]

Good luck!	**Powodzenia!** [pɔvɔ'dzɛɲa!]
Say hi to ...	**Pozdrów ...** ['pɔzdruf ...]

Foreign language

I don't understand.	**Nie rozumiem.** [ɲɛ rɔ'zumʲɛm]
Write it down, please.	**Czy może pan /pani/ to napisać?** [tʃi 'mɔʒɛ pan /'paɲi/ tɔ na'pʲisatɕ?]
Do you speak ...?	**Czy mówi pan /pani/ po ...?** [tʃi 'muvʲi pan /'paɲi/ pɔ ...?]

I speak a little bit of ...	**Mówię troszkę po ...** ['muvʲɛ 'trɔʃkɛ pɔ ...]
English	**angielsku** [a'ngʲɛlsku]
Turkish	**turecku** [tu'rɛtsku]
Arabic	**arabsku** [a'rapsku]
French	**francusku** [fran'tsusku]

German	**niemiecku** [ɲɛ'mʲɛtsku]
Italian	**włosku** ['vwɔsku]
Spanish	**hiszpańsku** [xi'ʃpaɲsku]
Portuguese	**portugalsku** [pɔrtu'galsku]
Chinese	**chińsku** ['xiɲsku]
Japanese	**japońsku** [ja'pɔɲsku]

Can you repeat that, please.	**Czy może pan /pani/ powtórzyć?** [tʃi 'mɔʒɛ pan /'paɲi/ pɔ'ftuʒitɕ?]
I understand.	**Rozumiem.** [rɔ'zumʲɛm]
I don't understand.	**Nie rozumiem.** [ɲɛ rɔ'zumʲɛm]
Please speak more slowly.	**Proszę mówić wolniej.** ['prɔʃɛ 'muvʲitɕ 'vɔlɲɛj]

Is that correct? (Am I saying it right?)	**Czy jest poprawne?** [tʃi 'jɛst pɔ'pravnɛ?]
What is this? (What does this mean?)	**Co to znaczy?** ['tsɔ tɔ 'znatʃi?]

Apologies

Excuse me, please.	**Przepraszam.** [pʃɛ'praʃam]
I'm sorry.	**Przepraszam.** [pʃɛ'praʃam]
I'm really sorry.	**Bardzo przepraszam.** ['bardzɔ pʃɛ'praʃam]
Sorry, it's my fault.	**Przepraszam, to moja wina.** [pʃɛ'praʃam, tɔ 'mɔja 'vʲina]
My mistake.	**Mój błąd.** [muj 'bwɔnt]
May I ...?	**Czy mogę ...?** [ʧɨ 'mɔgɛ ...?]
Do you mind if I ...?	**Czy ma pan /pani/ coś przeciwko gdybym ...?** [ʧɨ ma pan /'paɲi/ 'tsɔɕ pʃɛ'ʨifkɔ 'gdɨbɨm ...?]
It's OK.	**Nic się nie stało.** ['ɲits ɕiɛ ɲɛ 'stawɔ]
It's all right.	**Wszystko w porządku.** ['fʃɨstkɔ f pɔ'ʒɔntku]
Don't worry about it.	**Nic nie szkodzi.** ['ɲits ɲɛ 'ʃkɔdʑi]

Agreement

Yes.

Tak.
[tak]

Yes, sure.

Tak, oczywiście.
[tak, ɔtʃɨ'vʲiɕtɕɛ]

OK (Good!)

Dobrze!
['dɔbʒɛ!]

Very well.

Bardzo dobrze.
['bardzɔ 'dɔbʒɛ]

Certainly!

Oczywiście!
[ɔtʃɨ'vʲiɕtɕɛ!]

I agree.

Zgadzam się.
['zgadzam ɕɛ]

That's correct.

Dokładnie tak.
[dɔ'kwadɲɛ 'tak]

That's right.

Zgadza się.
['zgadza ɕɛ]

You're right.

Ma pan /pani/ rację.
[ma pan /'paɲi/ 'ratsjɛ]

I don't mind.

Nie mam nic przeciwko.
[ɲɛ 'mam 'ɲits pʃɛ'tɕifkɔ]

Absolutely right.

Bardzo poprawnie.
['bardzɔ pɔ'pravɲɛ]

It's possible.

To możliwe.
[tɔ mɔ'ʒʎivɛ]

That's a good idea.

To dobry pomysł.
[tɔ 'dɔbrɨ 'pɔmɨs]

I can't say no.

Nie mogę odmówić.
[ɲɛ 'mɔgɛ ɔ'dmuvʲitɕ]

I'd be happy to.

Z radością.
[z ra'dɔɕtɕiɔ̃]

With pleasure.

Z przyjemnością.
[s pʃɨjɛ'mnɔɕtɕiɔ̃]

Refusal. Expressing doubt

No.	**Nie.** [ɲɛ]
Certainly not.	**Z pewnością nie.** [s pɛ'vnɔɕtɕiɔ̃ 'ɲɛ]

I don't agree.	**Nie zgadzam się.** [ɲɛ 'zgadzam ɕiɛ]
I don't think so.	**Nie wydaje mi się.** [ɲɛ vɨ'dajɛ mʲi ɕiɛ]
It's not true.	**To nie prawda.** [tɔ ɲɛ 'pravda]

You are wrong.	**Nie ma pan /pani/ racji.** [ɲɛ ma pan /'paɲi/ 'ratsji]
I think you are wrong.	**Myślę że nie ma pan /pani/ racji.** ['mɨɕlɛ 'ʒɛ ɲɛ ma pan /'paɲi/ 'ratsji]

I'm not sure.	**Nie jestem pewien /pewna/.** [ɲɛ 'jɛstɛm 'pɛvʲɛn /'pɛvna/]
It's impossible.	**To niemożliwe.** [tɔ ɲɛmɔ'ʒʎivɛ]
Nothing of the kind (sort)!	**Nic podobnego!** ['ɲits pɔdɔ'bnɛgɔ!]

The exact opposite.	**Dokładnie odwrotnie.** [dɔ'kwadɲɛ ɔ'dvrɔtɲɛ]
I'm against it.	**Nie zgadzam się.** [ɲɛ 'zgadzam ɕiɛ]
I don't care.	**Wszystko mi jedno.** ['fʃistkɔ mʲi 'jɛdnɔ]
I have no idea.	**Nie mam pojęcia.** [ɲɛ 'mam pɔ'jɛntɕa]
I doubt that.	**Wątpię w to.** ['vɔntpʲiɛ f 'tɔ]

Sorry, I can't.	**Przepraszam, nie mogę.** [pʃɛ'praʃam, ɲɛ 'mɔgɛ]
Sorry, I don't want to.	**Przepraszam, nie chcę.** [pʃɛ'praʃam, ɲɛ 'xtsɛ]

Thank you, but I don't need this.	**Dziękuję, ale nie potrzebuję tego.** [dʑiɛɲ'kujɛ, 'alɛ ɲɛ pɔtʃɛ'bujɛ 'tɛgɔ]
It's late.	**Robi się późno.** ['rɔbʲi ɕiɛ 'puʒnɔ]

I have to get up early.

Muszę wstać wcześnie.
['muʃɛ 'fstatɕ 'ftʃɛɕɲɛ]

I don't feel well.

Źle się czuję.
[ʑlɛ ɕɛ 'tʃujɛ]

Expressing gratitude

Thank you.	**Dziękuję.** [dʑiɛŋ'kujɛ]
Thank you very much.	**Dziękuję bardzo.** [dʑiɛŋ'kujɛ 'bardzɔ]
I really appreciate it.	**Naprawdę to doceniam.** [na'pravdɛ tɔ dɔ'tsɛɲam]
I'm really grateful to you.	**Jestem naprawdę wdzięczny /wdzięczna/.** ['jɛstɛm na'pravdɛ 'vdʑiɛntʃni /'vdʑiɛntʃna/]
We are really grateful to you.	**Jesteśmy naprawdę wdzięczni.** [jɛs'tɛɕmi na'pravdɛ 'vdʑiɛntʃɲi]
Thank you for your time.	**Dziękuję za poświęcony czas.** [dʑiɛŋ'kujɛ za pɔɕvʲiɛn'tsɔni 'tʃas]
Thanks for everything.	**Dziękuję za wszystko.** [dʑiɛŋ'kujɛ za 'fʃistkɔ]
Thank you for ...	**Dziękuję za ...** [dʑiɛŋ'kujɛ za ...]
your help	**pańską pomoc** ['paɲskɔ̃ 'pɔmɔts]
a nice time	**miłe chwile** ['mʲiwɛ 'xvʲilɛ]
a wonderful meal	**doskonałą potrawę** [dɔskɔ'nawɔ̃ pɔ'travɛ]
a pleasant evening	**miły wieczór** ['mʲiwi 'vʲetʃur]
a wonderful day	**wspaniały dzień** [fspa'ɲawi 'dʑɛɲ]
an amazing journey	**miła podróż** ['mʲiwa 'pɔdruʒ]
Don't mention it.	**Nie ma za co.** [ɲɛ ma za 'tsɔ]
You are welcome.	**Proszę.** ['prɔʃɛ]
Any time.	**Zawsze do usług.** ['zafʃɛ dɔ 'uswuk]
My pleasure.	**Cała przyjemność po mojej stronie.** [tsawa pʃi'jɛmnɔɕtɕ pɔ 'mɔjɛj 'strɔɲɛ]

Forget it. It's alright.　　　　**Nie ma o czy mówić.**
　　　　　　　　　　　　　　[ɲɛ ma ɔ ʧi 'muvʲiʨ]

Don't worry about it.　　　　**Nic nie szkodzi.**
　　　　　　　　　　　　　　['ɲits ɲɛ 'ʃkɔdʑi]

Congratulations. Best wishes

Congratulations!

Happy birthday!

Gratulacje!
[gratu'latsjɛ!]

**Wszystkiego najlepszego
z okazji urodzin!**
[fʃi'stkʲɛgɔ najlɛ'pʃɛgɔ
z ɔ'kazji u'rɔdzin!]

Merry Christmas!

Happy New Year!

Wesołych Świąt!
[vɛ'sɔwɨx 'ɕvʲiɔnt!]

Szczęśliwego Nowego Roku!
[ʃtʃɛ̃ɕʎi'vɛgɔ nɔ'vɛgɔ 'rɔku!]

Happy Easter!

Happy Hanukkah!

Wesołych Świąt Wielkanocnych!
[vɛ'sɔwɨx 'ɕvʲiɔnt vʲɛlka'nɔtsnɨx!]

Szczęśliwego Chanuka!
[ʃtʃɛ̃ɕʎi'vɛgɔ 'xanuka!]

I'd like to propose a toast.

Cheers!

Let's drink to ...!

To our success!

To your success!

Chciałbym wznieść toast.
['xtɕawbɨm 'vzɲɛɕtɕ 'tɔast]

Na zdrowie!
[na 'zdrɔvʲɛ!]

Wypijmy za ...!
[vɨ'pʲijmɨ za ...!]

Za naszą pomyślność!
[za 'naʃɔ̃ pɔ'mɨɕlnɔɕtɕ!]

Za Państwa pomyślność!
[za 'paɲstfa pɔ'mɨɕlnɔɕtɕ!]

Good luck!

Have a nice day!

Have a good holiday!

Have a safe journey!

I hope you get better soon!

Powodzenia!
[pɔvɔ'dzɛɲa!]

Miłego dnia!
['mʲiwɛgɔ 'dɲa!]

Miłych wakacji!
['mʲiwɨx va'katsji!]

Bezpiecznej podróży!
[bɛ'spʲɛtʃnɛj pɔ'druʒɨ!]

Szybkiego powrotu do zdrowia!
[ʃɨ'pkʲɛgɔ pɔ'vrɔtu dɔ 'zdrɔvʲa!]

Socializing

Why are you sad?

Dlaczego jest pani smutna?
[dla'tʃɛgɔ 'jɛst 'paɲi 'smutna?]

Smile! Cheer up!

**Proszę się uśmiechnąć,
głowa do góry!**
['prɔʃɛ ɕɛ u'ɕmʲɛxnɔntɕ,
'gwɔva dɔ 'guri!]

Are you free tonight?

Czy ma pani czas dzisiaj wieczorem?
[tʃi ma 'paɲi 'tʃaz 'dʑiɕaj vʲɛ'tʃɔrɛm?]

May I offer you a drink?

Czy mogę zaproponować pani drinka?
[tʃi 'mɔgɛ zaprɔpɔ'nɔvatɕ 'paɲi 'drinka?]

Would you like to dance?

Czy mogę prosić do tańca?
[tʃi 'mɔgɛ 'prɔɕitɕ dɔ 'taɲtsa?]

Let's go to the movies.

Może pójdziemy do kina?
['mɔʒɛ pu'jdʑɛmi dɔ 'kʲina?]

May I invite you to ...?

Czy mogę zaprosić pani ...?
[tʃi 'mɔgɛ za'prɔɕitɕ 'paɲi ...?]

a restaurant

do restauracji
[dɔ rɛsta'wratsji]

the movies

do kina
[dɔ 'kʲina]

the theater

do teatru
[dɔ tɛ'atru]

go for a walk

na spacer
[na 'spatsɛr]

At what time?

O której godzinie?
[ɔ 'kturɛj gɔ'dʑiɲɛ?]

tonight

dziś wieczorem
['dʑiɕ vʲɛ'tʃɔrɛm]

at six

o szóstej
[ɔ 'ʃustɛj]

at seven

o siódmej
[ɔ 'ɕudmɛj]

at eight

o ósmej
[ɔ 'usmɛj]

at nine

o dziewiątej
[ɔ dʑɛ'vʲiɔntɛj]

Do you like it here?

Czy podoba się panu /pani/ tutaj?
[tʃi pɔ'dɔba ɕɛ 'panu /'paɲi/ 'tutaj?]

Are you here with someone?

Czy jest tu pani z kimś?
[tʃi 'jɛst tu 'paɲi s 'kʲimɕ?]

I'm with my friend.	**Jestem z przyjacielem /przyjaciółką/.**
	['jɛstɛm s pʃija'tɕɛlɛm /pʃija'tɕuwkɔ̃/]
I'm with my friends.	**Jestem z przyjaciółmi.**
	['jɛstɛm s pʃija'tɕuwmʲi]
No, I'm alone.	**Nie, jestem sam /sama/.**
	[ɲɛ, 'jɛstɛm 'sam /'sama/]

Do you have a boyfriend?	**Czy masz chłopaka?**
	[tʃi 'maʃ xwɔ'paka?]
I have a boyfriend.	**Mam chłopaka.**
	[mam xwɔ'paka]
Do you have a girlfriend?	**Czy masz dziewczynę?**
	[tʃi 'maʃ dʑɛ'ftʃinɛ?]
I have a girlfriend.	**Mam dziewczynę.**
	[mam dʑɛ'ftʃinɛ]

Can I see you again?	**Czy mogę cię jeszcze zobaczyć?**
	[tʃi 'mɔgɛ tɕiɛ 'jɛʃtʃɛ zɔ'batʃitɕ?]
Can I call you?	**Czy mogę do ciebie zadzwonić?**
	[tʃi 'mɔgɛ dɔ 'tɕɛbʲɛ za'dzvɔɲitɕ?]
Call me. (Give me a call.)	**Zadzwoń do mnie.**
	['zadzvɔɲ dɔ 'mɲɛ]
What's your number?	**Jaki masz numer?**
	['jakʲi 'maʃ 'numɛr?]
I miss you.	**Tęsknię za Tobą.**
	['tɛ̃skɲiɛ za 'tɔbɔ̃]

You have a beautiful name.	**Ma pan /pani/ piękne imię.**
	[ma pan /'paɲi/ 'pʲiɛŋknɛ 'imʲiɛ]
I love you.	**Kocham cię.**
	['kɔxam tɕiɛ]
Will you marry me?	**Czy wyjdziesz za mnie?**
	[tʃi 'vijdʑɛʃ za 'mɲɛ?]
You're kidding!	**Żartuje pan /pani/!**
	[ʒar'tujɛ pan /'paɲi/!]
I'm just kidding.	**Żartuję.**
	[ʒar'tujɛ]

Are you serious?	**Czy mówi pan /pani/ poważnie?**
	[tʃi 'muvʲi pan /'paɲi/ pɔ'vaʒɲɛ?]
I'm serious.	**Mówię poważnie.**
	['muvʲiɛ pɔ'vaʒɲɛ]
Really?!	**Naprawdę?!**
	[na'pravdɛ?!]
It's unbelievable!	**To niemożliwe!**
	[tɔ ɲɛmɔ'ʒʎivɛ!]
I don't believe you.	**Nie wierzę.**
	[ɲɛ 'vʲɛʒɛ]
I can't.	**Nie mogę.**
	[ɲɛ 'mɔgɛ]
I don't know.	**Nie wiem.**
	[ɲɛ 'vʲɛm]

I don't understand you.

Nie rozumiem.
[ɲɛ rɔ'zum^jɛm]

Please go away.

Proszę odejść.
['prɔʃɛ 'ɔdɛjɕtɕ]

Leave me alone!

Proszę zostawić mnie w spokoju!
['prɔʃɛ zɔ'stav^jitɕ 'mɲɛ f spɔ'kɔju!]

I can't stand him.

Nie znoszę go.
[ɲɛ 'znɔʃɛ 'gɔ]

You are disgusting!

Jest pan obrzydliwy!
['jɛst pan ɔbʒi'dʎivi!]

I'll call the police!

Zadzwonię po policję!
[za'dzvɔɲiɛ pɔ pɔ'ʎitsjɛ!]

Sharing impressions. Emotions

I like it.	**Podoba mi się to.** [pɔ'dɔba mʲi ɕiɛ 'tɔ]
Very nice.	**Bardzo ładne.** ['bardzɔ 'wadnɛ]
That's great!	**Wspaniale!** [fspa'ɲalɛ!]
It's not bad.	**Nieźle.** ['ɲɛʑlɛ]

I don't like it.	**Nie podoba mi się to.** [ɲɛ pɔ'dɔba mʲi ɕiɛ 'tɔ]
It's not good.	**Nieładnie.** [ɲɛ'wadɲɛ]
It's bad.	**To jest złe.** [tɔ 'jɛsd 'zwɛ]
It's very bad.	**To bardzo złe.** [tɔ 'bardzɔ 'zwɛ]
It's disgusting.	**To obrzydliwe.** [tɔ ɔbʒɨ'dʎivɛ]

I'm happy.	**Jestem szczęśliwy /szczęśliwa/.** ['jɛstɛm ʃʧɛ'ɕʎivɨ /ʃʧɛ'ɕʎiva/]
I'm content.	**Jestem zadowolony /zadowolona/.** ['jɛstɛm zadɔvɔ'lɔnɨ /zadɔvɔ'lɔna/]
I'm in love.	**Jestem zakochany /zakochana/.** ['jɛstɛm zakɔ'xanɨ /zakɔ'xana/]
I'm calm.	**Jestem spokojny /spokojna/.** ['jɛstɛm spɔ'kɔjnɨ /spɔ'kɔjna/]
I'm bored.	**Jestem znudzony /znudzona/.** ['jɛstɛm znu'dzɔnɨ /znu'dzɔna/]

I'm tired.	**Jestem zmęczony /zmęczona/.** ['jɛstɛm zmɛ'nʧɔnɨ /zmɛ'nʧɔna/]
I'm sad.	**Jestem smutny /smutna/.** ['jɛstɛm 'smutnɨ /'smutna/]
I'm frightened.	**Jestem przestraszony /przestraszona/.** ['jɛstɛm pʃɛstra'ʃɔnɨ /pʃɛstra'ʃɔna/]
I'm angry.	**Jestem zły /zła/.** ['jɛstɛm 'zwɨ /'zwa/]
I'm worried.	**Martwię się.** ['martfiɛ ɕiɛ]

I'm nervous.

Jestem zdenerwowany /zdenerwowana/.
['jɛstɛm zdɛnɛrvɔ'vani /zdɛnɛrvɔ'vana/]

I'm jealous. (envious)

Jestem zazdrosny /zazdrosna/.
['jɛstɛm za'zdrɔsni /za'zdrɔsna/]

I'm surprised.

Jestem zaskoczony /zaskoczona/.
['jɛstɛm zaskɔ'ʧɔni /zaskɔ'ʧɔna/]

I'm perplexed.

Jestem zakłopotany /zakłopotana/.
['jɛstɛm zakwɔpɔ'tani /zakwɔpɔ'tana/]

Problems. Accidents

I've got a problem.

Mam problem.
[mam 'prɔblɛm]

We've got a problem.

Mamy problem.
['mamɨ 'prɔblɛm]

I'm lost.

Zgubiłem /Zgubiłam/ się.
[zgu'bʲiwɛm /zgu'bʲiwam/ ɕiɛ]

I missed the last bus (train).

Uciekł mi ostatni autobus (pociąg).
['utɕɛk mʲi ɔ'statɲi aw'tɔbus ('pɔtɕiɔŋk)]

I don't have any money left.

Nie mam ani grosza.
[ɲɛ 'mam 'aɲi 'grɔʃa]

I've lost my ...

Zgubiłem /Zgubiłam/ ...
[zgu'bʲiwɛm /zgu'bʲiwam/ ...]

Someone stole my ...

Ktoś ukradł ...
['ktɔɕ 'ukrat ...]

passport

mój paszport
[muj 'paʃpɔrt]

wallet

mój portfel
[muj 'pɔrtfɛl]

papers

moje dokumenty
['mɔjɛ dɔku'mɛntɨ]

ticket

mój bilet
[muj 'bʲilɛt]

money

moje pieniądze
['mɔjɛ pʲɛ'ɲiɔndzɛ]

handbag

moje torebkę
['mɔjɛ tɔ'rɛpkɛ]

camera

mój aparat fotograficzny
[muj a'parat fɔtɔgra'fitʃnɨ]

laptop

mój laptop
[muj 'laptɔp]

tablet computer

mój tablet
[muj 'tablɛt]

mobile phone

mój telefon
[muj tɛ'lefɔn]

Help me!

Pomocy!
[pɔ'mɔtsɨ!]

What's happened?

Co się stało?
['tsɔ ɕiɛ 'stawɔ?]

fire

pożar
['pɔʒar]

shooting	**strzał** ['stʃaw]
murder	**morderca** [mɔ'rdɛrtsa]
explosion	**wybuch** ['vɨbux]
fight	**bójka** ['bujka]

Call the police!	**Proszę zadzwonić na policję!** ['prɔʃɛ za'dzvɔɲitɕ na pɔ'ʎitsjɛ!]
Please hurry up!	**Proszę się pospieszyć!** ['prɔʃɛ ɕiɛ pɔ'spiɛʃitɕ!]
I'm looking for the police station.	**Szukam komendy policji.** ['ʃukam kɔ'mɛndɨ pɔ'ʎitsji]
I need to make a call.	**Muszę zadzwonić.** ['muʃɛ za'dzvɔɲitɕ]
May I use your phone?	**Czy mogę skorzystać z telefonu?** [tʃɨ 'mɔgɛ skɔ'ʒɨstatɕ s tɛle'fɔnu?]

I've been …	**Zostałem /Zostałam/ …** [zɔ'stawɛm /zɔ'stawam/ …]
mugged	**obrabowany /obrabowana/** [ɔbrabɔ'vanɨ /ɔbrabɔ'vana/]
robbed	**okradziony /okradziona/** [ɔkra'dzɔnɨ /ɔkra'dzɔna/]
raped	**zgwałcona** [zgva'wtsɔna]
attacked (beaten up)	**pobity /pobita/** [pɔ'biti /pɔ'bita/]

Are you all right?	**Czy wszystko w porządku?** [tʃɨ 'fʃistkɔ f pɔ'ʒɔntku?]
Did you see who it was?	**Czy widział pan /widziała pani/ kto to był?** [tʃɨ 'vidzaw pan /vi'dzawa 'paɲi/ 'ktɔ tɔ 'bɨw?]
Would you be able to recognize the person?	**Czy może pan /pani/ rozpoznać sprawcę?** [tʃɨ 'mɔʒɛ pan /paɲi/ rɔ'spɔznatɕ 'spraftsɛ?]
Are you sure?	**Jest pan pewny /pani pewna/?** ['jɛst pan 'pɛvnɨ /'paɲi 'pɛvna/?]

Please calm down.	**Proszę się uspokoić.** ['prɔʃɛ ɕiɛ uspɔ'kɔitɕ]
Take it easy!	**Spokojnie!** [spɔ'kɔjɲɛ!]
Don't worry!	**Proszę się nie martwić!** ['prɔʃɛ ɕiɛ ɲɛ 'martfitɕ!]
Everything will be fine.	**Wszystko będzie dobrze.** [fʃistkɔ 'bɛndʑɛ 'dɔbʒɛ]

Everything's all right.	**Wszystko jest w porządku.**
	[ffistkɔ 'jɛsd f pɔ'ʒɔntku]
Come here, please.	**Proszę tu podejść.**
	['prɔʃɛ tu 'pɔdɛjɕtɕ]
I have some questions for you.	**Mam kilka pytań.**
	[mam 'kʲiʎka 'pitaɲ]
Wait a moment, please.	**Proszę chwilę zaczekać.**
	['prɔʃɛ 'xvʲilɛ za'tʃɛkatɕ]
Do you have any I.D.?	**Czy ma pan /pani/ dowód tożsamości?**
	[tʃi ma pan /'paɲi/ 'dɔvut tɔʃsa'mɔɕtɕi?]
Thanks. You can leave now.	**Dziękuję. Może pan /pani/ odejść.**
	[dʑiɛŋ'kujɛ. 'mɔʒɛ pan /'paɲi/ 'ɔdɛjɕtɕ]
Hands behind your head!	**Ręce za głowę!**
	['rɛntsɛ za 'gwɔvɛ!]
You're under arrest!	**Jest pan aresztowany**
	/pani aresztowana/!
	['jɛst pan arɛʃtɔ'vani
	/'paɲi arɛʃtɔ'vana/!]

Health problems

Please help me.	**Proszę mi pomóc.** ['prɔʃɛ mʲi 'pɔmuts]
I don't feel well.	**Źle się czuję.** [ʑlɛ ɕiɛ 'tʃujɛ]
My husband doesn't feel well.	**Mój mąż nie czuje się dobrze.** [muj 'mɔ̃ʒ ɲɛ 'tʃujɛ ɕiɛ 'dɔbʒɛ]
My son ...	**Mój syn ...** [muj 'sɨn ...]
My father ...	**Mój ojciec ...** [muj 'ɔjtɕɛts ...]

My wife doesn't feel well.	**Moja żona nie czuje się dobrze.** ['mɔja 'ʒɔna ɲɛ 'tʃujɛ ɕiɛ 'dɔbʒɛ]
My daughter ...	**Moja córka ...** ['mɔja 'tsurka ...]
My mother ...	**Moja matka ...** ['mɔja 'matka ...]

I've got a ...	**Boli mnie ...** ['bɔʎi 'mɲɛ ...]
headache	**głowa** ['gwɔva]
sore throat	**gardło** ['gardwɔ]
stomach ache	**brzuch** ['bʒux]
toothache	**ząb** ['zɔmp]

I feel dizzy.	**Kręci mi się w głowie.** ['krɛntɕi mʲi ɕiɛ v 'gwɔvʲɛ]
He has a fever.	**On ma gorączkę.** [ɔn ma gɔ'rɔntʃkɛ]
She has a fever.	**Ona ma gorączkę.** ['ɔna ma gɔ'rɔntʃkɛ]
I can't breathe.	**Nie mogę oddychać.** [ɲɛ 'mɔgɛ ɔ'ddɨxatɕ]

I'm short of breath.	**Mam krótki oddech.** [mam 'krutkʲi 'ɔddɛx]
I am asthmatic.	**Jestem astmatykiem.** ['jɛstɛm astma'tɨkʲɛm]
I am diabetic.	**Jestem diabetykiem.** ['jɛstɛm diabɛ'tɨkʲɛm]

I can't sleep.	**Mam problemy ze snem.** [mam prɔ'blɛmɨ zɛ 'snɛm]
food poisoning	**Zatrułem się jedzeniem** [za'truwɛm ɕiɛ jɛ'dzɛɲɛm]

It hurts here.	**Boli mnie tu.** ['bɔʎi 'mɲɛ 'tu]
Help me!	**Pomocy!** [pɔ'mɔtsi!]
I am here!	**Jestem tu!** ['jɛstɛm 'tu!]
We are here!	**Tu jesteśmy!** [tu jɛ'stɛɕmɨ!]
Get me out of here!	**Wyjmijcie mnie stąd!** [vɨ'jmʲijtɕɛ 'mɲɛ 'stɔnt!]
I need a doctor.	**Potrzebuję lekarza.** [pɔtʃɛ'bujɛ lɛ'kaʒa]
I can't move.	**Nie mogę się ruszać.** [ɲɛ 'mɔgɛ ɕiɛ 'ruʃatɕ]
I can't move my legs.	**Nie mogę się ruszać nogami.** [ɲɛ 'mɔgɛ ɕiɛ 'ruʃatɕ nɔ'gamʲi]

I have a wound.	**Jestem ranny /ranna/.** ['jɛstɛm 'rannɨ /'ranna/]
Is it serious?	**Czy to poważne?** [tʃɨ tɔ pɔ'vaʒnɛ?]
My documents are in my pocket.	**Moje dokumenty są w kieszeni.** ['mɔjɛ dɔku'mɛntɨ 'sɔ̃ f kʲɛ'ʃɛɲi]
Calm down!	**Proszę się uspokoić.** ['prɔʃɛ ɕiɛ uspɔ'kɔitɕ]
May I use your phone?	**Czy mogę skorzystać z telefonu?** [tʃɨ 'mɔgɛ skɔ'ʒistatɕ s tɛlɛ'fɔnu?]

Call an ambulance!	**Proszę wezwać karetkę!** ['prɔʃɛ 'vɛzvatɕ ka'rɛtkɛ!]
It's urgent!	**To pilne!** [tɔ 'pʲilnɛ!]
It's an emergency!	**To nagłe!** [tɔ 'nagwɛ!]
Please hurry up!	**Proszę się pospieszyć!** ['prɔʃɛ ɕiɛ pɔ'spʲɛʃitɕ!]
Would you please call a doctor?	**Czy może pan /pani/ zadzwonić po lekarza?** [tʃɨ 'mɔʒɛ pan /'paɲi/ za'dzvɔɲitɕ pɔ lɛ'kaʒa?]
Where is the hospital?	**Gdzie jest szpital?** [gdʑɛ 'jɛst ʃpʲi'tal?]

How are you feeling?	**Jak się pan /pani/ czuje?** ['jak ɕiɛ pan /'paɲi/ 'tʃujɛ?]
Are you all right?	**Czy wszystko w porządku?** [tʃɨ 'fʃistkɔ f pɔ'ʒɔntku?]

What's happened?

Co się stało?
['tsɔ ɕiɛ 'stawɔ?]

I feel better now.

Czuję się już lepiej.
['ʧujɛ ɕiɛ 'juʒ 'lɛpʲɛj]

It's OK.

W porządku.
[f pɔ'ʒɔntku]

It's all right.

Wszystko w porządku.
['fʃistkɔ f pɔ'ʒɔntku]

At the pharmacy

pharmacy (drugstore)	**apteka** [a'ptɛka]
24-hour pharmacy	**apteka całodobowa** [a'ptɛka tsawɔdɔ'bɔva]
Where is the closest pharmacy?	**Gdzie jest najbliższa apteka?** [gdzɛ 'jɛst najb'ʎiʃʃa a'ptɛka?]

Is it open now?	**Czy jest teraz otwarta?** [tʃɨ 'jɛst 'tɛraz ɔ'tfarta?]
At what time does it open?	**Od której jest czynne?** [ɔt 'kturɛj 'jɛst 'tʃinnɛ?]
At what time does it close?	**Do której jest czynne?** [dɔ 'kturɛj 'jɛst 'tʃinnɛ?]

Is it far?	**Czy to daleko?** [tʃɨ tɔ da'lɛkɔ?]
Can I get there on foot?	**Czy mogę tam dojść pieszo?** [tʃɨ 'mɔgɛ tam 'dɔjɕtɕ 'pʲɛʃɔ?]
Can you show me on the map?	**Czy może mi pan /pani/ pokazać na mapie?** [tʃɨ 'mɔʒɛ mʲi pan /'paɲi/ pɔ'kazatɕ na 'mapʲɛ?]

Please give me something for ...	**Proszę coś na ...** ['prɔʃɛ 'tsɔɕ na ...]
a headache	**ból głowy** [bul 'gwɔvɨ]
a cough	**kaszel** ['kaʃɛl]
a cold	**przeziębienie** [pʃɛziɛm'bʲɛɲɛ]
the flu	**grypę** ['grɨpɛ]

a fever	**gorączkę** [gɔ'rɔntʃkɛ]
a stomach ache	**ból brzucha** [bul 'bʒuxa]
nausea	**nudności** [nu'dnɔɕtɕi]
diarrhea	**rozwolnienie** [rɔzvɔ'lɲɛɲɛ]
constipation	**zatwardzenie** [zatfar'dzɛɲɛ]

pain in the back	**ból pleców** [bul 'plɛtsuf]
chest pain	**ból w klatce piersiowej** [bul f 'klattsɛ pʲɛ'rɕɔvɛj]
side stitch	**kolkę** ['kɔʎkɛ]
abdominal pain	**ból brzucha** [bul 'bʒuxa]

pill	**tabletka** [ta'blɛtka]
ointment, cream	**maść** ['maɕtɕ]
syrup	**syrop** ['sɨrɔp]
spray	**spray** ['sprai̯]
drops	**drażetki** [dra'ʒɛtkʲi]

You need to go to the hospital.	**Musi pan /pani/ iść do szpitala.** ['muɕi pan /'paɲi/ 'iɕtɕ dɔ ʃpʲi'tala]
health insurance	**polisa na życie** [pɔ'ʎisa na 'ʒitɕɛ]
prescription	**recepta** [rɛ'tsɛpta]
insect repellant	**środek na owady** ['ɕrɔdɛk na ɔ'vadɨ]
Band Aid	**plaster** ['plastɛr]

The bare minimum

Excuse me, ...	**Przepraszam, ...** [pʃɛ'praʃam, ...]
Hello.	**Witam.** ['vʲitam]
Thank you.	**Dziękuję.** [dʑiɛŋ'kujɛ]
Good bye.	**Do widzenia.** [dɔ vʲi'dzɛɲa]
Yes.	**Tak.** [tak]
No.	**Nie.** [ɲɛ]
I don't know.	**Nie wiem.** [ɲɛ 'vʲɛm]
Where? | Where to? | When?	**Gdzie? | Dokąd? | Kiedy?** [gdʑɛ? | 'dɔkɔnt? | 'kʲɛdi?]

I need ...	**Potrzebuję ...** [pɔtʃɛ'bujɛ ...]
I want ...	**Chcę ...** ['xtsɛ ...]
Do you have ...?	**Czy jest ...?** [tʃi 'jɛst ...?]
Is there a ... here?	**Czy jest tutaj ...?** [tʃi 'jɛst 'tutaj ...?]
May I ...?	**Czy mogę ...?** [tʃi 'mɔgɛ ...?]
..., please (polite request)	**..., poproszę** [..., pɔ'prɔʃɛ]

I'm looking for ...	**Szukam ...** ['ʃukam ...]
restroom	**toalety** [tɔa'lɛti]
ATM	**bankomatu** [bankɔ'matu]
pharmacy (drugstore)	**apteki** [a'ptɛkʲi]
hospital	**szpitala** [ʃpʲi'tala]
police station	**komendy policji** [kɔ'mɛndɨ pɔ'ʎitsji]
subway	**metra** ['mɛtra]

taxi	**taksówki** [ta'ksufkʲi]
train station	**dworca kolejowego** ['dvɔrtsa kɔlɛjɔ'vɛgɔ]

My name is …	**Mam na imię …** [mam na 'imʲiɛ …]
What's your name?	**Jak pan /pani/ ma na imię?** ['jak pan /'paɲi/ ma na 'imʲiɛ?]
Could you please help me?	**Czy może pan /pani/ mi pomóc?** [tʃi 'mɔʒɛ pan /'paɲi/ mʲi 'pɔmuts?]
I've got a problem.	**Mam problem.** [mam 'prɔblɛm]
I don't feel well.	**Źle się czuję.** [zlɛ ɕiɛ 'tʃujɛ]
Call an ambulance!	**Proszę wezwać karetkę!** ['prɔʃɛ 'vɛzvatɕ ka'rɛtkɛ!]
May I make a call?	**Czy mogę zadzwonić?** [tʃi 'mɔgɛ za'dzvɔɲitɕ?]

I'm sorry.	**Przepraszam.** [pʃɛ'praʃam]
You're welcome.	**Proszę bardzo.** ['prɔʃɛ 'bardzɔ]

I, me	**ja** ['ja]
you (inform.)	**ty** ['ti]
he	**on** [ɔn]
she	**ona** ['ɔna]
they (masc.)	**oni** ['ɔɲi]
they (fem.)	**one** ['ɔnɛ]
we	**my** ['mɨ]
you (pl)	**wy** ['vɨ]
you (sg, form.)	**pan /pani/** [pan /'paɲi/]

ENTRANCE	**WEJŚCIE** ['vɛjɕtɕɛ]
EXIT	**WYJŚCIE** ['vɨjɕtɕɛ]
OUT OF ORDER	**NIECZYNNY** [ɲɛ'tʃɨnnɨ]
CLOSED	**ZAMKNIĘTE** [za'mkɲiɛntɛ]

OPEN	**OTWARTE** [ɔ'tfartɛ]
FOR WOMEN	**PANIE** ['paɲɛ]
FOR MEN	**PANOWIE** [pa'nɔvʲɛ]

TOPICAL
VOCABULARY

This section contains more
than 3,000 of the most
important words.
The dictionary will provide
invaluable assistance while
traveling abroad, because
frequently individual words
are enough for you to be
understood.
The dictionary includes a
convenient transcription of
each foreign word

VOCABULARY
CONTENTS

Basic concepts	75
Numbers. Miscellaneous	81
Colours. Units of measurement	85
Main verbs	89
Time. Calendar	95
Travel. Hotel	101
Transportation	105
City	111
Clothing & Accessories	119
Everyday experience	125
Meals. Restaurant	133
Personal information. Family	143
Human body. Medicine	147
Apartment	155
The Earth. Weather	161
Fauna	173
Flora	181
Countries of the world	187

T&P Books Publishing

T&P BOOKS

BASIC CONCEPTS

1. Pronouns
2. Greetings. Salutations
3. Questions
4. Prepositions
5. Function words. Adverbs. Part 1
6. Function words. Adverbs. Part 2

T&P Books Publishing

1. Pronouns

I, me	**ja**	[ja]
you	**ty**	[tɨ]
he	**on**	[ɔn]
she	**ona**	['ɔna]
it	**ono**	['ɔnɔ]
we	**my**	[mɨ]
you (to a group)	**wy**	[vɨ]
they	**one**	['ɔnɛ]

2. Greetings. Salutations

Hello! (fam.)	**Dzień dobry!**	[dʒeɲ 'dɔbrɨ]
Hello! (form.)	**Dzień dobry!**	[dʒeɲ 'dɔbrɨ]
Good morning!	**Dzień dobry!**	[dʒeɲ 'dɔbrɨ]
Good afternoon!	**Dzień dobry!**	[dʒeɲ 'dɔbrɨ]
Good evening!	**Dobry wieczór!**	[dɔbrɨ 'vetʃur]
to say hello	**witać się**	['vitatʃ ɕɛ̃]
Hi! (hello)	**Cześć!**	[tʃɛɕtʃ]
greeting (n)	**pozdrowienia** (l.mn.)	[pɔzdrɔ'veɲa]
to greet (vt)	**witać**	['vitatʃ]
How are you?	**Jak się masz?**	[jak ɕɛ̃ maʃ]
What's new?	**Co nowego?**	[tsɔ nɔ'vɛgɔ]
Bye-Bye! Goodbye!	**Do widzenia!**	[dɔ vi'dzɛɲa]
See you soon!	**Do zobaczenia!**	[dɔ zɔbat'ʃɛɲa]
Farewell! (to a friend)	**Żegnaj!**	['ʒɛgnaj]
Farewell! (form.)	**Żegnam!**	['ʒɛgnam]
to say goodbye	**żegnać się**	['ʒɛgnatʃ ɕɛ̃]
So long!	**Na razie!**	[na 'raʒe]
Thank you!	**Dziękuję!**	[dʒɛ̃'kue]
Thank you very much!	**Bardzo dziękuję!**	[bardzɔ dʒɛ̃'kuɛ̃]
You're welcome	**Proszę**	['prɔʃɛ̃]
Don't mention it!	**To drobiazg**	[tɔ 'drɔbʲazk]
It was nothing	**Nie ma za co**	['ne ma 'za tsɔ]
Excuse me, ...	**Przepraszam!**	[pʃɛp'raʃam]
to excuse (forgive)	**wybaczać**	[vɨ'batʃatʃ]
to apologize (vi)	**przepraszać**	[pʃɛp'raʃatʃ]

My apologies	Przepraszam!	[pʃɛp'raʃam]
I'm sorry!	Przepraszam!	[pʃɛp'raʃam]
to forgive (vt)	wybaczać	[vɨ'batʃatʃ]
please (adv)	proszę	['proʃɛ]

Don't forget!	Nie zapomnijcie!	[ne zapɔm'nijtʃe]
Certainly!	Oczywiście!	[ɔtʃɨ'victʃe]
Of course not!	Oczywiście, że nie!	[ɔtʃivictʃe ʒɛ 'ne]
Okay! (I agree)	Zgoda!	['zgɔda]
That's enough!	Dosyć!	['dɔsɨtʃ]

3. Questions

Who?	Kto?	[ktɔ]
What?	Co?	[tsɔ]
Where? (at, in)	Gdzie?	[gdʒe]
Where (to)?	Dokąd?	['dɔkɔ̃t]
From where?	Skąd?	[skɔ̃t]
When?	Kiedy?	['kedɨ]
Why? (What for?)	Dlaczego?	[dʎat'ʃɛgɔ]
Why? (reason)	Czemu?	['tʃɛmu]

What for?	Do czego?	[dɔ 'tʃɛgɔ]
How? (in what way)	Jak?	[jak]
What? (What kind of ...?)	Jaki?	['jaki]
Which?	Który?	['kturɨ]

About whom?	O kim?	['ɔ kim]
About what?	O czym?	['ɔ tʃɨm]
With whom?	Z kim?	[s kim]

| How many? How much? | Ile? | ['ile] |
| Whose? | Czyj? | [tʃɨj] |

4. Prepositions

with (accompanied by)	z	[z]
without	bez	[bɛz]
to (indicating direction)	do	[dɔ]
about (talking ~ ...)	o	[ɔ]
before (in time)	przed	[pʃɛt]
in front of ...	przed	[pʃɛt]

under (beneath, below)	pod	[pɔt]
above (over)	nad	[nat]
on (atop)	na	[na]
from (off, out of)	z ... , ze ...	[z], [zɛ]
of (made from)	z ... , ze ...	[z], [zɛ]

| in (e.g., ~ ten minutes) | za | [za] |
| over (across the top of) | przez | [pʃɛs] |

5. Function words. Adverbs. Part 1

Where? (at, in)	Gdzie?	[gdʒe]
here (adv)	tu	[tu]
there (adv)	tam	[tam]

| somewhere (to be) | gdzieś | [gdʒeɕ] |
| nowhere (not anywhere) | nigdzie | ['nigdʒe] |

| by (near, beside) | koło, przy | ['kɔwɔ], [pʃi] |
| by the window | przy oknie | [pʃi 'ɔkne] |

Where (to)?	Dokąd?	['dɔkɔ̃t]
here (e.g., come ~!)	tutaj	['tutaj]
there (e.g., to go ~)	tam	[tam]
from here (adv)	stąd	[stɔ̃t]
from there (adv)	stamtąd	['stamtɔ̃t]

| close (adv) | blisko | ['bliskɔ] |
| far (adv) | daleko | [da'lɛkɔ] |

near (e.g., ~ Paris)	koło	['kɔwɔ]
nearby (adv)	obok	['ɔbɔk]
not far (adv)	niedaleko	[neda'lekɔ]

left (adj)	lewy	['levi]
on the left	z lewej	[z 'levɛj]
to the left	w lewo	[v 'levɔ]

right (adj)	prawy	['pravi]
on the right	z prawej	[s 'pravɛj]
to the right	w prawo	[f 'pravɔ]

in front (adv)	z przodu	[s 'pʃɔdu]
front (as adj)	przedni	['pʃɛdni]
ahead (the kids ran ~)	naprzód	['napʃut]

behind (adv)	z tyłu	[s 'tiwu]
from behind	od tyłu	[ɔt 'tiwu]
back (towards the rear)	do tyłu	[dɔ 'tiwu]
middle	środek (m)	['ɕrɔdɛk]
in the middle	w środku	[f 'ɕrɔdku]

at the side	z boku	[z 'bɔku]
everywhere (adv)	wszędzie	['fʃɛdʒe]
around (in all directions)	dookoła	[dɔːˈkɔwa]
from inside	z wewnątrz	[z 'vɛvnɔ̃tʃ]

somewhere (to go)	dokąd	['dɔkɔ̃tɕ]
straight (directly)	na wprost	['na fprɔst]
back (e.g., come ~)	z powrotem	[s pɔv'rɔtɛm]

| from anywhere | skądkolwiek | [skɔ̃t'kɔʎvek] |
| from somewhere | skądś | [skɔ̃tɕ] |

firstly (adv)	po pierwsze	[pɔ 'perfʃɛ]
secondly (adv)	po drugie	[pɔ 'druge]
thirdly (adv)	po trzecie	[pɔ 'tʃɛtʃe]

suddenly (adv)	nagle	['nagle]
at first (at the beginning)	na początku	[na pɔt'ʃɔ̃tku]
for the first time	po raz pierwszy	[pɔ ras 'perfʃɨ]
long before ...	na długo przed ...	[na 'dwugɔ pʃɛt]
anew (over again)	od nowa	[ɔd 'nɔva]
for good (adv)	na zawsze	[na 'zafʃɛ]

never (adv)	nigdy	['nigdɨ]
again (adv)	znowu	['znɔvu]
now (adv)	teraz	['tɛras]
often (adv)	często	['tʃɛnstɔ]
then (adv)	wtedy	['ftɛdɨ]
urgently (quickly)	pilnie	['piʎne]
usually (adv)	zwykle	['zvikle]

by the way, ...	a propos	[a prɔ'pɔ]
possible (that is ~)	może, możliwe	['mɔʒɛ], [mɔʒ'livɛ]
probably (adv)	prawdopodobnie	[pravdɔpɔ'dɔbne]
maybe (adv)	być może	[bitʃ 'mɔʒɛ]
besides ...	poza tym	[pɔ'za tim]
that's why ...	dlatego	[dʎa'tɛgɔ]
in spite of ...	mimo że ...	['mimɔ ʒɛ]
thanks to ...	dzięki	['dʒɛ̃ki]

what (pron.)	co	[tsɔ]
that (conj.)	że	[ʒɛ]
something	coś	[tsɔɕ]
anything (something)	cokolwiek	[tsɔ'kɔʎvek]
nothing	nic	[nits]

who (pron.)	kto	[ktɔ]
someone	ktoś	[ktɔɕ]
somebody	ktokolwiek	[ktɔ'kɔʎvek]

nobody	nikt	[nikt]
nowhere (a voyage to ~)	nigdzie	['nigdʒe]
nobody's	niczyj	['nitʃɨj]
somebody's	czyjkolwiek	[tʃɨj'kɔʎvek]
so (I'm ~ glad)	tak	[tak]
also (as well)	także	['tagʒɛ]
too (as well)	też	[tɛʃ]

6. Function words. Adverbs. Part 2

Why?	Dlaczego?	[dʎat'ʃɛgɔ]
for some reason	z jakiegoś powodu	[z ja'kegɔɕ pɔ'vɔdu]
because ...	dlatego, że ...	[dla'tɛgɔ], [ʒɛ]
for some purpose	po coś	['pɔ ʦɔɕ]

and	i	[i]
or	albo	['aʎbɔ]
but	ale	['ale]
for (e.g., ~ me)	dla	[dʎa]

too (~ many people)	zbyt	[zbɨt]
only (exclusively)	tylko	['tɨʎkɔ]
exactly (adv)	dokładnie	[dɔk'wadne]
about (more or less)	około	[ɔ'kɔwɔ]

approximately (adv)	w przybliżeniu	[f pʃɨbli'ʒɛny]
approximate (adj)	przybliżony	[pʃɨbli'ʒɔnɨ]
almost (adv)	prawie	[prave]
the rest	reszta (ż)	['rɛʃta]

each (adj)	każdy	['kaʒdɨ]
any (no matter which)	jakikolwiek	[jaki'kɔʎvjek]
many, much (a lot of)	dużo	['duʒɔ]
many people	wiele	['vele]
all (everyone)	wszystkie	['fʃistke]

in return for ...	w zamian za ...	[v 'zamʲan za]
in exchange (adv)	zamiast	['zamʲast]
by hand (made)	ręcznie	['rɛntʃne]
hardly (negative opinion)	ledwo, prawie	['ledvɔ], ['pravje]

probably (adv)	prawdopodobnie	[pravdɔpɔ'dɔbne]
on purpose (intentionally)	celowo	[ʦɛ'lɔvɔ]
by accident (adv)	przypadkiem	[pʃɨ'patkem]

very (adv)	bardzo	['bardzɔ]
for example (adv)	na przykład	[na 'pʃɨkwat]
between	między	['mendʑi]
among	wśród	[fɕrut]
so much (such a lot)	aż tyle	[aʒ 'tile]
especially (adv)	szczególnie	[ʃtʃɛ'guʎne]

T&P BOOKS

NUMBERS.
MISCELLANEOUS

7. Cardinal numbers. Part 1
8. Cardinal numbers. Part 2
9. Ordinal numbers

T&P Books Publishing

7. Cardinal numbers. Part 1

0 zero	**zero**	['zɛrɔ]
1 one	**jeden**	['edɛn]
2 two	**dwa**	[dva]
3 three	**trzy**	[tʃi]
4 four	**cztery**	['tʃtɛri]

5 five	**pięć**	[pɛ̃tʃ]
6 six	**sześć**	[ʃɛctʃ]
7 seven	**siedem**	['cedɛm]
8 eight	**osiem**	['ɔcem]
9 nine	**dziewięć**	['dʒevɛ̃tʃ]

10 ten	**dziesięć**	['dʒecɛ̃tʃ]
11 eleven	**jedenaście**	[edɛ'nactʃe]
12 twelve	**dwanaście**	[dva'nactʃe]
13 thirteen	**trzynaście**	[tʃi'nactʃe]
14 fourteen	**czternaście**	[tʃtɛr'nactʃe]

15 fifteen	**piętnaście**	[pɛ̃t'nactʃe]
16 sixteen	**szesnaście**	[ʃɛs'nactʃe]
17 seventeen	**siedemnaście**	[cedɛm'nactʃe]
18 eighteen	**osiemnaście**	[ɔcem'nactʃe]
19 nineteen	**dziewiętnaście**	[dʒevɛ̃t'nactʃe]

20 twenty	**dwadzieścia**	[dva'dʒectʃa]
21 twenty-one	**dwadzieścia jeden**	[dva'dʒectʃa 'edɛn]
22 twenty-two	**dwadzieścia dwa**	[dva'dʒectʃa dva]
23 twenty-three	**dwadzieścia trzy**	[dva'dʒectʃa tʃi]

30 thirty	**trzydzieści**	[tʃi'dʒectʃi]
31 thirty-one	**trzydzieści jeden**	[tʃi'dʒectʃi 'edɛn]
32 thirty-two	**trzydzieści dwa**	[tʃi'dʒectʃi dva]
33 thirty-three	**trzydzieści trzy**	[tʃi'dʒectʃi tʃi]

40 forty	**czterdzieści**	[tʃtɛr'dʒectʃi]
41 forty-one	**czterdzieści jeden**	[tʃtɛr'dʒectʃi 'edɛn]
42 forty-two	**czterdzieści dwa**	[tʃtɛr'dʒectʃi dva]
43 forty-three	**czterdzieści trzy**	[tʃtɛr'dʒectʃi tʃi]

50 fifty	**pięćdziesiąt**	[pɛ̃'dʒecɔ̃t]
51 fifty-one	**pięćdziesiąt jeden**	[pɛ̃'dʒecɔ̃t 'edɛn]
52 fifty-two	**pięćdziesiąt dwa**	[pɛ̃'dʒecɔ̃t dva]
53 fifty-three	**pięćdziesiąt trzy**	[pɛ̃'dʒecɔ̃t tʃi]
60 sixty	**sześćdziesiąt**	[ʃɛc'dʒecɔ̃t]

61 sixty-one	sześćdziesiąt jeden	[ʃɛɕ'dʒɛɕɔt 'edɛn]
62 sixty-two	sześćdziesiąt dwa	[ʃɛɕ'dʒɛɕɔt dva]
63 sixty-three	sześćdziesiąt trzy	[ʃɛɕ'dʒɛɕɔt tʃɨ]

70 seventy	siedemdziesiąt	[ɕedɛm'dʒɛɕɔt]
71 seventy-one	siedemdziesiąt jeden	[ɕedɛm'dʒɛɕɔt 'edɛn]
72 seventy-two	siedemdziesiąt dwa	[ɕedɛm'dʒɛɕɔt dva]
73 seventy-three	siedemdziesiąt trzy	[ɕedɛm'dʒɛɕɔt tʃɨ]

80 eighty	osiemdziesiąt	[ɔɕem'dʒɛɕɔt]
81 eighty-one	osiemdziesiąt jeden	[ɔɕem'dʒɛɕɔt 'edɛn]
82 eighty-two	osiemdziesiąt dwa	[ɔɕem'dʒɛɕɔt dva]
83 eighty-three	osiemdziesiąt trzy	[ɔɕem'dʒɛɕɔt tʃɨ]

90 ninety	dziewięćdziesiąt	[dʒevɛ̃'dʒɛɕɔt]
91 ninety-one	dziewięćdziesiąt jeden	[dʒevɛ̃'dʒɛɕɔt edɛn]
92 ninety-two	dziewięćdziesiąt dwa	[dʒevɛ̃'dʒɛɕɔt dva]
93 ninety-three	dziewięćdziesiąt trzy	[dʒevɛ̃'dʒɛɕɔt tʃɨ]

8. Cardinal numbers. Part 2

100 one hundred	sto	[stɔ]
200 two hundred	dwieście	['dvɛɕtʃe]
300 three hundred	trzysta	['tʃɨsta]
400 four hundred	czterysta	['tʃtɛrista]
500 five hundred	pięćset	['pɛ̃tʃsɛt]

600 six hundred	sześćset	['ʃɛɕtʃsɛt]
700 seven hundred	siedemset	['ɕedɛmsɛt]
800 eight hundred	osiemset	[ɔ'ɕemsɛt]
900 nine hundred	dziewięćset	['dʒevɛ̃tʃsɛt]

1000 one thousand	tysiąc	['tiɕɔ̃ts]
2000 two thousand	dwa tysiące	[dva tiɕɔ̃tsɛ]
3000 three thousand	trzy tysiące	[tʃɨ tiɕɔ̃tsɛ]
10000 ten thousand	dziesięć tysięcy	['dʒeɕɛ̃tʃ ti'ɕentsi]
one hundred thousand	sto tysięcy	[stɔ ti'ɕentsi]
million	milion	['miʎjɔn]
billion	miliard	['miʎjart]

9. Ordinal numbers

first (adj)	pierwszy	['perfʃɨ]
second (adj)	drugi	['drugi]
third (adj)	trzeci	['tʃɛtʃi]
fourth (adj)	czwarty	['tʃfarti]
fifth (adj)	piąty	[pɔ̃ti]
sixth (adj)	szósty	['ʃusti]

seventh (adj)	**siódmy**	['ɕudmɨ]
eighth (adj)	**ósmy**	['usmɨ]
ninth (adj)	**dziewiąty**	[dʒevɔ̃ti]
tenth (adj)	**dziesiąty**	[dʒeɕɔ̃ti]

COLOURS. UNITS OF MEASUREMENT

10. Colors
11. Units of measurement
12. Containers

T&P Books Publishing

10. Colors

color	kolor (m)	['kɔlɜr]
shade (tint)	odcień (m)	['ɔtɕeɲ]
hue	ton (m)	[tɔn]
rainbow	tęcza (ż)	['tɛntʃa]

white (adj)	biały	['bʲawɨ]
black (adj)	czarny	['tʃarnɨ]
gray (adj)	szary	['ʃarɨ]

green (adj)	zielony	[ʑe'lɜnɨ]
yellow (adj)	żółty	['ʒuwtɨ]
red (adj)	czerwony	[tʃɛr'vɔnɨ]
blue (adj)	ciemny niebieski	['tɕɛmnɨ ne'beski]
light blue (adj)	niebieski	[ne'beski]
pink (adj)	różowy	[ru'ʒɔvɨ]
orange (adj)	pomarańczowy	[pɔmaraɲt'ʃɔvɨ]
violet (adj)	fioletowy	[fʲɔle'tɔvɨ]
brown (adj)	brązowy	[brɔ̃'zɔvɨ]

golden (adj)	złoty	['zwɔtɨ]
silvery (adj)	srebrzysty	[srɛb'ʒɨstɨ]
beige (adj)	beżowy	[bɛ'ʒɔvɨ]
cream (adj)	kremowy	[krɛ'mɔvɨ]
turquoise (adj)	turkusowy	[turku'sɔvɨ]
cherry red (adj)	wiśniowy	[viɕ'nɜvɨ]
lilac (adj)	liliowy	[li'ʎjɔvɨ]
crimson (adj)	malinowy	[mali'nɔvɨ]

light (adj)	jasny	['jasnɨ]
dark (adj)	ciemny	['tɕemnɨ]
bright, vivid (adj)	jasny	['jasnɨ]

colored (pencils)	kolorowy	[kɔlɜ'rɔvɨ]
color (e.g., ~ film)	kolorowy	[kɔlɜ'rɔvɨ]
black-and-white (adj)	czarno-biały	['tʃarnɔ 'bʲawɨ]
plain (one-colored)	jednokolorowy	['ednɔkɔlɜ'rɔvɨ]
multicolored (adj)	różnokolorowy	['ruʒnɔkɔlɜ'rɔvɨ]

11. Units of measurement

weight	ciężar (m)	['tʃenʒar]
length	długość (ż)	['dwugɔɕtʃ]

86

width	szerokość (ż)	[ʃɛ'rɔkɔɕtʃ]
height	wysokość (ż)	[vɨ'sɔkɔɕtʃ]
depth	głębokość (ż)	[gwɛ̃'bɔkɔɕtʃ]
volume	objętość (ż)	[ɔbʰ'entɔɕtʃ]
area	powierzchnia (ż)	[pɔ'veʃhɲa]

gram	gram (m)	[gram]
milligram	miligram (m)	[mi'ligram]
kilogram	kilogram (m)	[ki'lɜgram]
ton	tona (ż)	['tɔna]
pound	funt (m)	[funt]
ounce	uncja (ż)	['unˈtsʰja]

meter	metr (m)	[mɛtr]
millimeter	milimetr (m)	[mi'limɛtr]
centimeter	centymetr (m)	[tsɛn'timɛtr]
kilometer	kilometr (m)	[ki'lɜmɛtr]
mile	mila (ż)	['miʎa]

inch	cal (m)	[tsaʎ]
foot	stopa (ż)	['stɔpa]
yard	jard (m)	['jart]

square meter	metr (m) kwadratowy	[mɛtr kfadra'tɔvɨ]
hectare	hektar (m)	['hɛktar]
liter	litr (m)	[litr]
degree	stopień (m)	['stɔpeɲ]
volt	wolt (m)	[vɔʎt]
ampere	amper (m)	[am'pɛr]
horsepower	koń (m) mechaniczny	[kɔɲ mɛha'nitʃnɨ]

quantity	ilość (ż)	['ilɜɕtʃ]
a little bit of ...	niedużo ...	[ne'duʒɔ]
half	połowa (ż)	[pɔ'wɔva]
dozen	tuzin (m)	['tuʒin]
piece (item)	sztuka (ż)	['ʃtuka]

size	rozmiar (m)	['rɔzmʲar]
scale (map ~)	skala (ż)	['skaʎa]

minimal (adj)	minimalny	[mini'maʎnɨ]
the smallest (adj)	najmniejszy	[najm'nejʃɨ]
medium (adj)	średni	['ɕrɛdni]
maximal (adj)	maksymalny	[maksɨ'maʎnɨ]
the largest (adj)	największy	[naj'veŋkʃɨ]

12. Containers

canning jar (glass ~)	słoik (m)	['swɔik]
can	puszka (ż)	['puʃka]

bucket	**wiadro** (n)	['vʲadrɔ]
barrel	**beczka** (ż)	['bɛtʃka]

wash basin (e.g., plastic ~)	**miednica** (ż)	[med'nitsa]
tank (100 - 200L water ~)	**zbiornik** (m)	['zbɔrnik]
hip flask	**piersiówka** (ż)	[per'ɕyvka]
jerrycan	**kanister** (m)	[ka'nistɛr]
tank (e.g., tank car)	**cysterna** (ż)	[tsis'tɛrna]

mug	**kubek** (m)	['kubɛk]
cup (of coffee, etc.)	**filiżanka** (ż)	[fili'ʒaŋka]
saucer	**spodek** (m)	['spɔdɛk]
glass (tumbler)	**szklanka** (ż)	['ʃkʎaŋka]
wine glass	**kielich** (m)	['kelih]
stock pot (soup pot)	**garnek** (m)	['garnɛk]

bottle (~ of wine)	**butelka** (ż)	[bu'tɛʎka]
neck (of the bottle, etc.)	**szyjka** (ż)	['ʃijka]

carafe	**karafka** (ż)	[ka'rafka]
pitcher	**dzbanek** (m)	['dzbanɛk]
vessel (container)	**naczynie** (n)	[nat'ʃine]
pot (crock, stoneware ~)	**garnek** (m)	['garnɛk]
vase	**wazon** (m)	['vazɔn]

bottle (perfume ~)	**flakon** (m)	[fʎa'kɔn]
vial, small bottle	**fiolka** (ż)	[fʲɔʎka]
tube (of toothpaste)	**tubka** (ż)	['tupka]

sack (bag)	**worek** (m)	['vɔrɛk]
bag (paper ~, plastic ~)	**torba** (ż)	['tɔrba]
pack (of cigarettes, etc.)	**paczka** (ż)	['patʃka]

box (e.g., shoebox)	**pudełko** (n)	[pu'dɛwkɔ]
crate	**skrzynka** (ż)	['skʃiŋka]
basket	**koszyk** (m)	['kɔʃik]

MAIN VERBS

13. The most important verbs. Part 1
14. The most important verbs. Part 2
15. The most important verbs. Part 3
16. The most important verbs. Part 4

T&P Books Publishing

to advise (vt)	radzić	['radʒitʃ]
to agree (say yes)	zgadzać się	['zgadzatʃ ɕɛ̃]
to answer (vi, vt)	odpowiadać	[ɔtpɔ'vʲadatʃ]
to apologize (vi)	przepraszać	[pʃɛp'raʃatʃ]
to arrive (vi)	przyjeżdżać	[pʃi'eʒdʒatʃ]

to ask (~ oneself)	pytać	['pitatʃ]
to ask (~ sb to do sth)	prosić	['prɔɕitʃ]
to be (vi)	być	[bitʃ]

to be afraid	bać się	[batʃ ɕɛ̃]
to be hungry	chcieć jeść	[htʃetʃ ectʃ]
to be interested in ...	interesować się	[intɛrɛ'sɔvatʃ ɕɛ̃]
to be needed	być potrzebnym	[bitʃ pɔt'ʃɛbnim]
to be surprised	dziwić się	['dʒivitʃ ɕɛ̃]

to be thirsty	chcieć pić	[htʃetʃ pitʃ]
to begin (vt)	rozpoczynać	[rɔspɔt'ʃinatʃ]
to belong to ...	należeć	[na'leʒɛtʃ]

| to boast (vi) | chwalić się | ['hfalitʃ ɕɛ̃] |
| to break (split into pieces) | psuć | [psutʃ] |

to call (~ for help)	wołać	['vɔwatʃ]
can (v aux)	móc	[muts]
to catch (vt)	łowić	['wɔvitʃ]

| to change (vt) | zmienić | ['zmenitʃ] |
| to choose (select) | wybierać | [vi'beratʃ] |

to come down (the stairs)	schodzić	['shɔdʒitʃ]
to compare (vt)	porównywać	[pɔruv'nivatʃ]
to complain (vi, vt)	skarżyć się	['skarʒitʃ ɕɛ̃]
to confuse (mix up)	mylić	['militʃ]

| to continue (vt) | kontynuować | [kɔntinu'ɔvatʃ] |
| to control (vt) | kontrolować | [kɔntrɔ'lɜvatʃ] |

to cook (dinner)	gotować	[gɔ'tɔvatʃ]
to cost (vt)	kosztować	[kɔʃ'tɔvatʃ]
to count (add up)	liczyć	['litʃitʃ]
to count on ...	liczyć na ...	['litʃitʃ na]
to create (vt)	stworzyć	['stfɔʒitʃ]
to cry (weep)	płakać	['pwakatʃ]

14. The most important verbs. Part 2

to deceive (vi, vt)	oszukiwać	[ɔʃu'kivatʃ]
to decorate (tree, street)	ozdabiać	[ɔz'dabʲatʃ]
to defend (a country, etc.)	bronić	['brɔnitʃ]
to demand (request firmly)	zażądać	[za'ʒɔ̃datʃ]
to dig (vt)	kopać	['kɔpatʃ]
to discuss (vt)	omawiać	[ɔ'mavʲatʃ]
to do (vt)	robić	['rɔbitʃ]
to doubt (have doubts)	wątpić	['vɔ̃tpitʃ]
to drop (let fall)	upuszczać	[u'puʃtʃatʃ]
to enter	wchodzić	['fhɔdʑitʃ]
(room, house, etc.)		
to exist (vi)	istnieć	['istnetʃ]
to expect (foresee)	przewidzieć	[pʃɛ'vidʑetʃ]
to explain (vt)	objaśniać	[ɔbʰʲaɕɲatʃ]
to fall (vi)	spadać	['spadatʃ]
to find (vt)	znajdować	[znaj'dɔvatʃ]
to finish (vt)	kończyć	['kɔntʃitʃ]
to fly (vi)	lecieć	['letʃetʃ]
to follow ... (come after)	podążać	[pɔ'dɔ̃ʒatʃ]
to forget (vi, vt)	zapominać	[zapɔ'minatʃ]
to forgive (vt)	przebaczać	[pʃɛ'batʃatʃ]
to give (vt)	dawać	['davatʃ]
to give a hint	czynić aluzje	['tʃinitʃ a'lyzʰe]
to go (on foot)	iść	[iɕtʃ]
to go for a swim	kąpać się	['kɔ̃patʃ ɕɛ̃]
to go out (for dinner, etc.)	wychodzić	[viʰ'hɔdʑitʃ]
to guess (the answer)	odgadnąć	[ɔd'gadnɔ̃tʃ]
to have (vt)	mieć	[metʃ]
to have breakfast	jeść śniadanie	[eɕtʃ ɕɲa'dane]
to have dinner	jeść kolację	[eɕtʃ kɔ'ʎatsʰɛ̃]
to have lunch	jeść obiad	[eɕtʃ 'ɔbʲat]
to hear (vt)	słyszeć	['swiʃɛtʃ]
to help (vt)	pomagać	[pɔ'magatʃ]
to hide (vt)	chować	['hɔvatʃ]
to hope (vi, vt)	mieć nadzieję	[metʃ na'dʑeɛ̃]
to hunt (vi, vt)	polować	[pɔ'lɔvatʃ]
to hurry (vi)	śpieszyć się	['ɕpeʃitʃ ɕɛ̃]

15. The most important verbs. Part 3

to inform (vt)	informować	[infɔr'mɔvatʃ]
to insist (vi, vt)	nalegać	[na'legatʃ]

to insult (vt)	znieważać	[zne'vaʒatʃ]
to invite (vt)	zapraszać	[zap'raʃatʃ]
to joke (vi)	żartować	[ʒar'tɔvatʃ]

to keep (vt)	zachowywać	[zaho'vivatʃ]
to keep silent	milczeć	['miʎtʃɛtʃ]
to kill (vt)	zabijać	[za'bijatʃ]
to know (sb)	znać	[znatʃ]
to know (sth)	wiedzieć	['vedʒetʃ]
to laugh (vi)	śmiać się	['ɕmʲatʃ ɕɛ̃]

to liberate (city, etc.)	wyzwalać	[viz'vaʎatʃ]
to like (I like ...)	podobać się	[pɔ'dɔbatʃ ɕɛ̃]
to look for ... (search)	szukać	['ʃukatʃ]
to love (sb)	kochać	['kɔhatʃ]
to make a mistake	mylić się	['militʃ ɕɛ̃]

to manage, to run	kierować	[ke'rɔvatʃ]
to mean (signify)	znaczyć	['znatʃitʃ]
to mention (talk about)	wspominać	[fspɔ'minatʃ]
to miss (school, etc.)	opuszczać	[ɔ'puʃtʃatʃ]
to notice (see)	zauważać	[zau'vaʒatʃ]

to object (vi, vt)	sprzeciwiać się	[spʃɛ'tʃivʲatʃ ɕɛ̃]
to observe (see)	obserwować	[ɔbsɛr'vɔvatʃ]
to open (vt)	otwierać	[ɔt'feratʃ]
to order (meal, etc.)	zamawiać	[za'mavʲatʃ]
to order (mil.)	rozkazywać	[rɔska'zivatʃ]
to own (possess)	posiadać	[pɔ'ɕadatʃ]

to participate (vi)	uczestniczyć	[utʃɛst'nitʃitʃ]
to pay (vi, vt)	płacić	['pwatʃitʃ]
to permit (vt)	zezwalać	[zɛz'vaʎatʃ]
to plan (vt)	planować	[pʎa'nɔvatʃ]
to play (children)	grać	[gratʃ]

to pray (vi, vt)	modlić się	['mɔdlitʃ ɕɛ̃]
to prefer (vt)	woleć	['vɔletʃ]
to promise (vt)	obiecać	[ɔ'betsatʃ]
to pronounce (vt)	wymawiać	[vi'mavʲatʃ]
to propose (vt)	proponować	[prɔpɔ'nɔvatʃ]
to punish (vt)	karać	['karatʃ]

16. The most important verbs. Part 4

to read (vi, vt)	czytać	['tʃitatʃ]
to recommend (vt)	polecać	[pɔ'letsatʃ]
to refuse (vi, vt)	odmawiać	[ɔd'mavʲatʃ]
to regret (be sorry)	żałować	[ʒa'wɔvatʃ]
to rent (sth from sb)	wynajmować	[vinaj'mɔvatʃ]

to repeat (say again)	powtarzać	[pɔfˈtaʒatʃ]
to reserve, to book	rezerwować	[rɛzɛrˈvɔvatʃ]
to run (vi)	biec	[bets]
to save (rescue)	ratować	[raˈtɔvatʃ]
to say (~ thank you)	powiedzieć	[pɔˈvedʒetʃ]

to scold (vt)	besztać	[ˈbɛʃtatʃ]
to see (vt)	widzieć	[ˈvidʒetʃ]
to sell (vt)	sprzedawać	[spʃɛˈdavatʃ]
to send (vt)	wysyłać	[vɨˈsɨwatʃ]
to shoot (vi)	strzelać	[ˈstʃɛʎatʃ]

to shout (vi)	krzyczeć	[ˈkʃɨtʃɛtʃ]
to show (vt)	pokazywać	[pɔkaˈzɨvatʃ]
to sign (document)	podpisywać	[pɔtpiˈsɨvatʃ]
to sit down (vi)	siadać	[ˈɕadatʃ]

to smile (vi)	uśmiechać się	[uɕˈmehatʃ ɕɛ̃]
to speak (vi, vt)	rozmawiać	[rɔzˈmavʲatʃ]
to steal (money, etc.)	kraść	[kraɕtʃ]
to stop (for pause, etc.)	zatrzymywać się	[zatʃɨˈmɨvatʃ ɕɛ̃]
to stop (please ~ calling me)	przestawać	[pʃɛsˈtavatʃ]

to study (vt)	studiować	[studʰˈɔvatʃ]
to swim (vi)	pływać	[ˈpwɨvatʃ]
to take (vt)	brać	[bratʃ]
to think (vi, vt)	myśleć	[ˈmɨɕletʃ]
to threaten (vt)	grozić	[ˈgrɔʑitʃ]

to touch (with hands)	dotykać	[dɔˈtɨkatʃ]
to translate (vt)	tłumaczyć	[twuˈmatʃɨtʃ]
to trust (vt)	ufać	[ˈufatʃ]
to try (attempt)	próbować	[pruˈbɔvatʃ]
to turn (e.g., ~ left)	skręcać	[ˈskrɛntsatʃ]

to underestimate (vt)	nie doceniać	[nedɔˈtsɛɲatʃ]
to understand (vt)	rozumieć	[rɔˈzumetʃ]
to unite (vt)	łączyć	[ˈwɔ̃tʃɨtʃ]
to wait (vt)	czekać	[ˈtʃɛkatʃ]

to want (wish, desire)	chcieć	[htʃetʃ]
to warn (vt)	ostrzegać	[ɔstʃˈɛgatʃ]
to work (vi)	pracować	[praˈtsɔvatʃ]
to write (vt)	pisać	[ˈpisatʃ]
to write down	zapisywać	[zapiˈsɨvatʃ]

TIME. CALENDAR

17. Weekdays
18. Hours. Day and night
19. Months. Seasons

T&P Books Publishing

17. Weekdays

Monday	**poniedziałek** (m)	[pɔne'dʒʲawɛk]
Tuesday	**wtorek** (m)	['ftɔrɛk]
Wednesday	**środa** (ż)	['ɕrɔda]
Thursday	**czwartek** (m)	['tʃfartɛk]
Friday	**piątek** (m)	[pɔ̃tɛk]
Saturday	**sobota** (ż)	[sɔ'bɔta]
Sunday	**niedziela** (ż)	[ne'dʒeʎa]
today (adv)	**dzisiaj**	['dʒiɕaj]
tomorrow (adv)	**jutro**	['jutrɔ]
the day after tomorrow	**pojutrze**	[pɔ'jutʃɛ]
yesterday (adv)	**wczoraj**	['ftʃɔraj]
the day before yesterday	**przedwczoraj**	[pʃɛtft'ʃɔraj]
day	**dzień** (m)	[dʒeɲ]
working day	**dzień** (m) **roboczy**	[dʒeɲ rɔ'bɔtʃi]
public holiday	**dzień** (m) **świąteczny**	[dʒeɲ ɕfɔ̃'tɛtʃni]
day off	**dzień** (m) **wolny**	[dʒeɲ 'vɔʎni]
weekend	**weekend** (m)	[u'ikɛnt]
all day long	**cały dzień**	['tsawɨ dʒeɲ]
the next day (adv)	**następnego dnia**	[nastɛ̃p'nɛgɔ dɲa]
two days ago	**dwa dni temu**	[dva dni 'tɛmu]
the day before	**w przeddzień**	[f 'pʃɛddʒeɲ]
daily (adj)	**codzienny**	[tsɔ'dʒeɲi]
every day (adv)	**codziennie**	[tsɔ'dʒeɲe]
week	**tydzień** (m)	['tɨdʒeɲ]
last week (adv)	**w zeszłym tygodniu**	[v 'zɛʃwim tɨ'gɔdny]
next week (adv)	**w następnym tygodniu**	[v nas'tɛ̃pnim tɨ'gɔdny]
weekly (adj)	**tygodniowy**	[tɨgɔd'nɔvi]
every week (adv)	**co tydzień**	[tsɔ tɨ'dʒeɲ]
twice a week	**dwa razy w tygodniu**	[dva 'razi v tɨ'gɔdny]
every Tuesday	**co wtorek**	[tsɔ 'ftɔrek]

18. Hours. Day and night

morning	**ranek** (m)	['ranɛk]
in the morning	**rano**	['ranɔ]
noon, midday	**południe** (n)	[pɔ'wudne]
in the afternoon	**po południu**	[pɔ pɔ'wudny]
evening	**wieczór** (m)	['vetʃur]

in the evening	wieczorem	[vet'ʃɔrɛm]
night	noc (ż)	[nɔts]
at night	w nocy	[v 'nɔtsi]
midnight	północ (ż)	['puwnɔts]

second	sekunda (ż)	[sɛ'kunda]
minute	minuta (ż)	[mi'nuta]
hour	godzina (ż)	[gɔ'dʒina]
half an hour	pół godziny	[puw gɔ'dʒini]
a quarter-hour	kwadrans (m)	['kfadrans]
fifteen minutes	piętnaście minut	[pɛ̃t'naɕtʃe 'minut]
24 hours	doba (ż)	['dɔba]

sunrise	wschód (m) słońca	[fshut 'swɔɲtsa]
dawn	świt (m)	[ɕfit]
early morning	wczesny ranek (m)	['ftʃɛsni 'ranɛk]
sunset	zachód (m)	['zahut]

early in the morning	wcześnie rano	['ftʃɛɕne 'ranɔ]
this morning	dzisiaj rano	['dʒiɕaj 'ranɔ]
tomorrow morning	jutro rano	['jutrɔ 'ranɔ]

this afternoon	dzisiaj w dzień	['dʒiɕaj v dʒeɲ]
in the afternoon	po południu	[pɔ pɔ'wudny]
tomorrow afternoon	jutro popołudniu	[jutrɔ pɔpɔ'wudny]

| tonight (this evening) | dzisiaj wieczorem | [dʒiɕaj vet'ʃɔrɛm] |
| tomorrow night | jutro wieczorem | ['jutrɔ vet'ʃɔrɛm] |

at 3 o'clock sharp	równo o trzeciej	['ruvnɔ ɔ 'tʃɛtʃej]
about 4 o'clock	około czwartej	[ɔ'kɔwɔ 'tʃfartɛj]
by 12 o'clock	na dwunastą	[na dvu'nastɔ̃]

in 20 minutes	za dwadzieścia minut	[za dva'dʒeɕtʃa 'minut]
in an hour	za godzinę	[za gɔ'dʒinɛ̃]
on time (adv)	na czas	[na tʃas]

a quarter of ...	za kwadrans	[za 'kfadrans]
within an hour	w ciągu godziny	[f tʃɔ̃gu gɔ'dʒini]
every 15 minutes	co piętnaście minut	[tsɔ pɛ̃t'naɕtʃe 'minut]
round the clock	całą dobę	['tsawɔ̃ 'dɔbɛ̃]

19. Months. Seasons

January	styczeń (m)	['stitʃɛɲ]
February	luty (m)	['lyti]
March	marzec (m)	['maʒɛts]
April	kwiecień (m)	['kfetʃeɲ]
May	maj (m)	[maj]
June	czerwiec (m)	['tʃɛrvets]

July	lipiec (m)	['lipɛts]
August	sierpień (m)	['ɕerpɛɲ]
September	wrzesień (m)	['vʒɛɕeɲ]
October	październik (m)	[paʑ'dʒernik]
November	listopad (m)	[lis'tɔpat]
December	grudzień (m)	['grudʒeɲ]

spring	wiosna (ż)	['vɔsna]
in spring	wiosną	['vɔsnɔ̃]
spring (as adj)	wiosenny	[vɔ'sɛɲɨ]

summer	lato (n)	['ʎatɔ]
in summer	latem	['ʎatɛm]
summer (as adj)	letni	['letni]

fall	jesień (ż)	['eɕeɲ]
in fall	jesienią	[e'ɕenɔ̃]
fall (as adj)	jesienny	[e'ɕeɲɨ]

winter	zima (ż)	['ʒima]
in winter	zimą	['ʒimɔ̃]
winter (as adj)	zimowy	[ʒi'mɔvɨ]

month	miesiąc (m)	['meɕɔ̃ts]
this month	w tym miesiącu	[f tɨm me'ɕɔ̃tsu]
next month	w przyszłym miesiącu	[v 'pʃisʃwɨm me'ɕɔ̃tsu]
last month	w zeszłym miesiącu	[v 'zɛʃwɨm me'ɕɔ̃tsu]

a month ago	miesiąc temu	['meɕɔ̃ts 'tɛmu]
in a month (a month later)	za miesiąc	[za 'meɕɔ̃ts]
in 2 months (2 months later)	za dwa miesiące	[za dva me'ɕɔ̃tse]
the whole month	przez cały miesiąc	[pʃɛs 'tsawɨ 'meɕɔ̃ts]
all month long	cały miesiąc	['tsawɨ 'meɕɔ̃ts]

monthly (~ magazine)	comiesięczny	[tsɔme'ɕentʃnɨ]
monthly (adv)	comiesięcznie	[tsɔme'ɕentʃne]
every month	co miesiąc	[tsɔ 'meɕɔ̃ts]
twice a month	dwa razy w miesiącu	[dva 'razɨ v meɕɔ̃tsu]

year	rok (m)	[rɔk]
this year	w tym roku	[f tɨm 'rɔku]
next year	w przyszłym roku	[v 'pʃisʃwɨm 'rɔku]
last year	w zeszłym roku	[v 'zɛʃwɨm 'rɔku]

a year ago	rok temu	[rɔk 'tɛmu]
in a year	za rok	[za rɔk]
in two years	za dwa lata	[za dva 'ʎata]
the whole year	cały rok	['tsawɨ rɔk]
all year long	cały rok	['tsawɨ rɔk]
every year	co roku	[tsɔ 'rɔku]
annual (adj)	coroczny	[tsɔ'rɔtʃnɨ]

| annually (adv) | corocznie | [tsɔ'rɔtʃne] |
| 4 times a year | cztery razy w roku | ['tʃtɛrɨ 'razɨ v 'rɔku] |

date (e.g., today's ~)	data (ż)	['data]
date (e.g., ~ of birth)	data (ż)	['data]
calendar	kalendarz (m)	[ka'lendaʃ]

half a year	pół roku	[puw 'rɔku]
six months	półrocze (n)	[puw'rɔtʃɛ]
season (summer, etc.)	sezon (m)	['sɛzɔn]
century	wiek (m)	[vek]

TRAVEL. HOTEL

20. Trip. Travel
21. Hotel
22. Sightseeing

T&P Books Publishing

tourism, travel	turystyka (ż)	[tu'ristika]
tourist	turysta (m)	[tu'rista]
trip, voyage	podróż (ż)	['podruʃ]
adventure	przygoda (ż)	[pʃi'gɔda]
trip, journey	podróż (ż)	['podruʃ]

vacation	urlop (m)	['urlɔp]
to be on vacation	być na urlopie	[bitʃ na ur'lɔpe]
rest	wypoczynek (m)	[vipɔt'ʃinɛk]

train	pociąg (m)	['pɔtʃɔ̃k]
by train	pociągiem	[pɔtʃɔ̃gem]
airplane	samolot (m)	[sa'mɔlɔt]
by airplane	samolotem	[samɔ'lɔtɛm]
by car	samochodem	[samɔ'hɔdɛm]
by ship	statkiem	['statkem]

luggage	bagaż (m)	['bagaʃ]
suitcase	walizka (ż)	[va'liska]
luggage cart	wózek (m) bagażowy	['vuzɛk baga'ʒɔvi]
passport	paszport (m)	['paʃpɔrt]
visa	wiza (ż)	['viza]
ticket	bilet (m)	['bilet]
air ticket	bilet (m) lotniczy	['bilet lɔt'nitʃi]

guidebook	przewodnik (m)	[pʃɛ'vɔdnik]
map (tourist ~)	mapa (ż)	['mapa]
area (rural ~)	miejscowość (ż)	[mejs'tsɔvɔɕtʃ]
place, site	miejsce (n)	['mejstsɛ]

exotica (n)	egzotyka (ż)	[ɛg'zɔtika]
exotic (adj)	egzotyczny	[ɛgzɔ'titʃni]
amazing (adj)	zadziwiający	[zadʒivjaɔ̃tsi]

group	grupa (ż)	['grupa]
excursion, sightseeing tour	wycieczka (ż)	[vi'tʃetʃka]
guide (person)	przewodnik (ż)	[pʃɛ'vɔdnik]

| hotel | hotel (m) | ['hɔtɛʎ] |
| motel | motel (m) | ['mɔtɛʎ] |

three-star	trzy gwiazdki	[tʃi 'gviaztki]
five-star	pięć gwiazdek	[pɛ̃tʃ 'gviazdɛk]
to stay (in hotel, etc.)	zatrzymać się	[zat'ʃimatʃ ɕɛ̃]

room	pokój (m)	['pɔkuj]
single room	pokój (m) jednoosobowy	['pɔkuj ednɔ:sɔ'bɔvi]
double room	pokój (m) dwuosobowy	['pɔkuj dvuɔsɔ'bɔvi]
to book a room	rezerwować pokój	[rɛzɛr'vɔvatʃ 'pɔkuj]

| half board | wyżywienie (n) Half Board | [viʑi'vene haf bɔrd] |
| full board | pełne (n) wyżywienie | ['pɛwnɛ viʑivi'ene] |

with bath	z łazienką	[z wa'ʒenkɔ̃]
with shower	z prysznicem	[z priʃ'nitsɛm]
satellite television	telewizja (z) satelitarna	[tɛle'vizʰja satɛli'tarna]
air-conditioner	klimatyzator (m)	[klimati'zatɔr]
towel	ręcznik (m)	['rɛntʃnik]
key	klucz (m)	[klytʃ]

administrator	administrator (m)	[administ'ratɔr]
chambermaid	pokojówka (z)	[pɔkɔ'jufka]
porter, bellboy	tragarz (m)	['tragaʃ]
doorman	odźwierny (m)	[ɔd'vjerni]

restaurant	restauracja (z)	[rɛstau'ratsʰja]
pub, bar	bar (m)	[bar]
breakfast	śniadanie (n)	[ɕɲa'dane]
dinner	kolacja (z)	[kɔ'ʎatsʰja]
buffet	szwedzki stół (m)	['ʃfɛtski stuw]

elevator	winda (z)	['vinda]
DO NOT DISTURB	NIE PRZESZKADZAĆ	[ne pʃɛʃ'kadzatʃ]
NO SMOKING	ZAKAZ PALENIA!	['zakas pa'leɲa]

22. Sightseeing

monument	pomnik (m)	['pɔmnik]
fortress	twierdza (z)	['tfer dza]
palace	pałac (m)	['pawats]
castle	zamek (m)	['zamɛk]
tower	wieża (z)	['veʒa]
mausoleum	mauzoleum (n)	[mauzɔ'leum]

architecture	architektura (z)	[arhitɛk'tura]
medieval (adj)	średniowieczny	[ɕrɛdnɔ'vetʃni]
ancient (adj)	zabytkowy	[zabit'kɔvi]
national (adj)	narodowy	[narɔ'dɔvi]
well-known (adj)	znany	['znani]
tourist	turysta (m)	[tu'rista]
guide (person)	przewodnik (m)	[pʃɛ'vɔdnik]

excursion, sightseeing tour	**wycieczka** (ż)	[vi'tʃetʃka]
to show (vt)	**pokazywać**	[pɔka'zɨvatʃ]
to tell (vt)	**opowiadać**	[ɔpɔ'vʲadatʃ]
to find (vt)	**znaleźć**	['znaleɕtʃ]
to get lost (lose one's way)	**zgubić się**	['zgubitʃ ɕɛ̃]
map (e.g., subway ~)	**plan** (m)	[pʎan]
map (e.g., city ~)	**plan** (m)	[pʎan]
souvenir, gift	**pamiątka** (ż)	[pamɔ̃tka]
gift shop	**sklep** (m) **z upominkami**	[sklep s upɔmi'ŋkami]
to take pictures	**robić zdjęcia**	['rɔbitʃ 'zdʰɛ̃tʃa]
to have one's picture taken	**fotografować się**	[fɔtɔgra'fɔvatʃ ɕɛ̃]

T&P BOOKS

TRANSPORTATION

23. Airport
24. Airplane
25. Train
26. Ship

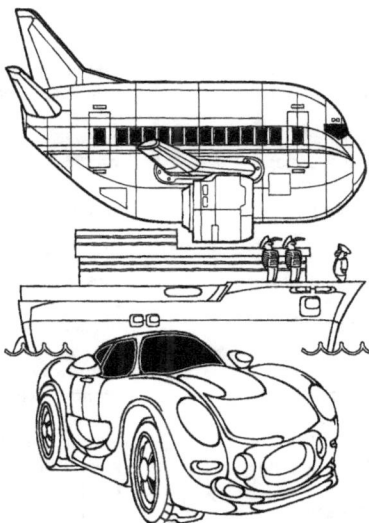

T&P Books Publishing

23. Airport

airport	port (m) lotniczy	[pɔrt lɜt'nitʃi]
airplane	samolot (m)	[sa'mɔlɜt]
airline	linie (l.mn.) lotnicze	['linje lɜt'nitʃɛ]
air traffic controller	kontroler (m) lotów	[kɔnt'rɔler 'lɜtuf]
departure	odlot (m)	['ɔdlɜt]
arrival	przylot (m)	['pʃilɜt]
to arrive (by plane)	przylecieć	[pʃi'letʃetʃ]
departure time	godzina (z) odlotu	[gɔ'dʑina ɔd'lɜtu]
arrival time	godzina (z) przylotu	[gɔ'dʑina pʃi'lɜtu]
to be delayed	opóźniać się	[ɔ'puʑjnatʃ ɕɛ̃]
flight delay	opóźnienie (n) odlotu	[ɔpuʑ'nene ɔd'lɜtu]
information board	tablica (z) informacyjna	[tab'litsa informa'tsijna]
information	informacja (z)	[infɔr'matshja]
to announce (vt)	ogłaszać	[ɔg'waʃatʃ]
flight (e.g., next ~)	lot (m)	['lɜt]
customs	urząd (m) celny	['uʒɔ̃t 'tsɛʎni]
customs officer	celnik (m)	['tsɛʎnik]
customs declaration	deklaracja (z)	[dɛkʎa'ratshja]
to fill out the declaration	wypełnić deklarację	[vi'pɛwnitʃ dɛkʎa'ratshɛ̃]
passport control	odprawa (z) paszportowa	[ɔtp'rava paʃpɔr'tɔva]
luggage	bagaż (m)	['bagaʃ]
hand luggage	bagaż (m) podręczny	['bagaʃ pɔd'rɛntʃni]
Lost Luggage Desk	poszukiwanie (n) bagażu	[pɔʃuki'vane ba'gaʒu]
luggage cart	wózek (m) bagażowy	['vuzɛk baga'ʒɔvi]
landing	lądowanie (n)	[lɔ̃dɔ'vane]
landing strip	pas (m) startowy	[pas star'tɔvi]
to land (vi)	lądować	[lɔ̃'dɔvatʃ]
airstairs	schody (l.mn.) do samolotu	['shɔdɨ dɔ samɔ'lɜtu]
check-in	odprawa (z) biletowa	[ɔtp'rava bile'tɔva]
check-in desk	stanowisko (n) odprawy	[stanɔ'viskɔ ɔtp'ravi]
to check-in (vi)	zgłosić się do odprawy	['zgwɔɕitʃ ɕɛ̃ dɔ ɔtp'ravi]
boarding pass	karta (z) pokładowa	['karta pɔkwa'dɔva]
departure gate	wyjście (n) do odprawy	['vijɕtʃe dɔ ɔtp'ravi]
transit	tranzyt (m)	['tranzɨt]
to wait (vt)	czekać	['tʃɛkatʃ]

departure lounge	poczekalnia (ż)	[pɔtʃɛ'kaʎɲa]
to see off	odprowadzać	[ɔtprɔ'vadzatʃ]
to say goodbye	żegnać się	['ʒɛgnatʃ ɕɛ̃]

24. Airplane

airplane	samolot (m)	[sa'mɔlɔt]
air ticket	bilet (m) lotniczy	['bilet lɔt'nitʃi]
airline	linie (l.mn.) lotnicze	['liɲje lɔt'nitʃɛ]
airport	port (m) lotniczy	[pɔrt lɔt'nitʃi]
supersonic (adj)	ponaddźwiękowy	[pɔnaddʑ'vɛ̃'kɔvi]

captain	kapitan (m) statku	[ka'pitan 'statku]
crew	załoga (ż)	[za'wɔga]
pilot	pilot (m)	['pilɔt]
flight attendant	stewardessa (ż)	[stɛva'rdɛssa]
navigator	nawigator (m)	[navi'gatɔr]

wings	skrzydła (l.mn.)	['skʃidwa]
tail	ogon (m)	['ɔgɔn]
cockpit	kabina (ż)	[ka'bina]
engine	silnik (m)	['ɕiʎnik]
undercarriage (landing gear)	podwozie (n)	[pɔd'vɔʒe]
turbine	turbina (ż)	[tur'bina]

propeller	śmigło (n)	['ɕmigwɔ]
black box	czarna skrzynka (ż)	['tʃarna 'skʃiŋka]
yoke (control column)	wolant (m)	['vɔʎant]
fuel	paliwo (n)	[pa'livɔ]
safety card	instrukcja (ż)	[inst'rukts^hja]
oxygen mask	maska (ż) tlenowa	['maska tle'nɔva]
uniform	uniform (m)	[u'nifɔrm]
life vest	kamizelka (ż) ratunkowa	[kami'zɛʎka ratu'ŋkɔva]
parachute	spadochron (m)	[spa'dɔhrɔn]

takeoff	start (m)	[start]
to take off (vi)	startować	[star'tɔvatʃ]
runway	pas (m) startowy	[pas star'tɔvi]

visibility	widoczność (ż)	[vi'dɔtʃnɔɕtʃ]
flight (act of flying)	lot (m)	['lɔt]
altitude	wysokość (ż)	[vi'sɔkɔɕtʃ]
air pocket	dziura (ż) powietrzna	['dʑyra pɔ'vetʃna]

seat	miejsce (n)	['mejstsɛ]
headphones	słuchawki (l.mn.)	[swu'hafki]
folding tray (tray table)	stolik (m) rozkładany	['stɔlik rɔskwa'danɨ]
airplane window	iluminator (m)	[ilymi'natɔr]
aisle	przejście (n)	['pʃɛjɕtʃe]

25. Train

train	pociąg (m)	['pɔtʃɔ̃k]
commuter train	pociąg (m) podmiejski	['pɔtʃɔk pɔd'mejski]
express train	pociąg (m) pośpieszny	['pɔtʃɔk pɔɕ'peʃni]
diesel locomotive	lokomotywa (z)	[lɔkɔmɔ'tiva]
steam locomotive	parowóz (m)	[pa'rɔvus]
passenger car	wagon (m)	['vagɔn]
dining car	wagon (m) restauracyjny	['vagɔn rɛstaura'tsijni]
rails	szyny (l.mn.)	['ʃini]
railroad	kolej (z)	['kɔlej]
railway tie	podkład (m)	['pɔtkwat]
platform (railway ~)	peron (m)	['pɛrɔn]
track (~ 1, 2, etc.)	tor (m)	[tɔr]
semaphore	semafor (m)	[sɛ'mafɔr]
station	stacja (z)	['statsʰja]
engineer (train driver)	maszynista (m)	[maʃi'nista]
porter (of luggage)	tragarz (m)	['tragaʃ]
car attendant	konduktor (m)	[kɔn'duktɔr]
passenger	pasażer (m)	[pa'saʒɛr]
conductor	kontroler (m)	[kɔnt'rɔler]
(ticket inspector)		
corridor (in train)	korytarz (m)	[kɔ'ritaʃ]
emergency brake	hamulec (m) bezpieczeństwa	[ha'mulets bɛzpet'ʃɛɲstfa]
compartment	przedział (m)	['pʃɛdʒʲaw]
berth	łóżko (n)	['wuʃkɔ]
upper berth	łóżko (n) górne	['wuʃkɔ 'gurnɛ]
lower berth	łóżko (n) dolne	['wuʃkɔ 'dɔʎnɛ]
bed linen, bedding	pościel (z)	['pɔɕtʃeʎ]
ticket	bilet (m)	['bilet]
schedule	rozkład (m) jazdy	['rɔskwad 'jazdi]
information display	tablica (z) informacyjna	[tab'litsa informa'tsijna]
to leave, to depart	odjeżdżać	[ɔdʰ'eʒdʒatʃ]
departure (of train)	odjazd (m)	['ɔdʰjast]
to arrive (ab. train)	wjeżdżać	['vʰeʒdʒatʃ]
arrival	przybycie (n)	[pʃi'bitʃe]
to arrive by train	przyjechać pociągiem	[pʃi'ehatʃ pɔtʃɔ̃gem]
to get on the train	wsiąść do pociągu	[fɕɔ̃ɕtʃ dɔ pɔtʃɔ̃gu]
to get off the train	wysiąść z pociągu	['viɕɔ̃ɕtʃ s pɔtʃɔ̃gu]
train wreck	katastrofa (z)	[katast'rɔfa]
steam locomotive	parowóz (m)	[pa'rɔvus]

stoker, fireman	palacz (m)	['paʌatʃ]
firebox	palenisko (n)	[pale'niskɔ]
coal	węgiel (m)	['vɛŋeʌ]

26. Ship

| ship | statek (m) | ['statɛk] |
| vessel | okręt (m) | ['ɔkrɛ̃t] |

steamship	parowiec (m)	[pa'rɔvets]
riverboat	motorowiec (m)	[mɔtɔ'rɔvets]
cruise ship	liniowiec (m)	[li'njɔvets]
cruiser	krążownik (m)	[krɔ̃'ʒɔvnik]

yacht	jacht (m)	[jaht]
tugboat	holownik (m)	[hɔ'lɔvnik]
barge	barka (ż)	['barka]
ferry	prom (m)	[prɔm]

| sailing ship | żaglowiec (m) | [ʒag'lɔvets] |
| brigantine | brygantyna (ż) | [brigan'tina] |

| ice breaker | lodołamacz (m) | [lɔdɔ'wamatʃ] |
| submarine | łódź (ż) podwodna | [wutʃ pɔd'vɔdna] |

boat (flat-bottomed ~)	łódź (ż)	[wutʃ]
dinghy	szalupa (ż)	[ʃa'lypa]
lifeboat	szalupa (ż)	[ʃa'lypa]
motorboat	motorówka (ż)	[mɔtɔ'rufka]

captain	kapitan (m)	[ka'pitan]
seaman	marynarz (m)	[ma'rinaʃ]
sailor	marynarz (m)	[ma'rinaʃ]
crew	załoga (ż)	[za'wɔga]

boatswain	bosman (m)	['bɔsman]
ship's boy	chłopiec (m) okrętowy	['hwɔpets ɔkrɛ̃'tɔvi]
cook	kucharz (m) okrętowy	['kuhaʃ ɔkrɛ̃'tɔvi]
ship's doctor	lekarz (m) okrętowy	['lekaʃ ɔkrɛ̃'tɔvi]

deck	pokład (m)	['pɔkwat]
mast	maszt (m)	[maʃt]
sail	żagiel (m)	['ʒageʌ]

hold	ładownia (ż)	[wa'dɔvɲa]
bow (prow)	dziób (m)	[dʒyp]
stern	rufa (ż)	['rufa]
oar	wiosło (n)	['vɔswɔ]
screw propeller	śruba (ż) napędowa	['ɕruba napɛ̃'dɔva]
cabin	kajuta (ż)	[ka'juta]

wardroom	mesa (ż)	['mɛsa]
engine room	maszynownia (ż)	[maʃi'nɔvɲa]
bridge	mostek (m) kapitański	['mɔstɛk kapi'taɲski]
radio room	radiokabina (ż)	[radʰɔka'bina]
wave (radio)	fala (ż)	['faʎa]
logbook	dziennik (m) pokładowy	['dʑɛŋik pɔkwa'dɔvɨ]

spyglass	luneta (ż)	[ly'nɛta]
bell	dzwon (m)	[dzvɔn]
flag	bandera (ż)	[ban'dɛra]

rope (mooring ~)	lina (ż)	['lina]
knot (bowline, etc.)	węzeł (m)	['vɛnzɛw]

deckrails	poręcz (ż)	['pɔrɛ̃tʃ]
gangway	trap (m)	[trap]

anchor	kotwica (ż)	[kɔt'fiʦa]
to weigh anchor	podnieść kotwicę	['pɔdnɛɕtʃ kɔt'fiʦɛ̃]
to drop anchor	zarzucić kotwicę	[za'ʒutʃitʃ kɔt'fiʦɛ̃]
anchor chain	łańcuch (m) kotwicy	['waɲʦuh kɔt'fiʦɨ]

port (harbor)	port (m)	[pɔrt]
quay, wharf	nabrzeże (n)	[nab'ʒɛʒɛ]
to berth (moor)	cumować	[ʦu'mɔvatʃ]
to cast off	odbijać	[ɔd'bijatʃ]

trip, voyage	podróż (ż)	['pɔdruʃ]
cruise (sea trip)	podróż (ż) morska	['pɔdruʃ 'mɔrska]
course (route)	kurs (m)	[kurs]
route (itinerary)	trasa (ż)	['trasa]

fairway	tor (m) wodny	[tɔr 'vɔdnɨ]
shallows	mielizna (ż)	[me'lizna]
to run aground	osiąść na mieliźnie	['ɔɕɔ̃ɕtʃ na me'liʑne]

storm	sztorm (m)	[ʃtɔrm]
signal	sygnał (m)	['sɨgnaw]
to sink (vi)	tonąć	['tɔɔ̃ntʃ]
SOS (distress signal)	SOS	[ɛs ɔ ɛs]
ring buoy	koło (n) ratunkowe	['kɔwɔ ratu'ŋkɔvɛ]

T&P BOOKS

CITY

27. Urban transportation
28. City. Life in the city
29. Urban institutions
30. Signs
31. Shopping

T&P Books Publishing

27. Urban transportation

bus	**autobus** (m)	[au'tɔbus]
streetcar	**tramwaj** (m)	['tramvaj]
trolley bus	**trolejbus** (m)	[trɔ'lejbus]
route (of bus, etc.)	**trasa** (z)	['trasa]
number (e.g., bus ~)	**numer** (m)	['numɛr]
to go by ...	**jechać w ...**	['ehatʃ v]
to get on (~ the bus)	**wsiąść**	[fɕɔ̃ɕtʃ]
to get off ...	**zsiąść z ...**	[zɕɔ̃ɕtʃ z]
stop (e.g., bus ~)	**przystanek** (m)	[pʃis'tanɛk]
next stop	**następny przystanek** (m)	[nas'tɛ̃pnɨ pʃis'tanɛk]
terminus	**stacja** (z) **końcowa**	['statsʰja kɔɲ'tsɔva]
schedule	**rozkład** (m) **jazdy**	['rɔskwad 'jazdɨ]
to wait (vt)	**czekać**	['tʃɛkatʃ]
ticket	**bilet** (m)	['bilet]
fare	**cena** (z) **biletu**	['tsɛna bi'letu]
cashier (ticket seller)	**kasjer** (m), **kasjerka** (z)	['kasʰer], [kasʰ'erka]
ticket inspection	**kontrola** (z) **biletów**	[kɔnt'rɔʎa bi'letɔf]
ticket inspector	**kontroler** (m) **biletów**	[kɔnt'rɔler bi'letɔf]
to be late (for ...)	**spóźniać się**	['spuʑʲɲatʃ ɕɛ̃]
to miss (~ the train, etc.)	**spóźnić się**	['spuʑʲnitʃ ɕɛ̃]
to be in a hurry	**śpieszyć się**	['ɕpeʃɨtʃ ɕɛ̃]
taxi, cab	**taksówka** (z)	[tak'sufka]
taxi driver	**taksówkarz** (m)	[tak'sufkaʃ]
by taxi	**taksówką**	[tak'sufkɔ̃]
taxi stand	**postój** (m) **taksówek**	['pɔstuj tak'suvɛk]
to call a taxi	**wezwać taksówkę**	['vɛzvatʃ tak'sufkɛ̃]
to take a taxi	**wziąć taksówkę**	[vʑɔ̃tʃ tak'sufkɛ̃]
traffic	**ruch** (m) **uliczny**	[ruh u'litʃnɨ]
traffic jam	**korek** (m)	['kɔrɛk]
rush hour	**godziny** (l.mn.) **szczytu**	[gɔ'dʑinɨ 'ʃtʃɨtu]
to park (vi)	**parkować**	[par'kɔvatʃ]
to park (vt)	**parkować**	[par'kɔvatʃ]
parking lot	**parking** (m)	['parkiŋk]
subway	**metro** (n)	['mɛtrɔ]
station	**stacja** (z)	['statsʰja]
to take the subway	**jechać metrem**	['ehatʃ 'mɛtrɛm]

train	pociąg (m)	['pɔtɕɔ̃k]
train station	dworzec (m)	['dvɔʒɛts]

28. City. Life in the city

city, town	miasto (n)	['mʲastɔ]
capital city	stolica (z)	[stɔ'litsa]
village	wieś (z)	[veɕ]

city map	plan (m) miasta	[pʎan 'mʲasta]
downtown	centrum (n) miasta	['tsɛntrum 'mʲasta]
suburb	dzielnica (z) podmiejska	[dʒɛʎ'nitsa pɔd'mejska]
suburban (adj)	podmiejski	[pɔd'mejski]

outskirts	peryferie (l.mn.)	[pɛri'fɛrʰe]
environs (suburbs)	okolice (l.mn.)	[ɔkɔ'litsɛ]
city block	osiedle (n)	[ɔ'ɕedle]
residential block (area)	osiedle (n) mieszkaniowe	[ɔ'ɕedle meʃka'nɜvɛ]

traffic	ruch (m) uliczny	[ruh u'litʃnɨ]
traffic lights	światła (l.mn.)	['ɕfʲatwa]
public transportation	komunikacja (z) publiczna	[kɔmuni'katsʰja pub'litʃna]
intersection	skrzyżowanie (n)	[skʃɨʒɔ'vane]

crosswalk	przejście (n)	['pʃɛjɕtʃe]
pedestrian underpass	przejście (n) podziemne	['pʃɛjɕtʃe pɔ'dʒemnɛ]
to cross (~ the street)	przechodzić	[pʃɛ'hɔdʒitʃ]
pedestrian	pieszy (m)	['peʃɨ]
sidewalk	chodnik (m)	['hɔdnik]

bridge	most (m)	[mɔst]
embankment (river walk)	nadbrzeże (n)	[nadb'ʒɛʒɛ]
fountain	fontanna (z)	[fɔn'taŋa]

allée (garden walkway)	aleja (z)	[a'leja]
park	park (m)	[park]
boulevard	bulwar (m)	['buʎvar]
square	plac (m)	[pʎats]
avenue (wide street)	aleja (z)	[a'leja]
street	ulica (z)	[u'litsa]
side street	zaułek (m)	[za'uwɛk]
dead end	ślepa uliczka (z)	['ɕlepa u'litʃka]

house	dom (m)	[dɔm]
building	budynek (m)	[bu'dinɛk]
skyscraper	wieżowiec (m)	[ve'ʒɔvets]

facade	fasada (z)	[fa'sada]
roof	dach (m)	[dah]

window	okno (n)	['ɔknɔ]
arch	łuk (m)	[wuk]
column	kolumna (ż)	[kɔ'lymna]
corner	róg (m)	[ruk]

store window	witryna (ż)	[vit'rina]
signboard (store sign, etc.)	szyld (m)	[ʃiʎt]
poster	afisz (m)	['afiʃ]
advertising poster	plakat (m) reklamowy	['pʎakat rɛkʎa'mɔvɨ]
billboard	billboard (m)	['biʎbɔrt]

garbage, trash	śmiecie (l.mn.)	['ɕmetʃe]
trashcan (public ~)	kosz (m) na śmieci	[kɔʃ na 'ɕmetʃi]
to litter (vi)	śmiecić	['ɕmetʃitʃ]
garbage dump	wysypisko (n) śmieci	[vɨsipiskɔ 'ɕmetʃi]

phone booth	budka (ż) telefoniczna	['butka tɛlefɔ'nitʃna]
lamppost	słup (m) oświetleniowy	[swup ɔɕvetle'nɔvɨ]
bench (park ~)	ławka (ż)	['wafka]

police officer	policjant (m)	[pɔ'litsʰjant]
police	policja (ż)	[pɔ'litsʰja]
beggar	żebrak (m)	['ʒɛbrak]
homeless (n)	bezdomny (m)	[bɛz'dɔmnɨ]

29. Urban institutions

store	sklep (m)	[sklep]
drugstore, pharmacy	apteka (ż)	[ap'tɛka]
eyeglass store	optyk (m)	['ɔptik]
shopping mall	centrum (n) handlowe	['tsɛntrum hand'lɔvɛ]
supermarket	supermarket (m)	[supɛr'markɛt]

bakery	sklep (m) z pieczywem	[sklep s pet'ʃivɛm]
baker	piekarz (m)	['pekaʃ]
candy store	cukiernia (ż)	[tsu'kerɲa]
grocery store	sklep (m) spożywczy	[sklep spɔ'ʒivtʃi]
butcher shop	sklep (m) mięsny	[sklep 'mensnɨ]

| produce store | warzywniak (m) | [va'ʒivɲak] |
| market | targ (m) | [tark] |

coffee house	kawiarnia (ż)	[ka'vʲarɲa]
restaurant	restauracja (ż)	[rɛstau'ratsʰja]
pub, bar	piwiarnia (ż)	[pi'vʲarɲa]
pizzeria	pizzeria (ż)	[pi'tserʰja]

hair salon	salon (m) fryzjerski	['salɔn frizʰ'erski]
post office	poczta (ż)	['pɔtʃta]
dry cleaners	pralnia (ż) chemiczna	['praʎɲa hɛ'mitʃna]

photo studio	zakład (m) fotograficzny	['zakwat fɔtɔgra'fitʃni]
shoe store	sklep (m) obuwniczy	[sklep ɔbuv'nitʃi]
bookstore	księgarnia (z)	[kɕɛ̃'garɲa]
sporting goods store	sklep (m) sportowy	[sklep spɔr'tɔvi]

clothes repair shop	reperacja (z) odzieży	[rɛpɛ'ratsʰja ɔ'dʑeʒi]
formal wear rental	wypożyczanie (n) strojów okazjonalnych	[vipɔʒi'tʃane strɔ'juv ɔkazʲɔ'naʎnih]
video rental store	wypożyczalnia (z) filmów	[vipɔʒit'ʃaʎɲa 'fiʎmuf]

circus	cyrk (m)	[tsirk]
zoo	zoo (n)	['zɔ:]
movie theater	kino (n)	['kinɔ]
museum	muzeum (n)	[mu'zɛum]
library	biblioteka (z)	[biblʲɔ'tɛka]
theater	teatr (m)	['tɛatr]
opera (opera house)	opera (z)	['ɔpɛra]
nightclub	klub nocny (m)	[klyp 'nɔtsni]
casino	kasyno (n)	[ka'sinɔ]

mosque	meczet (m)	['mɛtʃɛt]
synagogue	synagoga (z)	[sina'gɔga]
cathedral	katedra (z)	[ka'tɛdra]
temple	świątynia (z)	[ɕfɔ̃'tiɲa]
church	kościół (m)	['kɔʃtʃow]

college	instytut (m)	[ins'titut]
university	uniwersytet (m)	[uni'vɛrsitɛt]
school	szkoła (z)	['ʃkɔwa]

prefecture	urząd (m) dzielnicowy	['uʒɔ̃d dʑeʎnitsɔvi]
city hall	urząd (m) miasta	['uʒɔ̃t 'mʲasta]
hotel	hotel (m)	['hɔtɛʎ]
bank	bank (m)	[baŋk]

embassy	ambasada (z)	[amba'sada]
travel agency	agencja (z) turystyczna	[a'gɛntsʰja turis'titʃna]
information office	informacja (z)	[infɔr'matsʰja]
currency exchange	kantor (m)	['kantɔr]

| subway | metro (n) | ['mɛtrɔ] |
| hospital | szpital (m) | ['ʃpitaʎ] |

| gas station | stacja (z) benzynowa | ['statsʰja bɛnzi'nɔva] |
| parking lot | parking (m) | ['parkiŋk] |

30. Signs

| signboard (store sign, etc.) | szyld (m) | [ʃiʎt] |
| notice (door sign, etc.) | napis (m) | ['napis] |

poster	plakat (m)	['pʎakat]
direction sign	drogowskaz (m)	[drɔ'gɔfskas]
arrow (sign)	strzałka (ż)	['stʃawka]

caution	ostrzeżenie (n)	[ɔstʃɛ'ʒɛne]
warning sign	przestroga (ż)	[pʃɛst'rɔga]
to warn (vt)	ostrzegać	[ɔst'ʃɛgatʃ]

rest day (weekly ~)	dzień (m) wolny	[dʒeɲ 'vɔʎnɨ]
timetable (schedule)	rozkład (m) jazdy	['rɔskwad 'jazdɨ]
opening hours	godziny (l.mn.) pracy	[gɔ'dʒinɨ 'pratsɨ]

WELCOME!	WITAMY!	[vi'tamɨ]
ENTRANCE	WEJŚCIE	['vɛjɕtʃe]
EXIT	WYJŚCIE	['vɨjɕtʃe]

PUSH	PCHAĆ	[phatʃ]
PULL	CIĄGNĄĆ	[tʃɔ̃gnɔɲtʃ]
OPEN	OTWARTE	[ɔt'fartɛ]
CLOSED	ZAMKNIĘTE	[zamk'nentɛ]

| WOMEN | DLA PAŃ | [dʎa paɲ] |
| MEN | DLA MĘŻCZYZN | [dʎa 'mɛ̃ʒtʃizn] |

| DISCOUNTS | ZNIŻKI | ['zniʃki] |
| SALE | WYPRZEDAŻ | [vɨp'ʃɛdaʃ] |

| NEW! | NOWOŚĆ! | ['nɔvɔɕtʃ] |
| FREE | GRATIS | ['gratis] |

ATTENTION!	UWAGA!	[u'vaga]
NO VACANCIES	BRAK MIEJSC	[brak mejsts]
RESERVED	REZERWACJA	[rɛzɛr'vatsʰja]

| ADMINISTRATION | ADMINISTRACJA | [administ'ratsʰja] |
| STAFF ONLY | WEJŚCIE SŁUŻBOWE | ['vɛjɕtʃe swuʒ'bɔvɛ] |

BEWARE OF THE DOG!	UWAGA! ZŁY PIES	[u'vaga zwɨ pes]
NO SMOKING	ZAKAZ PALENIA!	['zakas pa'leɲa]
DO NOT TOUCH!	NIE DOTYKAĆ!	[ne dɔ'tikatʃ]

DANGEROUS	NIEBEZPIECZNY	[nebɛs'petʃnɨ]
DANGER	NIEBEZPIECZEŃSTWO	[nebɛspetʃɛɲstfɔ]
HIGH VOLTAGE	WYSOKIE NAPIĘCIE	[vɨsɔke napɛ̃tʃe]

| NO SWIMMING! | KĄPIEL WZBRONIONA | [kɔmpeʎ vzbrɔnɔ̃a] |
| OUT OF ORDER | NIECZYNNE | [netʃiɲɛ] |

FLAMMABLE	ŁATWOPALNE	[vatvɔ'paʎnɛ]
FORBIDDEN	ZAKAZ	['zakas]
NO TRESPASSING!	ZAKAZ PRZEJŚCIA	['zakas 'pʃɛjɕtʃʲa]
WET PAINT	ŚWIEŻO MALOWANE	['ɕfeʒɔ malɜ'vanɛ]

31. Shopping

to buy (purchase)	kupować	[ku'povatʃ]
purchase	zakup (m)	['zakup]
to go shopping	robić zakupy	['robitʃ za'kupɨ]
shopping	zakupy (l.mn.)	[za'kupɨ]

to be open (ab. store)	być czynnym	[bɨtʃ 'tʃɨnɨm]
to be closed	być nieczynnym	[bɨtʃ net'ʃɨnɨm]

footwear, shoes	obuwie (n)	[ɔ'buve]
clothes, clothing	odzież (ż)	['ɔdʒeʃ]
cosmetics	kosmetyki (l.mn.)	[kɔs'mɛtɨki]
food products	artykuły (l.mn.) spożywcze	[artɨ'kuwɨ spɔ'ʒiftʃɛ]
gift, present	prezent (m)	['prɛzɛnt]

salesman	ekspedient (m)	[ɛks'pɛdʰent]
saleswoman	ekspedientka (ż)	[ɛkspedʰ'entka]

check out, cash desk	kasa (ż)	['kasa]
mirror	lustro (n)	['lystrɔ]
counter (store ~)	lada (ż)	['ʎada]
fitting room	przymierzalnia (ż)	[pʃime'ʒaʎɲa]

to try on	przymierzyć	[pʃi'meʒitʃ]
to fit (ab. dress, etc.)	pasować	[pa'sɔvatʃ]
to like (I like ...)	podobać się	[pɔ'dɔbatʃ ɕɛ̃]

price	cena (ż)	['tsɛna]
price tag	metka (ż)	['mɛtka]
to cost (vt)	kosztować	[kɔʃ'tɔvatʃ]
How much?	Ile kosztuje?	['ile kɔʃ'tue]
discount	zniżka (ż)	['zniʃka]

inexpensive (adj)	niedrogi	[ned'rɔgi]
cheap (adj)	tani	['tani]
expensive (adj)	drogi	['drɔgi]
It's expensive	To dużo kosztuje	[tɔ 'duʒɔ kɔʃ'tue]

rental (n)	wypożyczalnia (ż)	[vɨpɔʒit'ʃaʎɲa]
to rent (~ a tuxedo)	wypożyczyć	[vɨpɔ'ʒitʃitʃ]
credit (trade credit)	kredyt (m)	['krɛdɨt]
on credit (adv)	na kredyt	[na 'krɛdɨt]

T&P BOOKS

CLOTHING & ACCESSORIES

32. Outerwear. Coats
33. Men's & women's clothing
34. Clothing. Underwear
35. Headwear
36. Footwear
37. Personal accessories
38. Clothing. Miscellaneous
39. Personal care. Cosmetics
40. Watches. Clocks

T&P Books Publishing

32. Outerwear. Coats

clothes	odzież (ż)	['ɔdʒeʃ]
outerwear	wierzchnie okrycie (n)	['veʃhne ɔk'ritʃe]
winter clothing	odzież (ż) zimowa	['ɔdʒeʒ ʒi'mɔva]
coat (overcoat)	palto (n)	['paʎtɔ]
fur coat	futro (n)	['futrɔ]
fur jacket	futro (n) krótkie	['futrɔ 'krɔtkɛ]
down coat	kurtka (ż) puchowa	['kurtka pu'hɔva]
jacket (e.g., leather ~)	kurtka (ż)	['kurtka]
raincoat (trenchcoat, etc.)	płaszcz (m)	[pwaʃtʃ]
waterproof (adj)	nieprzemakalny	[nepʃɛma'kaʎni]

33. Men's & women's clothing

shirt (button shirt)	koszula (ż)	[kɔ'ʃuʎa]
pants	spodnie (l.mn.)	['spɔdne]
jeans	dżinsy (l.mn.)	['dʒinsi]
suit jacket	marynarka (ż)	[mari'narka]
suit	garnitur (m)	[gar'nitur]
dress (frock)	sukienka (ż)	[su'keŋka]
skirt	spódnica (ż)	[spud'nitsa]
blouse	bluzka (ż)	['blyska]
knitted jacket (cardigan, etc.)	sweterek (m)	[sfɛ'tɛrɛk]
jacket (of woman's suit)	żakiet (m)	['ʒaket]
T-shirt	koszulka (ż)	[kɔ'ʃuʎka]
shorts (short trousers)	spodenki (l.mn.)	[spɔ'dɛŋki]
tracksuit	dres (m)	[drɛs]
bathrobe	szlafrok (m)	['ʃʎafrɔk]
pajamas	pidżama (ż)	[pi'dʒama]
sweater	sweter (m)	['sfɛtɛr]
pullover	pulower (m)	[pu'lɔvɛr]
vest	kamizelka (ż)	[kami'zɛʎka]
tailcoat	frak (m)	[frak]
tuxedo	smoking (m)	['smɔkiŋk]
uniform	uniform (m)	[u'nifɔrm]
workwear	ubranie (n) robocze	[ub'rane rɔ'bɔtʃɛ]

| overalls | kombinezon (m) | [kɔmbi'nɛzɔn] |
| coat (e.g., doctor's smock) | kitel (m) | ['kitɛʎ] |

34. Clothing. Underwear

underwear	bielizna (ż)	[be'lizna]
undershirt (A-shirt)	podkoszulek (m)	[pɔtkɔ'ʃulek]
socks	skarpety (l.mn.)	[skar'pɛti]

nightgown	koszula (ż) nocna	[kɔ'ʃuʎa 'nɔtsna]
bra	biustonosz (m)	[bys'tɔnɔʃ]
knee highs	podkolanówki (l.mn.)	[pɔdkɔʎa'nufki]
(knee-high socks)		

pantyhose	rajstopy (l.mn.)	[rajs'tɔpi]
stockings (thigh highs)	pończochy (l.mn.)	[pɔnt'ʃɔhi]
bathing suit	kostium (m) kąpielowy	['kɔstʰjum kɔ̃pelɔvi]

35. Headwear

hat	czapka (ż)	['tʃapka]
fedora	kapelusz (m) fedora	[ka'pɛlyʃ fɛ'dɔra]
baseball cap	bejsbolówka (ż)	[bɛjsbɔ'lyfka]
flatcap	kaszkiet (m)	['kaʃket]

beret	beret (m)	['bɛrɛt]
hood	kaptur (m)	['kaptur]
panama hat	panama (ż)	[pa'nama]

| headscarf | chustka (ż) | ['hustka] |
| women's hat | kapelusik (m) | [kapɛ'lyɕik] |

hard hat	kask (m)	[kask]
garrison cap	furażerka (ż)	[fura'ʒɛrka]
helmet	hełm (m)	[hɛwm]

| derby | melonik (m) | [mɛ'lɔnik] |
| top hat | cylinder (m) | [tsi'lindɛr] |

36. Footwear

footwear	obuwie (n)	[ɔ'buve]
shoes (men's shoes)	buty (l.mn.)	['buti]
shoes (women's shoes)	pantofle (l.mn.)	[pan'tɔfle]
boots (cowboy ~)	kozaki (l.mn.)	[kɔ'zaki]
slippers	kapcie (l.mn.)	['kaptʃe]
tennis shoes (e.g., Nike ~)	adidasy (l.mn.)	[adi'dasi]

| sneakers (e.g., Converse ~) | tenisówki (l.mn.) | [tɛni'sufki] |
| sandals | sandały (l.mn.) | [san'dawɨ] |

cobbler (shoe repairer)	szewc (m)	[ʃɛfts]
heel	obcas (m)	['ɔbtsas]
pair (of shoes)	para (ż)	['para]

shoestring	sznurowadło (n)	[ʃnurɔ'vadwɔ]
to lace (vt)	sznurować	[ʃnu'rɔvatʃ]
shoehorn	łyżka (ż) do butów	['wɨʒka dɔ 'butuf]
shoe polish	pasta (ż) do butów	['pasta dɔ 'butuf]

37. Personal accessories

gloves	rękawiczki (l.mn.)	[rɛ̃ka'vitʃki]
mittens	rękawiczki (l.mn.)	[rɛ̃ka'vitʃki]
scarf (muffler)	szalik (m)	['ʃalik]

glasses (eyeglasses)	okulary (l.mn.)	[ɔku'ʎarɨ]
frame (eyeglass ~)	oprawka (ż)	[ɔp'rafka]
umbrella	parasol (m)	[pa'rasɔʎ]
walking stick	laska (ż)	['ʎaska]
hairbrush	szczotka (ż) do włosów	['ʃtʃotka dɔ 'vwɔsuv]
fan	wachlarz (m)	['vahʎaʃ]

tie (necktie)	krawat (m)	['kravat]
bow tie	muszka (ż)	['muʃka]
suspenders	szelki (l.mn.)	['ʃɛʎki]
handkerchief	chusteczka (ż) do nosa	[hus'tɛtʃka dɔ 'nɔsa]

comb	grzebień (m)	['gʒɛbeɲ]
barrette	spinka (ż)	['spiŋka]
hairpin	szpilka (ż)	['ʃpiʎka]
buckle	sprzączka (ż)	['spʃõtʃka]

| belt | pasek (m) | ['pasɛk] |
| shoulder strap | pasek (m) | ['pasɛk] |

bag (handbag)	torba (ż)	['tɔrba]
purse	torebka (ż)	[tɔ'rɛpka]
backpack	plecak (m)	['pletsak]

38. Clothing. Miscellaneous

fashion	moda (ż)	['mɔda]
in vogue (adj)	modny	['mɔdnɨ]
fashion designer	projektant (m) mody	[prɔ'ektant 'mɔdɨ]

collar	kołnierz (m)	['kɔwneʃ]
pocket	kieszeń (ż)	['keʃɛɲ]
pocket (as adj)	kieszonkowy	[keʃɔ'ŋkɔvɨ]
sleeve	rękaw (m)	['rɛŋkaf]
hanging loop	wieszak (m)	['veʃak]
fly (on trousers)	rozporek (m)	[rɔs'pɔrɛk]

zipper (fastener)	zamek (m) błyskawiczny	['zamɛk bwiska'vitʃnɨ]
fastener	zapięcie (m)	[za'pɛ̃tʃe]
button	guzik (m)	['guʒik]
buttonhole	dziurką (ż) na guzik	['dʒɨrka na gu'ʒik]
to come off (ab. button)	urwać się	['urvatʃ çɛ̃]

to sew (vi, vt)	szyć	[ʃitʃ]
to embroider (vi, vt)	haftować	[haf'tɔvatʃ]
embroidery	haft (m)	[haft]
sewing needle	igła (ż)	['igwa]
thread	nitka (ż)	['nitka]
seam	szew (m)	[ʃɛf]

to get dirty (vi)	wybrudzić się	[vɨb'rudʒitʃ çɛ̃]
stain (mark, spot)	plama (ż)	['pʎama]
to crease, crumple (vi)	zmiąć się	[zmɔ̃tʃ çɛ̃]
to tear, to rip (vt)	rozerwać	[rɔ'zɛrvatʃ]
clothes moth	mól (m)	[muʎ]

39. Personal care. Cosmetics

toothpaste	pasta (ż) do zębów	['pasta dɔ 'zɛ̃buf]
toothbrush	szczoteczka (ż) do zębów	[ʃtʃɔ'tɛtʃka dɔ 'zɛ̃buf]
to brush one's teeth	myć zęby	[mitʃ 'zɛ̃bɨ]

razor	maszynka (ż) do golenia	[ma'ʃiŋka dɔ gɔ'leɲa]
shaving cream	krem (m) do golenia	[krɛm dɔ gɔ'leɲa]
to shave (vi)	golić się	['gɔlitʃ çɛ̃]

| soap | mydło (n) | ['midwɔ] |
| shampoo | szampon (m) | ['ʃampɔn] |

scissors	nożyczki (l.mn.)	[nɔ'ʒitʃki]
nail file	pilnik (m) do paznokci	['piʎnik dɔ paz'nɔktʃi]
nail clippers	cążki (l.mn.) do paznokci	['tsɔ̃ʃki dɔ paz'nɔktʃi]
tweezers	pinceta (ż)	[pin'tsɛta]

cosmetics	kosmetyki (l.mn.)	[kɔs'mɛtɨki]
face mask	maseczka (ż)	[ma'sɛtʃka]
manicure	manikiur (m)	[ma'nikyr]
to have a manicure	robić manikiur	['rɔbitʃ ma'nikyr]
pedicure	pedikiur (m)	[pɛ'dikyr]
make-up bag	kosmetyczka (ż)	[kɔsmɛ'titʃka]

face powder	puder (m)	['pudɛr]
powder compact	puderniczka (ż)	[pudɛr'nitʃka]
blusher	róż (m)	[ruʃ]

perfume (bottled)	perfumy (l.mn.)	[pɛr'fumi]
toilet water (perfume)	woda (ż) toaletowa	['vɔda tɔale'tɔva]
lotion	płyn (m) kosmetyczny	[pwin kɔsmɛ'titʃni]
cologne	woda (ż) kolońska	['vɔda kɔ'lɔɲska]

eyeshadow	cienie (l.mn.) do powiek	['tʃene dɔ 'pɔvek]
eyeliner	kredka (ż) do oczu	['krɛtka dɔ 'ɔtʃu]
mascara	tusz (m) do rzęs	[tuʃ dɔ ʒɛ̃s]

lipstick	szminka (ż)	['ʃmiɲka]
nail polish, enamel	lakier (m) do paznokci	['ʎaker dɔ paz'nɔktʃi]
hair spray	lakier (m) do włosów	['ʎaker dɔ 'vwɔsuv]
deodorant	dezodorant (m)	[dɛzɔ'dɔrant]

cream	krem (m)	[krɛm]
face cream	krem (m) do twarzy	[krɛm dɔ 'tfaʒi]
hand cream	krem (m) do rąk	[krɛm dɔ rɔ̃k]
day (as adj)	na dzień	['na dʒeɲ]
night (as adj)	nocny	['nɔtsni]

tampon	tampon (m)	['tampɔn]
toilet paper	papier (m) toaletowy	['paper tɔale'tɔvi]
hair dryer	suszarka (ż) do włosów	[su'ʃarka dɔ 'vwɔsuv]

40. Watches. Clocks

watch (wristwatch)	zegarek (m)	[zɛ'garɛk]
dial	tarcza (ż) zegarowa	['tartʃa zɛga'rɔva]
hand (of clock, watch)	wskazówka (ż)	[fska'zɔfka]
metal watch band	bransoleta (ż)	[bransɔ'leta]
watch strap	pasek (m)	['pasɛk]

battery	bateria (ż)	[ba'tɛrʲja]
to be dead (battery)	wyczerpać się	[vit'ʃɛrpatʃ ɕɛ̃]
to change a battery	wymienić baterię	[vi'menitʃ ba'tɛrʲɛ̃]
to run fast	śpieszyć się	['ɕpeʃitʃ ɕɛ̃]
to run slow	spóźnić się	['spuʑnitʃ ɕɛ̃]

wall clock	zegar (m) ścienny	['zɛgar 'ɕtʃeɲi]
hourglass	klepsydra (ż)	[klɛp'sidra]
sundial	zegar (m) słoneczny	['zɛgar swɔ'nɛtʃni]
alarm clock	budzik (m)	['budʑik]
watchmaker	zegarmistrz (m)	[zɛ'garmistʃ]
to repair (vt)	naprawiać	[nap'ravʲatʃ]

T&P BOOKS

EVERYDAY EXPERIENCE

41. Money
42. Post. Postal service
43. Banking
44. Telephone. Phone conversation
45. Mobile telephone
46. Stationery
47. Foreign languages

T&P Books Publishing

money	**pieniądze** (l.mn.)	[pɛnɔ̃dzɛ]
currency exchange	**wymiana** (ż)	[viˈmʲana]
exchange rate	**kurs** (m)	[kurs]
ATM	**bankomat** (m)	[baˈŋkɔmat]
coin	**moneta** (ż)	[mɔˈnɛta]
dollar	**dolar** (m)	[ˈdɔʎar]
euro	**euro** (m)	[ˈɛurɔ]
lira	**lir** (m)	[lir]
Deutschmark	**marka** (ż)	[ˈmarka]
franc	**frank** (m)	[fraŋk]
pound sterling	**funt szterling** (m)	[funt ˈʃtɛrliŋk]
yen	**jen** (m)	[en]
debt	**dług** (m)	[dwuk]
debtor	**dłużnik** (m)	[ˈdwuʒnik]
to lend (money)	**pożyczyć**	[pɔˈʒɨtʃitʃ]
to borrow (vi, vt)	**pożyczyć od ...**	[pɔˈʒɨtʃitʃ ɔt]
bank	**bank** (m)	[baŋk]
account	**konto** (n)	[ˈkɔntɔ]
to deposit into the account	**wpłacić na konto**	[ˈvpwatʃitʃ na ˈkɔntɔ]
to withdraw (vt)	**podjąć z konta**	[ˈpɔdʰɔ̃tʃ s ˈkɔnta]
credit card	**karta** (ż) **kredytowa**	[ˈkarta krɛdiˈtɔva]
cash	**gotówka** (ż)	[gɔˈtufka]
check	**czek** (m)	[tʃɛk]
to write a check	**wystawić czek**	[visˈtavitʃ tʃɛk]
checkbook	**książeczka** (ż) **czekowa**	[kɕɔ̃ˈʒɛtʃka tʃɛˈkɔva]
wallet	**portfel** (m)	[ˈpɔrtfɛʎ]
change purse	**portmonetka** (ż)	[pɔrtmɔˈnɛtka]
billfold	**portmonetka** (ż)	[pɔrtmɔˈnɛtka]
safe	**sejf** (m)	[sɛjf]
heir	**spadkobierca** (m)	[spatkɔˈbertsa]
inheritance	**spadek** (m)	[ˈspadɛk]
fortune (wealth)	**majątek** (m)	[maɔ̃tɛk]
lease	**dzierżawa** (ż)	[dʑerˈʒava]
rent (money)	**czynsz** (m)	[tʃinʃ]
to rent (sth from sb)	**wynajmować**	[vinajˈmɔvatʃ]
price	**cena** (ż)	[ˈʦɛna]

| cost | wartość (ż) | ['vartɔçtʃ] |
| sum | suma (ż) | ['suma] |

to spend (vt)	wydawać	[vi'davatʃ]
expenses	wydatki (l.mn.)	[vi'datki]
to economize (vi, vt)	oszczędzać	[ɔʃt'ʃɛndzatʃ]
economical	ekonomiczny	[ɛkɔnɔ'mitʃni]

to pay (vi, vt)	płacić	['pwatʃitʃ]
payment	opłata (ż)	[ɔp'wata]
change (give the ~)	reszta (ż)	['rɛʃta]

tax	podatek (m)	[pɔ'datɛk]
fine	kara (ż)	['kara]
to fine (vt)	karać grzywną	['karatʃ 'gʒivnɔ̃]

42. Post. Postal service

post office	poczta (ż)	['pɔtʃta]
mail (letters, etc.)	poczta (ż)	['pɔtʃta]
mailman	listonosz (m)	[lis'tɔnɔʃ]
opening hours	godziny (l.mn.) pracy	[gɔ'dʒini 'pratsi]

letter	list (m)	[list]
registered letter	list (m) polecony	[list pɔle'tsɔni]
postcard	pocztówka (ż)	[pɔtʃ'tufka]
telegram	telegram (m)	[tɛ'legram]
package (parcel)	paczka (ż)	['patʃka]
money transfer	przekaz (m) pieniężny	['pʃɛkas pe'nenʒni]

to receive (vt)	odebrać	[ɔ'dɛbratʃ]
to send (vt)	wysłać	['viswatʃ]
sending	wysłanie (n)	[vis'wane]
address	adres (m)	['adrɛs]
ZIP code	kod (m) pocztowy	[kɔt pɔtʃ'tɔvi]
sender	nadawca (m)	[na'daftsa]
receiver	odbiorca (m)	[ɔd'bɜrtsa]

| name (first name) | imię (n) | ['imɛ̃] |
| surname (last name) | nazwisko (n) | [naz'viskɔ] |

postage rate	taryfa (ż)	[ta'rifa]
standard (adj)	zwykła	['zvikwa]
economical (adj)	oszczędna	[ɔʃt'ʃɛndna]

weight	ciężar (m)	['tʃenʒar]
to weigh (~ letters)	ważyć	['vaʒitʃ]
envelope	koperta (ż)	[kɔ'pɛrta]
postage stamp	znaczek (m)	['znatʃɛk]
to stamp an envelope	naklejać znaczek	[nak'lejatʃ 'znatʃɛk]

43. Banking

| bank | bank (m) | [baŋk] |
| branch (of bank, etc.) | filia (ż) | ['fiʎja] |

| bank clerk, consultant | konsultant (m) | [kɔn'suʎtant] |
| manager (director) | kierownik (m) | [ke'rɔvnik] |

bank account	konto (n)	['kɔntɔ]
account number	numer (m) konta	['numɛr 'kɔnta]
checking account	rachunek (m) bieżący	[ra'hunɛk be'ʒɔ̃tsi]
savings account	rachunek (m) oszczędnościowy	[ra'hunɛk ɔʃtʃɛ̃dnɔɕ'tʃɔvi]

to open an account	założyć konto	[za'wɔʒitʃ 'kɔntɔ]
to close the account	zamknąć konto	['zamknɔ̃tʃ 'kɔ̃tɔ]
to deposit into the account	wpłacić na konto	['vpwatʃitʃ na 'kɔntɔ]
to withdraw (vt)	podjąć z konta	['pɔdʰɔ̃tʃ s 'kɔnta]

deposit	wkład (m)	[fkwat]
to make a deposit	dokonać wpłaty	[dɔ'kɔnatʃ 'fpwati]
wire transfer	przelew (m)	['pʃɛlev]
to wire, to transfer	dokonać przelewu	[dɔ'kɔnatʃ pʃɛ'levu]
sum	suma (ż)	['suma]
How much?	Ile?	['ile]

| signature | podpis (m) | ['pɔdpis] |
| to sign (vt) | podpisać | [pɔd'pisatʃ] |

credit card	karta (ż) kredytowa	['karta krɛdi'tɔva]
code (PIN code)	kod (m)	[kɔd]
credit card number	numer (m) karty kredytowej	['numɛr 'karti krɛdi'tɔvɛj]
ATM	bankomat (m)	[ba'ŋkɔmat]

check	czek (m)	[tʃɛk]
to write a check	wystawić czek	[vis'tavitʃ tʃɛk]
checkbook	książeczka (ż) czekowa	[kɕɔ̃'ʒɛtʃka tʃɛ'kɔva]

loan (bank ~)	kredyt (m)	['krɛdit]
to apply for a loan	wystąpić o kredyt	[vis'tɔ̃pitʃ ɔ 'krɛdit]
to get a loan	brać kredyt	[bratʃ 'krɛdit]
to give a loan	udzielać kredytu	[u'dʑeʎatʃ krɛ'ditu]
guarantee	gwarancja (ż)	[gva'rantsʰja]

44. Telephone. Phone conversation

| telephone | telefon (m) | [tɛ'lefɔn] |
| mobile phone | telefon (m) komórkowy | [tɛ'lefɔn kɔmur'kɔvi] |

answering machine	sekretarka (ż)	[sɛkrɛ'tarka]
to call (by phone)	dzwonić	['dzvɔniʧ]
phone call	telefon (m)	[tɛ'lefɔn]

to dial a number	wybrać numer	['vɨbraʧ 'numɛr]
Hello!	Halo!	['halɔ]
to ask (vt)	zapytać	[za'pɨtaʧ]
to answer (vi, vt)	odpowiedzieć	[ɔtpɔ'vedʑeʧ]

to hear (vt)	słyszeć	['swɨʃɛʧ]
well (adv)	dobrze	['dɔbʒɛ]
not well (adv)	źle	[ʑle]
noises (interference)	zakłócenia (l.mn.)	[zakwu'ʦɛɲa]

receiver	słuchawka (ż)	[swu'hafka]
to pick up (~ the phone)	podnieść słuchawkę	['pɔdneɕʧ swu'hafkɛ̃]
to hang up (~ the phone)	odłożyć słuchawkę	[ɔd'wɔʒɨʧ swu'hafkɛ̃]

busy (adj)	zajęty	[za'entɨ]
to ring (ab. phone)	dzwonić	['dzvɔniʧ]
telephone book	książka (ż) telefoniczna	[kɕɔ̃ʃka tɛlefɔ'niʧna]

local (adj)	miejscowy	[mejs'tsɔvɨ]
long distance (~ call)	międzymiastowy	[mɛ̃dʑɨmʲas'tɔvɨ]
international (adj)	międzynarodowy	[mɛ̃dʑɨnarɔ'dɔvɨ]

45. Mobile telephone

mobile phone	telefon (m) komórkowy	[tɛ'lefɔn kɔmur'kɔvɨ]
display	wyświetlacz (m)	[vɨɕ'fetʌaʧ]
button	klawisz (m)	['kʌaviʃ]
SIM card	karta (ż) SIM	['karta sim]

battery	bateria (ż)	[ba'tɛrʰja]
to be dead (battery)	rozładować się	[rɔzwa'dɔvaʧ ɕɛ̃]
charger	ładowarka (ż)	[wadɔ'varka]

menu	menu (n)	['menu]
settings	ustawienia (l.mn.)	[usta'veɲa]
tune (melody)	melodia (ż)	[mɛ'lɔdʰja]
to select (vt)	wybrać	['vɨbraʧ]

| calculator | kalkulator (m) | [kaʌku'ʌatɔr] |
| voice mail | sekretarka (ż) | [sɛkrɛ'tarka] |

| alarm clock | budzik (m) | ['budʑik] |
| contacts | kontakty (l.mn.) | [kɔn'taktɨ] |

| SMS (text message) | SMS (m) | [ɛs ɛm ɛs] |
| subscriber | abonent (m) | [a'bɔnɛnt] |

46. Stationery

| ballpoint pen | długopis (m) | [dwu'gɔpis] |
| fountain pen | pióro (n) | ['pyrɔ] |

pencil	ołówek (m)	[ɔ'wuvɛk]
highlighter	marker (m)	['markɛr]
felt-tip pen	flamaster (m)	[fʎa'mastɛr]

| notepad | notes (m) | ['nɔtɛs] |
| agenda (diary) | kalendarz (m) | [ka'lendaʃ] |

ruler	linijka (ż)	[li'nijka]
calculator	kalkulator (m)	[kaʎku'ʎatɔr]
eraser	gumka (ż)	['gumka]
thumbtack	pinezka (ż)	[pi'nɛska]
paper clip	spinacz (m)	['spinatʃ]

glue	klej (m)	[klej]
stapler	zszywacz (m)	['sʃivatʃ]
hole punch	dziurkacz (m)	['dʒyrkatʃ]
pencil sharpener	temperówka (ż)	[tɛmpɛ'rufka]

47. Foreign languages

language	język (m)	['enzɨk]
foreign language	obcy język (m)	['ɔbtsɨ 'enzɨk]
to study (vt)	studiować	[studʰɔvatʃ]
to learn (language, etc.)	uczyć się	['utʃitʃ ɕɛ̃]

to read (vi, vt)	czytać	['tʃitatʃ]
to speak (vi, vt)	mówić	['muvitʃ]
to understand (vt)	rozumieć	[rɔ'zumetʃ]
to write (vt)	pisać	['pisatʃ]

fast (adv)	szybko	['ʃipkɔ]
slowly (adv)	wolno	['vɔʎnɔ]
fluently (adv)	swobodnie	[sfɔ'bɔdne]

rules	reguły (l.mn.)	[rɛ'guwɨ]
grammar	gramatyka (ż)	[gra'matika]
vocabulary	słownictwo (n)	[swɔv'nitstfɔ]
phonetics	fonetyka (ż)	[fɔ'nɛtika]

textbook	podręcznik (m)	[pɔd'rɛntʃnik]
dictionary	słownik (m)	['swɔvnik]
teach-yourself book	samouczek (m)	[samɔ'utʃɛk]
phrasebook	rozmówki (l.mn.)	[rɔz'mufki]
cassette	kaseta (ż)	[ka'sɛta]

videotape	kaseta (ż) wideo	[ka'sɛta vi'dɛɔ]
CD, compact disc	płyta CD (ż)	['pwita si'di]
DVD	płyta DVD (ż)	['pwita divi'di]

alphabet	alfabet (m)	[aʎ'fabɛt]
to spell (vt)	przeliterować	[pʃɛlite'rɔvatʃ]
pronunciation	wymowa (ż)	[vi'mɔva]

accent	akcent (m)	['aktsɛnt]
with an accent	z akcentem	[z ak'tsɛntɛm]
without an accent	bez akcentu	[bɛz ak'tsɛntu]

| word | wyraz (m), słowo (n) | ['viras], ['svɔvɔ] |
| meaning | znaczenie (n) | [zna'tʃɛnie] |

course (e.g., a French ~)	kurs (m)	[kurs]
to sign up	zapisać się	[za'pisatʃ ɕɛ̃]
teacher	wykładowca (m)	[vikwa'dɔftsa]

translation (process)	tłumaczenie (n)	[twumat'ʃɛne]
translation (text, etc.)	przekład (m)	['pʃɛkwat]
translator	tłumacz (m)	['twumatʃ]
interpreter	tłumacz (m)	['twumatʃ]

| polyglot | poliglota (m) | [pɔlig'lɔta] |
| memory | pamięć (ż) | ['pamɛ̃tʃ] |

T&P BOOKS

MEALS. RESTAURANT

48. Table setting
49. Restaurant
50. Meals
51. Cooked dishes
52. Food
53. Drinks
54. Vegetables
55. Fruits. Nuts
56. Bread. Candy
57. Spices

T&P Books Publishing

48. Table setting

spoon	łyżka (ż)	['wiʃka]
knife	nóż (m)	[nuʃ]
fork	widelec (m)	[vi'dɛlɛʦ]
cup (e.g., coffee ~)	filiżanka (ż)	[fili'ʒaŋka]
plate (dinner ~)	talerz (m)	['talɛʃ]
saucer	spodek (m)	['spɔdɛk]
napkin (on table)	serwetka (ż)	[sɛr'vɛtka]
toothpick	wykałaczka (ż)	[vika'watʃka]

49. Restaurant

restaurant	restauracja (ż)	[rɛstau'ratsʰja]
coffee house	kawiarnia (ż)	[ka'vʲarɲa]
pub, bar	bar (m)	[bar]
tearoom	herbaciarnia (ż)	[hɛrba'tʃʲarɲa]

waiter	kelner (m)	['kɛʎnɛr]
waitress	kelnerka (ż)	[kɛʎ'nɛrka]
bartender	barman (m)	['barman]
menu	menu (n)	['menu]
wine list	karta (ż) win	['karta vin]
to book a table	zarezerwować stolik	[zarɛzɛrvɔvatʃ 'stɔlik]

course, dish	danie (n)	['dane]
to order (meal)	zamówić	[za'muvitʃ]
to make an order	zamówić	[za'muvitʃ]

aperitif	aperitif (m)	[apɛri'tif]
appetizer	przystawka (ż)	[pʃis'tafka]
dessert	deser (m)	['dɛsɛr]

check	rachunek (m)	[ra'hunɛk]
to pay the check	zapłacić rachunek	[zap'watʃitʃ ra'hunɛk]
to give change	wydać resztę	['vidatʃ 'rɛʃtɛ̃]
tip	napiwek (m)	[na'pivɛk]

50. Meals

food	jedzenie (n)	[e'dzɛne]
to eat (vi, vt)	jeść	[eʨ]

breakfast	śniadanie (n)	[ɕɲa'dane]
to have breakfast	jeść śniadanie	[eɕtʃ ɕɲa'dane]
lunch	obiad (m)	['ɔbʲat]
to have lunch	jeść obiad	[eɕtʃ 'ɔbʲat]
dinner	kolacja (ż)	[kɔ'ʎatsʰja]
to have dinner	jeść kolację	[eɕtʃ kɔ'ʎatsʰɛ̃]

| appetite | apetyt (m) | [a'pɛtit] |
| Enjoy your meal! | Smacznego! | [smatʃ'nɛgɔ] |

to open (~ a bottle)	otwierać	[ɔt'feratʃ]
to spill (liquid)	rozlać	['rɔzʎatʃ]
to spill out (vi)	rozlać się	['rɔzʎatʃ ɕɛ̃]

to boil (vi)	gotować się	[gɔ'tɔvatʃ ɕɛ̃]
to boil (vt)	gotować	[gɔ'tɔvatʃ]
boiled (~ water)	gotowany	[gɔtɔ'vani]
to chill, cool down (vt)	ostudzić	[ɔs'tudʒitʃ]
to chill (vi)	stygnąć	['stignɔ̃tʃ]

| taste, flavor | smak (m) | [smak] |
| aftertaste | posmak (m) | ['pɔsmak] |

to slim down (lose weight)	odchudzać się	[ɔd'hudzatʃ ɕɛ̃]
diet	dieta (ż)	['dʰeta]
vitamin	witamina (ż)	[vita'mina]
calorie	kaloria (ż)	[ka'lɔrja]
vegetarian (n)	wegetarianin (m)	[vɛgɛtarʰ'janin]
vegetarian (adj)	wegetariański	[vɛgɛtarʰ'jaɲski]

fats (nutrient)	tłuszcze (l.mn.)	['twuʃtʃɛ]
proteins	białka (l.mn.)	['bʲawka]
carbohydrates	węglowodany (l.mn.)	[vɛnɛ̃ɜvɔ'danɨ]
slice (of lemon, ham)	plasterek (m)	[pʎas'tɛrɛk]
piece (of cake, pie)	kawałek (m)	[ka'vawɛk]
crumb (of bread, cake, etc.)	okruchek (m)	[ɔk'ruhɛk]

51. Cooked dishes

course, dish	danie (n)	['dane]
cuisine	kuchnia (ż)	['kuhɲa]
recipe	przepis (m)	['pʃɛpis]
portion	porcja (ż)	['pɔrtsʰja]

| salad | sałatka (ż) | [sa'watka] |
| soup | zupa (ż) | ['zupa] |

| clear soup (broth) | rosół (m) | ['rɔsuw] |
| sandwich (bread) | kanapka (ż) | [ka'napka] |

fried eggs	jajecznica (ż)	[jaetʃˈniʦa]
fried meatballs	kotlet (m)	[ˈkɔtlɛt]
hamburger (beefburger)	hamburger (m)	[hamˈburgɛr]
beefsteak	befsztyk (m)	[ˈbɛfʃtik]
stew	pieczeń (ż)	[ˈpetʃɛɲ]

side dish	dodatki (l.mn.)	[dɔˈdatki]
spaghetti	spaghetti (n)	[spaˈgɛtti]
pizza	pizza (ż)	[ˈpiʦa]
porridge (oatmeal, etc.)	kasza (ż)	[ˈkaʃa]
omelet	omlet (m)	[ˈɔmlɛt]

boiled (e.g., ~ beef)	gotowany	[gɔtɔˈvani]
smoked (adj)	wędzony	[vɛ̃ˈʣɔni]
fried (adj)	smażony	[smaˈʒɔni]
dried (adj)	suszony	[suˈʃɔni]
frozen (adj)	mrożony	[mrɔˈʒɔni]
pickled (adj)	marynowany	[marinɔˈvani]

sweet (sugary)	słodki	[ˈswɔtki]
salty (adj)	słony	[ˈswɔni]
cold (adj)	zimny	[ˈʒimni]
hot (adj)	gorący	[gɔˈrɔ̃ʦi]
bitter (adj)	gorzki	[ˈgɔʃki]
tasty (adj)	smaczny	[ˈsmatʃni]

to cook in boiling water	gotować	[gɔˈtɔvatʃ]
to cook (dinner)	gotować	[gɔˈtɔvatʃ]
to fry (vt)	smażyć	[ˈsmaʒitʃ]
to heat up (food)	odgrzewać	[ɔdgˈʒɛvatʃ]

to salt (vt)	solić	[ˈsɔlitʃ]
to pepper (vt)	pieprzyć	[ˈpepʃitʃ]
to grate (vt)	trzeć	[tʃɛtʃ]
peel (n)	skórka (ż)	[ˈskurka]
to peel (vt)	obierać	[ɔˈberatʃ]

52. Food

meat	mięso (n)	[ˈmensɔ]
chicken	kurczak (m)	[ˈkurtʃak]
Rock Cornish hen (poussin)	kurczak (m)	[ˈkurtʃak]

duck	kaczka (ż)	[ˈkatʃka]
goose	gęś (ż)	[gɛ̃ɕ]
game	dziczyzna (ż)	[ʣitʃˈizna]
turkey	indyk (m)	[ˈindik]

| pork | wieprzowina (ż) | [vepʃɔˈvina] |
| veal | cielęcina (ż) | [tʃelɛ̃ˈtʃina] |

lamb	baranina (ż)	[bara'nina]
beef	wołowina (ż)	[vɔwɔ'vina]
rabbit	królik (m)	['krulik]

sausage (bologna, pepperoni, etc.)	kiełbasa (ż)	[kew'basa]
vienna sausage (frankfurter)	parówka (ż)	[pa'rufka]
bacon	boczek (m)	['bɔtʃɛk]
ham	szynka (ż)	['ʃiŋka]
gammon	szynka (ż)	['ʃiŋka]

pâté	pasztet (m)	['paʃtɛt]
liver	wątróbka (ż)	[vɔ̃t'rupka]
lard	smalec (m)	['smaleʦ]
hamburger (ground beef)	farsz (m)	[farʃ]
tongue	ozór (m)	['ɔzur]

egg	jajko (n)	['jajkɔ]
eggs	jajka (l.mn.)	['jajka]
egg white	białko (n)	['bʲawkɔ]
egg yolk	żółtko (n)	['ʒuwtkɔ]

fish	ryba (ż)	['riba]
seafood	owoce (l.mn.) morza	[ɔ'vɔʦɛ 'mɔʒa]
caviar	kawior (m)	['kavɜr]

crab	krab (m)	[krap]
shrimp	krewetka (ż)	[krɛ'vɛtka]
oyster	ostryga (ż)	[ɔst'riga]
spiny lobster	langusta (ż)	[ʎa'ŋusta]
octopus	ośmiornica (ż)	[ɔɕmɜr'niʦa]
squid	kałamarnica (ż)	[kawamar'niʦa]

sturgeon	mięso (n) jesiotra	['mensɔ e'ɕɔtra]
salmon	łosoś (m)	['wɔsɔɕ]
halibut	halibut (m)	[ha'libut]

cod	dorsz (m)	[dɔrʃ]
mackerel	makrela (ż)	[mak'rɛla]
tuna	tuńczyk (m)	['tuɲtʃik]
eel	węgorz (m)	['vɛŋɔʃ]

trout	pstrąg (m)	[pstrɔ̃k]
sardine	sardynka (ż)	[sar'diŋka]
pike	szczupak (m)	['ʃtʃupak]
herring	śledź (m)	[ɕletɕ]

bread	chleb (m)	[hlep]
cheese	ser (m)	[sɛr]
sugar	cukier (m)	['ʦuker]
salt	sól (ż)	[suʎ]

rice	ryż (m)	[riʃ]
pasta	makaron (m)	[maˈkarɔn]
noodles	makaron (m)	[maˈkarɔn]

butter	masło (n) śmietankowe	[ˈmaswɔ ɕmetaˈŋkɔvɛ]
vegetable oil	olej (m) roślinny	[ˈɔlej rɔɕliɲi]
sunflower oil	olej (m) słonecznikowy	[ˈɔlej swɔnɛtʃnikɔvi]
margarine	margaryna (z)	[margaˈrina]

| olives | oliwki (ż, l.mn.) | [ɔˈlifki] |
| olive oil | olej (m) oliwkowy | [ˈɔlej ɔlifˈkɔvi] |

milk	mleko (n)	[ˈmlekɔ]
condensed milk	mleko skondensowane	[ˈmlekɔ skɔndɛnsɔˈvanɛ]
yogurt	jogurt (m)	[ʒgurt]
sour cream	śmietana (z)	[ɕmeˈtana]
cream (of milk)	śmietanka (z)	[ɕmeˈtaŋka]

| mayonnaise | majonez (m) | [maʒnɛs] |
| buttercream | krem (m) | [krɛm] |

cereal grains (wheat, etc.)	kasza (ż)	[ˈkaʃa]
flour	mąka (z)	[ˈmõka]
canned food	konserwy (l.mn.)	[kɔnˈsɛrvi]

cornflakes	płatki (l.mn.) kukurydziane	[ˈpwatki kukuriˈdʒˈanɛ]
honey	miód (m)	[myt]
jam	dżem (m)	[dʒɛm]
chewing gum	guma (z) do żucia	[ˈguma dɔ ˈʒutʃˈa]

53. Drinks

water	woda (ż)	[ˈvɔda]
drinking water	woda (ż) pitna	[ˈvɔda ˈpitna]
mineral water	woda (ż) mineralna	[ˈvɔda minɛˈraʎna]

still (adj)	niegazowana	[negaˈzɔvana]
carbonated (adj)	gazowana	[gaˈzɔvana]
sparkling (adj)	gazowana	[gaˈzɔvana]
ice	lód (m)	[lyt]
with ice	z lodem	[z ˈlɜdɛm]

non-alcoholic (adj)	bezalkoholowy	[bɛzaʎkɔhɔˈlɜvi]
soft drink	napój (m) bezalkoholowy	[ˈnapuj bɛzalkɔhɔˈlɜvi]
refreshing drink	napój (m) orzeźwiający	[ˈnapuj ɔʒɛzˈvjaɔ̃tsi]
lemonade	lemoniada (z)	[lemɔˈɲjada]

liquors	napoje (l.mn.) alkoholowe	[naˈpɔe aʎkɔhɔˈlɜvɛ]
wine	wino (n)	[ˈvinɔ]
white wine	białe wino (n)	[ˈbˈawɛ ˈvinɔ]

red wine	czerwone wino (n)	[tʃɛr'vɔnɛ 'vinɔ]
liqueur	likier (m)	['liker]
champagne	szampan (m)	['ʃampan]
vermouth	wermut (m)	['vɛrmut]

whisky	whisky (ż)	[u'iski]
vodka	wódka (ż)	['vutka]
gin	dżin (m), gin (m)	[dʒin]
cognac	koniak (m)	['kɔɲjak]
rum	rum (m)	[rum]

coffee	kawa (ż)	['kava]
black coffee	czarna kawa (ż)	['tʃarna 'kava]
coffee with milk	kawa (ż) z mlekiem	['kava z 'mlekem]
cappuccino	cappuccino (n)	[kapu'tʃinɔ]
instant coffee	kawa (ż) rozpuszczalna	['kava rɔspuʃt'ʃaʎna]

milk	mleko (n)	['mlekɔ]
cocktail	koktajl (m)	['kɔktajʎ]
milkshake	koktajl (m) mleczny	['kɔktajʎ 'mletʃni]

juice	sok (m)	[sɔk]
tomato juice	sok (m) pomidorowy	[sɔk pɔmidɔ'rɔvi]
orange juice	sok (m) pomarańczowy	[sɔk pɔmaraɲt'ʃɔvi]
freshly squeezed juice	sok (m) ze świeżych owoców	[sɔk zɛ 'ɕfeʒih ɔ'vɔʦuf]

beer	piwo (n)	['pivɔ]
light beer	piwo (n) jasne	[pivɔ 'jasnɛ]
dark beer	piwo (n) ciemne	[pivɔ 'ʨemnɛ]

tea	herbata (ż)	[hɛr'bata]
black tea	czarna herbata (ż)	['tʃarna hɛr'bata]
green tea	zielona herbata (ż)	[ʒe'lɔna hɛr'bata]

54. Vegetables

| vegetables | warzywa (l.mn.) | [va'ʒiva] |
| greens | włoszczyzna (ż) | [vwɔʃt'ʃizna] |

tomato	pomidor (m)	[pɔ'midɔr]
cucumber	ogórek (m)	[ɔ'gurɛk]
carrot	marchew (ż)	['marhɛf]
potato	ziemniak (m)	[ʒem'ɲak]
onion	cebula (ż)	[ʦɛ'buʎa]
garlic	czosnek (m)	['tʃɔsnɛk]

cabbage	kapusta (ż)	[ka'pusta]
cauliflower	kalafior (m)	[ka'ʎafɜr]
Brussels sprouts	brukselka (ż)	[bruk'sɛʎka]

broccoli	brokuły (l.mn.)	[brɔ'kuwɨ]
beetroot	burak (m)	['burak]
eggplant	bakłażan (m)	[bak'waʒan]
zucchini	kabaczek (m)	[ka'batʃɛk]
pumpkin	dynia (ż)	['dɨɲa]
turnip	rzepa (ż)	['ʒɛpa]

parsley	pietruszka (ż)	[pet'ruʃka]
dill	koperek (m)	[kɔ'pɛrɛk]
lettuce	sałata (ż)	[sa'wata]
celery	seler (m)	['sɛler]
asparagus	szparagi (l.mn.)	[ʃpa'ragi]
spinach	szpinak (m)	['ʃpinak]

pea	groch (m)	[grɔh]
beans	bób (m)	[bup]
corn (maize)	kukurydza (ż)	[kuku'ridza]
kidney bean	fasola (ż)	[fa'sɔʎa]

bell pepper	słodka papryka (ż)	['swɔdka pap'rɨka]
radish	rzodkiewka (ż)	[ʒɔt'kefka]
artichoke	karczoch (m)	['kartʃɔh]

55. Fruits. Nuts

fruit	owoc (m)	['ɔvɔts]
apple	jabłko (n)	['jabkɔ]
pear	gruszka (ż)	['gruʃka]
lemon	cytryna (ż)	[tsɨt'rɨna]
orange	pomarańcza (ż)	[poma'raɲtʃa]
strawberry	truskawka (ż)	[trus'kafka]

mandarin	mandarynka (ż)	[manda'riŋka]
plum	śliwka (ż)	['ɕlifka]
peach	brzoskwinia (ż)	[bʒɔsk'fiɲa]
apricot	morela (ż)	[mɔ'rɛʎa]
raspberry	malina (ż)	[ma'lina]
pineapple	ananas (m)	[a'nanas]

banana	banan (m)	['banan]
watermelon	arbuz (m)	['arbus]
grape	winogrona (l.mn.)	[vinɔg'rɔna]
sour cherry	wiśnia (ż)	['viɕɲa]
sweet cherry	czereśnia (ż)	[tʃɛ'rɛɕɲa]
melon	melon (m)	['mɛlɔn]

grapefruit	grejpfrut (m)	['grɛjpfrut]
avocado	awokado (n)	[avɔ'kadɔ]
papaya	papaja (ż)	[pa'paja]
mango	mango (n)	['maŋɔ]

pomegranate	granat (m)	['granat]
redcurrant	czerwona porzeczka (ż)	[tʃɛr'vɔna pɔ'ʒɛtʃka]
blackcurrant	czarna porzeczka (ż)	['tʃarna pɔ'ʒɛtʃka]
gooseberry	agrest (m)	['agrɛst]
bilberry	borówka (ż) czarna	[bɔ'rɔfka 'tʃarna]
blackberry	jeżyna (ż)	[e'ʒina]

raisin	rodzynek (m)	[rɔ'dzinɛk]
fig	figa (ż)	['figa]
date	daktyl (m)	['daktɨl]

peanut	orzeszek (l.mn.) ziemny	[ɔ'ʒɛʃɛk 'ʒemnɛ]
almond	migdał (m)	['migdaw]
walnut	orzech (m) włoski	['ɔʒɛh 'vwɔski]
hazelnut	orzech (m) laskowy	['ɔʒɛh ʎas'kɔvɨ]
coconut	orzech (m) kokosowy	['ɔʒɛh kɔkɔ'sɔvɨ]
pistachios	fistaszki (l.mn.)	[fis'taʃki]

56. Bread. Candy

bakers' confectionery (pastry)	wyroby (l.mn.) cukiernicze	[vɨ'rɔbɨ tsuker'nitʃɛ]
bread	chleb (m)	[hlep]
cookies	herbatniki (l.mn.)	[hɛrbat'niki]

chocolate (n)	czekolada (ż)	[tʃɛkɔ'ʎada]
chocolate (as adj)	czekoladowy	[tʃɛkɔʎa'dɔvɨ]
candy	cukierek (m)	[tsu'kerɛk]
cake (e.g., cupcake)	ciastko (n)	['tʃastkɔ]
cake (e.g., birthday ~)	tort (m)	[tɔrt]

| pie (e.g., apple ~) | ciasto (n) | ['tʃastɔ] |
| filling (for cake, pie) | nadzienie (n) | [na'dʒene] |

whole fruit jam	konfitura (ż)	[kɔnfi'tura]
marmalade	marmolada (ż)	[marmɔ'ʎada]
waffles	wafle (l.mn.)	['vafle]
ice-cream	lody (l.mn.)	['lɔdɨ]

57. Spices

salt	sól (ż)	[suʎ]
salty (adj)	słony	['swɔnɨ]
to salt (vt)	solić	['sɔlitʃ]

black pepper	pieprz (m) czarny	[pepʃ 'tʃarnɨ]
red pepper (milled ~)	papryka (ż)	[pap'rɨka]
mustard	musztarda (ż)	[muʃ'tarda]

horseradish	chrzan (m)	[hʃan]
condiment	przyprawa (ż)	[pʃip'rava]
spice	przyprawa (ż)	[pʃip'rava]
sauce	sos (m)	[sɔs]
vinegar	ocet (m)	['ɔtset]

anise	anyż (m)	['aniʃ]
basil	bazylia (ż)	[ba'ziʎja]
cloves	goździki (l.mn.)	['gɔʑ'dʒiki]
ginger	imbir (m)	['imbir]
coriander	kolendra (ż)	[kɔ'lendra]
cinnamon	cynamon (m)	[tsi'namɔn]

sesame	sezam (m)	['sɛzam]
bay leaf	liść (m) laurowy	[liɕtʃ ʎau'rɔvi]
paprika	papryka (ż)	[pap'rika]
caraway	kminek (m)	['kminɛk]
saffron	szafran (m)	['ʃafran]

PERSONAL
INFORMATION. FAMILY

58. Personal information. Forms
59. Family members. Relatives
60. Friends. Coworkers

T&P Books Publishing

58. Personal information. Forms

name (first name)	imię (n)	['imɛ̃]
surname (last name)	nazwisko (n)	[naz'viskɔ]
date of birth	data (ż) urodzenia	['data urɔ'dʑɛɲa]
place of birth	miejsce (n) urodzenia	['mejstsɛ urɔ'dʑɛɲa]
nationality	narodowość (ż)	[narɔ'dɔvɔɕʧ]
place of residence	miejsce (n) zamieszkania	['mejstse zameʃ'kaɲa]
country	kraj (m)	[kraj]
profession (occupation)	zawód (m)	['zavut]
gender, sex	płeć (ż)	['pwɛʧ]
height	wzrost (m)	[vzrɔst]
weight	waga (ż)	['vaga]

59. Family members. Relatives

mother	matka (ż)	['matka]
father	ojciec (m)	['ɔjʧets]
son	syn (m)	[sin]
daughter	córka (ż)	['tsurka]
younger daughter	młodsza córka (ż)	['mwɔtʃa 'tsurka]
younger son	młodszy syn (m)	['mwɔtʃi sin]
eldest daughter	starsza córka (ż)	['starʃa 'tsurka]
eldest son	starszy syn (m)	['starʃi sin]
brother	brat (m)	[brat]
sister	siostra (ż)	['ɕɔstra]
cousin (masc.)	kuzyn (m)	['kuzin]
cousin (fem.)	kuzynka (ż)	[ku'zinka]
mom, mommy	mama (ż)	['mama]
dad, daddy	tata (m)	['tata]
parents	rodzice (l.mn.)	[rɔ'dʑitsɛ]
child	dziecko (n)	['dʑetskɔ]
children	dzieci (l.mn.)	['dʑeʧi]
grandmother	babcia (ż)	['babʧʲa]
grandfather	dziadek (m)	['dʑʲadɛk]
grandson	wnuk (m)	[vnuk]
granddaughter	wnuczka (ż)	['vnuʧka]
grandchildren	wnuki (l.mn.)	['vnuki]

uncle	wujek (m)	['vuek]
aunt	ciocia (ż)	['tʃotʃ'a]
nephew	bratanek (m),	[bra'tanɛk],
	siostrzeniec (m)	[sɜst'ʃɛnɛts]
niece	bratanica (ż),	[brata'nitsa],
	siostrzenica (ż)	[sɜst'ʃɛnitsa]

mother-in-law (wife's mother)	teściowa (ż)	[tɛɕ'tʃova]
father-in-law (husband's father)	teść (m)	[tɛɕtʃ]
son-in-law (daughter's husband)	zięć (m)	[ʒɛ̃tʃ]
stepmother	macocha (ż)	[ma'tsɔha]
stepfather	ojczym (m)	['ɔjtʃim]

infant	niemowlę (n)	[ne'mɔvlɛ̃]
baby (infant)	niemowlę (n)	[ne'mɔvlɛ̃]
little boy, kid	maluch (m)	['malyh]

wife	żona (ż)	['ʒɔna]
husband	mąż (m)	[mɔ̃ʃ]
spouse (husband)	małżonek (m)	[maw'ʒɔnɛk]
spouse (wife)	małżonka (ż)	[maw'ʒɔŋka]

married (masc.)	żonaty	[ʒɔ'nati]
married (fem.)	zamężna	[za'mɛnʒna]
single (unmarried)	nieżonaty	[neʒɔ'nati]
bachelor	kawaler (m)	[ka'valer]
divorced (masc.)	rozwiedziony	[rɔzve'dʒɜni]
widow	wdowa (ż)	['vdɔva]
widower	wdowiec (m)	['vdɔvets]

relative	krewny (m)	['krɛvni]
close relative	bliski krewny (m)	['bliski 'krɛvni]
distant relative	daleki krewny (m)	[da'leki 'krɛvni]
relatives	rodzina (ż)	[rɔ'dʒina]

orphan (boy or girl)	sierota (ż)	[ɕe'rɔta]
guardian (of minor)	opiekun (m)	[ɔ'pekun]
to adopt (a boy)	zaadoptować	[za:dɔp'tɔvatʃ]
to adopt (a girl)	zaadoptować	[za:dɔp'tɔvatʃ]

60. Friends. Coworkers

friend (masc.)	przyjaciel (m)	[pʃi'jatʃeʎ]
friend (fem.)	przyjaciółka (ż)	[pʃija'tʃuwka]
friendship	przyjaźń (ż)	['pʃijaʑɲ]
to be friends	przyjaźnić się	[pʃi'jaʑnitʃ ɕɛ̃]
buddy (masc.)	kumpel (m)	['kumpɛʎ]

| buddy (fem.) | kumpela (ż) | [kum'pɛʎa] |
| partner | partner (m) | ['partnɛr] |

chief (boss)	szef (m)	[ʃɛf]
superior (n)	kierownik (m)	[ke'rɔvnik]
subordinate (n)	podwładny (m)	[pɔdv'wadnɨ]
colleague	koleżanka (ż)	[kɔle'ʒaŋka]

acquaintance (person)	znajomy (m)	[znaʒmɨ]
fellow traveler	towarzysz (m) podróży	[tɔ'vaʒiʃ pɔd'ruʒɨ]
classmate	kolega (m) z klasy	[kɔ'lega s 'kʎasɨ]

neighbor (masc.)	sąsiad (m)	['sɔ̃ɕat]
neighbor (fem.)	sąsiadka (ż)	[sɔ̃'ɕatka]
neighbors	sąsiedzi (l.mn.)	[sɔ̃'ɕedʒi]

HUMAN BODY.
MEDICINE

61. Head
62. Human body
63. Diseases
64. Symptoms. Treatments. Part 1
65. Symptoms. Treatments. Part 2
66. Symptoms. Treatments. Part 3
67. Medicine. Drugs. Accessories

T&P Books Publishing

61. Head

head	**głowa** (ż)	['gwɔva]
face	**twarz** (ż)	[tfaʃ]
nose	**nos** (m)	[nɔs]
mouth	**usta** (l.mn.)	['usta]
eye	**oko** (n)	['ɔkɔ]
eyes	**oczy** (l.mn.)	['ɔtʃi]
pupil	**źrenica** (ż)	[ʑ're'nitsa]
eyebrow	**brew** (ż)	[brɛf]
eyelash	**rzęsy** (l.mn.)	['ʒɛnsi]
eyelid	**powieka** (ż)	[pɔ'veka]
tongue	**język** (m)	['enzik]
tooth	**ząb** (m)	[zɔ̃mp]
lips	**wargi** (l.mn.)	['vargi]
cheekbones	**kości** (l.mn.) **policzkowe**	['kɔɕtʃi pɔlitʃ'kɔvɛ]
gum	**dziąsło** (n)	[dʑɔ̃swɔ]
palate	**podniebienie** (n)	[pɔdne'bene]
nostrils	**nozdrza** (l.mn.)	['nɔzdʒa]
chin	**podbródek** (m)	[pɔdb'rudek]
jaw	**szczęka** (ż)	['ʃtʃɛŋka]
cheek	**policzek** (m)	[pɔ'litʃɛk]
forehead	**czoło** (n)	['tʃɔwɔ]
temple	**skroń** (ż)	[skrɔɲ]
ear	**ucho** (n)	['uhɔ]
back of the head	**potylica** (ż)	[pɔti'litsa]
neck	**szyja** (ż)	['ʃija]
throat	**gardło** (n)	['gardwɔ]
hair	**włosy** (l.mn.)	['vwɔsi]
hairstyle	**fryzura** (ż)	[fri'zura]
haircut	**uczesanie** (n)	[utʃɛ'sane]
wig	**peruka** (ż)	[pɛ'ruka]
mustache	**wąsy** (l.mn.)	['vɔ̃si]
beard	**broda** (ż)	['brɔda]
to have (a beard, etc.)	**nosić**	['nɔɕitʃ]
braid	**warkocz** (m)	['varkɔtʃ]
sideburns	**baczki** (l.mn.)	['batʃki]
red-haired (adj)	**rudy**	['rudi]
gray (hair)	**siwy**	['ɕivi]

| bald (adj) | łysy | ['wisɨ] |
| bald patch | łysina (ż) | [wi'ɕina] |

| ponytail | koński ogon (m) | ['kɔɲski 'ɔgɔn] |
| bangs | grzywka (ż) | ['gʒɨfka] |

62. Human body

| hand | dłoń (ż) | [dwɔɲ] |
| arm | ręka (ż) | ['rɛŋka] |

finger	palec (m)	['palɛts]
thumb	kciuk (m)	['ktʃuk]
little finger	mały palec (m)	['mawɨ 'palɛts]
nail	paznokieć (m)	[paz'nɔketʃ]

fist	pięść (ż)	[pɛ̃ɕtʃ]
palm	dłoń (ż)	[dwɔɲ]
wrist	nadgarstek (m)	[nad'garstɛk]
forearm	przedramię (n)	[pʃɛd'ramɛ̃]
elbow	łokieć (n)	['wɔketʃ]
shoulder	ramię (n)	['ramɛ̃]

leg	noga (ż)	['nɔga]
foot	stopa (ż)	['stɔpa]
knee	kolano (n)	[kɔ'ʎanɔ]
calf (part of leg)	łydka (ż)	['wɨtka]

| hip | biodro (n) | ['bɔdrɔ] |
| heel | pięta (ż) | ['penta] |

body	ciało (n)	['tʃawɔ]
stomach	brzuch (m)	[bʒuh]
chest	pierś (ż)	[perɕ]
breast	piersi (l.mn.)	['perɕi]
flank	bok (m)	[bɔk]
back	plecy (l.mn.)	['plɛtsɨ]

| lower back | krzyż (m) | [kʃɨʃ] |
| waist | talia (ż) | ['taʎja] |

navel (belly button)	pępek (m)	['pɛ̃pɛk]
buttocks	pośladki (l.mn.)	[pɔɕ'ʎatki]
bottom	tyłek (m)	['tɨwɛk]

beauty mark	pieprzyk (m)	['pepʃik]
birthmark	znamię (n)	['znamɛ̃]
(café au lait spot)		
tattoo	tatuaż (m)	[ta'tuaʃ]
scar	blizna (ż)	['blizna]

63. Diseases

sickness	**choroba** (ż)	[hɔ'rɔba]
to be sick	**chorować**	[hɔ'rɔvatʃ]
health	**zdrowie** (n)	['zdrɔve]

runny nose (coryza)	**katar** (m)	['katar]
tonsillitis	**angina** (ż)	[aŋina]
cold (illness)	**przeziębienie** (n)	[pʃɛʒ̃'bene]
to catch a cold	**przeziębić się**	[pʃɛ'ʒembitʃ ɕɛ̃]

bronchitis	**zapalenie** (n) **oskrzeli**	[zapa'lɛne ɔsk'ʃɛli]
pneumonia	**zapalenie** (n) **płuc**	[zapa'lɛne pwuts]
flu, influenza	**grypa** (ż)	['grɨpa]

nearsighted (adj)	**krótkowzroczny**	[krutkɔvz'rɔtʃni]
farsighted (adj)	**dalekowzroczny**	[dalekɔvz'rɔtʃni]
strabismus (crossed eyes)	**zez** (m)	[zɛs]
cross-eyed (adj)	**zezowaty**	[zɛzɔ'vati]
cataract	**katarakta** (ż)	[kata'rakta]
glaucoma	**jaskra** (ż)	['jaskra]

stroke	**wylew** (m)	['vɨlef]
heart attack	**zawał** (m)	['zavaw]
myocardial infarction	**zawał** (m) **mięśnia sercowego**	['zavaw 'mɛ̃ɕɲa sɛrtsɔ'vɛgɔ]
paralysis	**paraliż** (m)	[pa'raliʃ]
to paralyze (vt)	**sparaliżować**	[sparali'ʒɔvatʃ]

allergy	**alergia** (ż)	[a'lergʰja]
asthma	**astma** (ż)	['astma]
diabetes	**cukrzyca** (ż)	[tsuk'ʃɨtsa]

toothache	**ból** (m) **zęba**	[buʎ 'zɛ̃ba]
caries	**próchnica** (ż)	[pruh'nitsa]

diarrhea	**rozwolnienie** (n)	[rɔzvɔʎ'nene]
constipation	**zaparcie** (n)	[za'partʃe]
stomach upset	**rozstrój** (m) **żołądka**	['rɔsstruj ʒɔ'wɔ̃tka]
food poisoning	**zatrucie** (n) **pokarmowe**	[zat'rutʃe pɔkar'mɔvɛ]
to get food poisoning	**zatruć się**	['zatrutʃ ɕɛ̃]

arthritis	**artretyzm** (m)	[art'rɛtizm]
rickets	**krzywica** (ż)	[kʃi'vitsa]
rheumatism	**reumatyzm** (m)	[rɛu'matizm]
atherosclerosis	**miażdżyca** (ż)	[mʲaʒ'dʒitsa]

gastritis	**nieżyt** (m) **żołądka**	['neʒit ʒɔ'wɔ̃tka]
appendicitis	**zapalenie** (n) **wyrostka robaczkowego**	[zapa'lene vɨ'rostka rɔbatʃkɔ'vɛgɔ]
ulcer	**wrzód** (m)	[vʒut]

measles	odra (ż)	['ɔdra]
rubella (German measles)	różyczka (ż)	[ru'ʒitʃka]
jaundice	żółtaczka (ż)	[ʒuw'tatʃka]
hepatitis	zapalenie (n) wątroby	[zapa'lene võt'rɔbi]

schizophrenia	schizofrenia (ż)	[shizɔf'rɛnʰja]
rabies (hydrophobia)	wścieklizna (ż)	[vɕtʃek'lizna]
neurosis	nerwica (ż)	[nɛr'vitsa]
concussion	wstrząs (m) mózgu	[fstʃõs 'muzgu]

cancer	rak (m)	[rak]
sclerosis	stwardnienie (n)	[stvard'nenie]
multiple sclerosis	stwardnienie (n) rozsiane	[stfard'nene rɔz'ɕanɛ]

alcoholism	alkoholizm (m)	[aʎkɔ'hɔlizm]
alcoholic (n)	alkoholik (m)	[aʎkɔ'hɔlik]
syphilis	syfilis (m)	[si'filis]
AIDS	AIDS (m)	[ɛjts]

tumor	nowotwór (m)	[nɔ'vɔtfur]
malignant (adj)	złośliwa	[zwɔɕ'liva]
benign (adj)	niezłośliwa	[nezwɔɕ'liva]

fever	febra (ż)	['fɛbra]
malaria	malaria (ż)	[ma'ʎarʰja]
gangrene	gangrena (ż)	[gaŋ'rɛna]
seasickness	choroba (ż) morska	[hɔ'rɔba 'mɔrska]
epilepsy	padaczka (ż)	[pa'datʃka]

epidemic	epidemia (ż)	[ɛpi'dɛmʰja]
typhus	tyfus (m)	['tifus]
tuberculosis	gruźlica (ż)	[gruʑ'litsa]
cholera	cholera (ż)	[hɔ'lera]
plague (bubonic ~)	dżuma (ż)	['dʒuma]

64. Symptoms. Treatments. Part 1

symptom	objaw (m)	['ɔbʰjaf]
temperature	temperatura (ż)	[tɛmpɛra'tura]
high temperature (fever)	gorączka (ż)	[gɔ'rõtʃka]
pulse	puls (m)	[puʎs]

dizziness (vertigo)	zawrót (m) głowy	['zavrut 'gwɔvi]
hot (adj)	gorący	[gɔ'rõtsi]
shivering	dreszcz (m)	['drɛʃtʃ]
pale (e.g., ~ face)	blady	['bʎadi]

cough	kaszel (m)	['kaʃɛʎ]
to cough (vi)	kaszleć	['kaʃletʃ]
to sneeze (vi)	kichać	['kihatʃ]

| faint | omdlenie (n) | [ɔmd'lene] |
| to faint (vi) | zemdleć | ['zɛmdletʃ] |

bruise (hématome)	siniak (m)	['ɕiɲak]
bump (lump)	guz (m)	[gus]
to bang (bump)	uderzyć się	[u'dɛʒitʃ ɕɛ̃]
contusion (bruise)	stłuczenie (n)	[stwut'ʃɛne]
to get a bruise	potłuc się	['pɔtwuts ɕɛ̃]

to limp (vi)	kuleć	['kuletʃ]
dislocation	zwichnięcie (n)	[zvih'nɛ̃tʃe]
to dislocate (vt)	zwichnąć	['zvihnɔ̃tʃ]
fracture	złamanie (n)	[zwa'mane]
to have a fracture	otrzymać złamanie	[ɔt'ʃimatʃ zwa'mane]

cut (e.g., paper ~)	skaleczenie (n)	[skalet'ʃɛne]
to cut oneself	skaleczyć się	[ska'letʃitʃ ɕɛ̃]
bleeding	krwotok (m)	['krfɔtɔk]

| burn (injury) | oparzenie (n) | [ɔpa'ʒɛne] |
| to get burned | poparzyć się | [pɔ'paʒitʃ ɕɛ̃] |

to prick (vt)	ukłuć	['ukwutʃ]
to prick oneself	ukłuć się	['ukwutʃ ɕɛ̃]
to injure (vt)	uszkodzić	[uʃ'kɔdʑitʃ]
injury	uszkodzenie (n)	[uʃkɔ'dzɛne]
wound	rana (ż)	['rana]
trauma	uraz (m)	['uras]

to be delirious	bredzić	['brɛdʑitʃ]
to stutter (vi)	jąkać się	[ɔ̃katʃ ɕɛ̃]
sunstroke	udar (m) słoneczny	['udar swɔ'nɛtʃnɨ]

65. Symptoms. Treatments. Part 2

| pain | ból (m) | [buʎ] |
| splinter (in foot, etc.) | drzazga (ż) | ['dʒazga] |

sweat (perspiration)	pot (m)	[pɔt]
to sweat (perspire)	pocić się	['pɔtʃitʃ ɕɛ̃]
vomiting	wymiotowanie (n)	[vɨmʲɔtɔ'vane]
convulsions	drgawki (l.mn.)	['drgavki]

pregnant (adj)	ciężarna (ż)	[tʃɛ̃'ʒarna]
to be born	urodzić się	[u'rɔdʑitʃ ɕɛ̃]
delivery, labor	poród (m)	['pɔrut]
to deliver (~ a baby)	rodzić	['rɔdʑitʃ]
abortion	aborcja (ż)	[a'bɔrtsʲja]
breathing, respiration	oddech (m)	['ɔddɛh]
in-breath (inhalation)	wdech (m)	[vdɛh]

out-breath (exhalation)	wydech (m)	['vidɛh]
to exhale (breathe out)	zrobić wydech	['zrɔbitʃ 'vidɛh]
to inhale (vi)	zrobić wdech	['zrɔbitʃ vdɛh]

disabled person	niepełnosprawny (m)	[nepɛwnɔsp'ravni]
cripple	kaleka (m, ż)	[ka'leka]
drug addict	narkoman (m)	[nar'kɔman]

deaf (adj)	niesłyszący, głuchy	[neswi'ʃɔtsi], ['gwuhi]
mute (adj)	niemy	['nemi]
deaf mute (adj)	głuchoniemy	[gwuhɔ'nemi]

mad, insane (adj)	zwariowany	[zvarʰɜ'vani]
madman	wariat (m)	['varʰjat]
(demented person)		
madwoman	wariatka (ż)	[varʰʲjatka]
to go insane	stracić rozum	['stratʃitʃ rɔzum]

gene	gen (m)	[gɛn]
immunity	odporność (ż)	[ɔt'pɔrnɔɕtʃ]
hereditary (adj)	dziedziczny	[dʒe'dʒitʃni]
congenital (adj)	wrodzony	[vrɔ'dzɔni]

virus	wirus (m)	['virus]
microbe	mikrob (m)	['mikrɔb]
bacterium	bakteria (ż)	[bak'tɛrʰja]
infection	infekcja (ż)	[in'fɛktsʰja]

66. Symptoms. Treatments. Part 3

hospital	szpital (m)	['ʃpitaʎ]
patient	pacjent (m)	['patsʰent]

diagnosis	diagnoza (ż)	[dʰjag'nɔza]
cure	leczenie (n)	[let'ʃɛne]
medical treatment	leczenie (n)	[let'ʃɛne]
to get treatment	leczyć się	['letʃitʃ ɕɛ̃]
to treat (~ a patient)	leczyć	['letʃitʃ]
to nurse (look after)	opiekować się	[ɔpe'kɔvatʃ ɕɛ̃]
care (nursing ~)	opieka (ż)	[ɔ'peka]

operation, surgery	operacja (ż)	[ɔpɛ'ratsʰja]
to bandage (head, limb)	opatrzyć	[ɔ'patʃitʃ]
bandaging	opatrunek (m)	[ɔpat'runɛk]

vaccination	szczepionka (m)	[ʃtʃɛ'pɔŋka]
to vaccinate (vt)	szczepić	['ʃtʃɛpitʃ]
injection, shot	zastrzyk (m)	['zastʃik]
to give an injection	robić zastrzyk	['rɔbitʃ 'zastʃik]
amputation	amputacja (ż)	[ampu'tatsʰja]

153

to amputate (vt)	amputować	[ampu'tɔvatʃ]
coma	śpiączka (ż)	[ɕpɔ̃tʃka]
to be in a coma	być w śpiączce	[bitʃ f ɕpɔ̃tʃse]
intensive care	reanimacja (ż)	[rɛani'matsʰja]

to recover (~ from flu)	wracać do zdrowia	['vratsatʃ dɔ 'zdrɔvʲa]
condition (patient's ~)	stan (m)	[stan]
consciousness	przytomność (ż)	[pʃi'tɔmnɔɕtʃ]
memory (faculty)	pamięć (ż)	['pamɛ̃tʃ]

to pull out (tooth)	usuwać	[u'suvatʃ]
filling	plomba (ż)	['plɔmba]
to fill (a tooth)	plombować	[plɔm'bɔvatʃ]

| hypnosis | hipnoza (ż) | [hip'nɔza] |
| to hypnotize (vt) | hipnotyzować | [hipnɔti'zɔvatʃ] |

67. Medicine. Drugs. Accessories

medicine, drug	lekarstwo (n)	[le'karstfɔ]
remedy	środek (m)	['ɕrɔdɛk]
to prescribe (vt)	zapisać	[za'pisatʃ]
prescription	recepta (ż)	[rɛ'tsɛpta]

tablet, pill	tabletka (ż)	[tab'letka]
ointment	maść (ż)	[maɕtʃ]
ampule	ampułka (ż)	[am'puwka]
mixture	mikstura (ż)	[miks'tura]
syrup	syrop (m)	['sirɔp]
pill	pigułka (ż)	[pi'guwka]
powder	proszek (m)	['prɔʃɛk]

gauze bandage	bandaż (m)	['bandaʃ]
cotton wool	wata (ż)	['vata]
iodine	jodyna (ż)	[ɜ'dina]
Band-Aid	plaster (m)	['pʎaster]
eyedropper	zakraplacz (m)	[zak'rapʎatʃ]
thermometer	termometr (m)	[tɛr'mɔmɛtr]
syringe	strzykawka (ż)	[stʃi'kafka]

| wheelchair | wózek (m) inwalidzki | ['vɔzɛk inva'lidzki] |
| crutches | kule (l.mn.) | ['kule] |

painkiller	środek (m) przeciwbólowy	['ɕrɔdɛk pʃɛtʃifbɔ'lɔvi]
laxative	środek (m) przeczyszczający	['ɕrɔdɛk pʃɛtʃiʃtʃaɔ̃tsi]
spirits (ethanol)	spirytus (m)	[spi'ritus]
medicinal herbs	zioła (l.mn.) lecznicze	[ʑi'ɔla lɛtʃ'nitʃɛ]
herbal (~ tea)	ziołowy	[ʑɜ'wɔvi]

T&P BOOKS

APARTMENT

68. Apartment
69. Furniture. Interior
70. Bedding
71. Kitchen
72. Bathroom
73. Household appliances

T&P Books Publishing

apartment	mieszkanie (n)	[meʃ'kane]
room	pokój (m)	['pɔkuj]
bedroom	sypialnia (ż)	[si'pʲaʎɲa]
dining room	jadalnia (ż)	[ja'daʎɲa]
living room	salon (m)	['salɜn]
study (home office)	gabinet (m)	[ga'binɛt]

entry room	przedpokój (m)	[pʃɛt'pɔkuj]
bathroom (room with	łazienka (ż)	[wa'ʒeŋka]
a bath or shower)		
half bath	toaleta (ż)	[tɔa'leta]

ceiling	sufit (m)	['sufit]
floor	podłoga (ż)	[pɔd'wɔga]
corner	kąt (m)	[kɔ̃t]

furniture	meble (l.mn.)	['mɛble]
table	stół (m)	[stɔw]
chair	krzesło (n)	['kʃɛswɔ]
bed	łóżko (n)	['wuʃkɔ]
couch, sofa	kanapa (ż)	[ka'napa]
armchair	fotel (m)	['fɔtɛʎ]

bookcase	biblioteczka (ż)	[bibʎjɔ'tɛtʃka]
shelf	półka (ż)	['puwka]
shelving unit	etażerka (ż)	[ɛta'ʒɛrka]

wardrobe	szafa (ż) ubraniowa	['ʃafa ubra'nɜva]
coat rack (wall-mounted ~)	wieszak (m)	['veʃak]
coat stand	wieszak (m)	['veʃak]

| bureau, dresser | komoda (ż) | [kɔ'mɔda] |
| coffee table | stolik (m) kawowy | ['stɔlik ka'vɔvi] |

mirror	lustro (n)	['lystrɔ]
carpet	dywan (m)	['divan]
rug, small carpet	dywanik (m)	[di'vanik]

| fireplace | kominek (m) | [kɔ'minɛk] |
| candle | świeca (ż) | ['ɕfetsa] |

candlestick	świecznik (m)	['ɕfetʃnik]
drapes	zasłony (l.mn.)	[zas'wɔni]
wallpaper	tapety (l.mn.)	[ta'pɛti]
blinds (jalousie)	żaluzje (l.mn.)	[ʒa'lyzʰe]

table lamp	lampka (ż) na stół	['ʎampka na stɔw]
wall lamp (sconce)	lampka (ż)	['ʎampka]
floor lamp	lampa (ż) stojąca	['ʎampa stɔ:tsa]
chandelier	żyrandol (m)	[ʒi'randɔʎ]

leg (of chair, table)	noga (ż)	['nɔga]
armrest	poręcz (ż)	['pɔrɛ̃tʃ]
back (backrest)	oparcie (n)	[ɔ'partʃe]
drawer	szuflada (ż)	[ʃuf'ʎada]

70. Bedding

bedclothes	pościel (ż)	['pɔɕtʃeʎ]
pillow	poduszka (ż)	[pɔ'duʃka]
pillowcase	poszewka (ż)	[pɔ'ʃɛfka]
duvet, comforter	kołdra (ż)	['kɔwdra]
sheet	prześcieradło (n)	[pʃɛɕtʃe'radwɔ]
bedspread	narzuta (ż)	[na'ʒuta]

71. Kitchen

kitchen	kuchnia (ż)	['kuhɲa]
gas	gaz (m)	[gas]
gas stove (range)	kuchenka (ż) gazowa	[ku'hɛŋka ga'zɔva]
electric stove	kuchenka (ż) elektryczna	[ku'hɛŋka ɛlekt'ritʃna]
oven	piekarnik (m)	[pe'karnik]
microwave oven	mikrofalówka (ż)	[mikrɔfa'lyfka]

refrigerator	lodówka (ż)	[lɔ'dufka]
freezer	zamrażarka (ż)	[zamra'ʒarka]
dishwasher	zmywarka (ż) do naczyń	[zmi'varka dɔ 'natʃiɲ]

meat grinder	maszynka (ż) do mięsa	[ma'ʃiŋka dɔ 'mensa]
juicer	sokowirówka (ż)	[sɔkɔvi'rufka]
toaster	toster (m)	['tɔstɛr]
mixer	mikser (m)	['miksɛr]

coffee machine	ekspres (m) do kawy	['ɛksprɛs dɔ 'kavi]
coffee pot	dzbanek (m) do kawy	['dzbanɛk dɔ 'kavi]
coffee grinder	młynek (m) do kawy	['mwinɛk dɔ 'kavi]

| kettle | czajnik (m) | ['tʃajnik] |
| teapot | czajniczek (m) | [tʃaj'nitʃɛk] |

| lid | pokrywka (ż) | [pɔk'rifka] |
| tea strainer | sitko (n) | ['ɕitkɔ] |

spoon	łyżka (ż)	['wiʃka]
teaspoon	łyżeczka (ż)	[wi'ʒɛtʃka]
soup spoon	łyżka (ż) stołowa	['wiʃka stɔ'wɔva]
fork	widelec (m)	[vi'dɛlɛts]
knife	nóż (m)	[nuʃ]

tableware (dishes)	naczynia (l.mn.)	[nat'ʃiɲa]
plate (dinner ~)	talerz (m)	['taleʃ]
saucer	spodek (m)	['spɔdɛk]

shot glass	kieliszek (m)	[ke'liʃɛk]
glass (tumbler)	szklanka (ż)	['ʃkʎaŋka]
cup	filiżanka (ż)	[fili'ʒaŋka]

sugar bowl	cukiernica (ż)	[tsuker'nitsa]
salt shaker	solniczka (ż)	[sɔʎ'nitʃka]
pepper shaker	pieprzniczka (ż)	[pepʃ'nitʃka]
butter dish	maselniczka (ż)	[masɛʎ'nitʃka]

stock pot (soup pot)	garnek (m)	['garnɛk]
frying pan (skillet)	patelnia (ż)	[pa'tɛʎɲa]
ladle	łyżka (ż) wazowa	['wiʃka va'zɔva]
colander	durszlak (m)	['durʃʎak]
tray (serving ~)	taca (ż)	['tatsa]

bottle	butelka (ż)	[bu'tɛʎka]
jar (glass)	słoik (m)	['swɔik]
can	puszka (ż)	['puʃka]

bottle opener	otwieracz (m) do butelek	[ɔt'feratʃ dɛ bu'tɛlek]
can opener	otwieracz (m) do puszek	[ɔt'feratʃ dɛ 'puʃɛk]
corkscrew	korkociąg (m)	[kɔr'kɔtʃɔ̃k]
filter	filtr (m)	[fiʎtr]
to filter (vt)	filtrować	[fiʎt'rɔvatʃ]

| trash, garbage (food waste, etc.) | odpadki (l.mn.) | [ɔt'patki] |
| trash can (kitchen ~) | kosz (m) na śmieci | [kɔʃ na 'ɕmetʃi] |

72. Bathroom

bathroom	łazienka (ż)	[wa'ʒeŋka]
water	woda (ż)	['vɔda]
faucet	kran (m)	[kran]
hot water	gorąca woda (ż)	[gɔ'rɔ̃tsa 'vɔda]
cold water	zimna woda (ż)	['ʒimna 'vɔda]
toothpaste	pasta (ż) do zębów	['pasta dɔ 'zɛ̃buf]

to brush one's teeth	myć zęby	[mitʃ 'zɛ̃bi]
to shave (vi)	golić się	['golitʃ ɕɛ̃]
shaving foam	pianka (z) do golenia	['pʲaŋka dɔ gɔ'leɲa]
razor	maszynka (z) do golenia	[ma'ʃɨŋka dɔ gɔ'leɲa]

to wash (one's hands, etc.)	myć	[mitʃ]
to take a bath	myć się	['mitʃ ɕɛ̃]
shower	prysznic (m)	['prɨʃɲits]
to take a shower	brać prysznic	[bratʃ 'prɨʃɲits]

bathtub	wanna (z)	['vaɲa]
toilet (toilet bowl)	sedes (m)	['sɛdɛs]
sink (washbasin)	zlew (m)	[zlef]

| soap | mydło (n) | ['mɨdwɔ] |
| soap dish | mydelniczka (z) | [mɨdɛʎ'nitʃka] |

sponge	gąbka (z)	['gɔ̃pka]
shampoo	szampon (m)	['ʃampɔn]
towel	ręcznik (m)	['rɛntʃɲik]
bathrobe	szlafrok (m)	['ʃʎafrɔk]

laundry (process)	pranie (n)	['prane]
washing machine	pralka (z)	['praʎka]
to do the laundry	prać	[pratʃ]
laundry detergent	proszek (m) do prania	['prɔʃɛk dɔ 'praɲa]

73. Household appliances

TV set	telewizor (m)	[tɛle'vizɔr]
tape recorder	magnetofon (m)	[magnɛ'tɔfɔn]
VCR (video recorder)	magnetowid (m)	[magnɛ'tɔvid]
radio	odbiornik (m)	[ɔd'bɔrnik]
player (CD, MP3, etc.)	odtwarzacz (m)	[ɔtt'vaʒatʃ]

video projector	projektor (m) wideo	[prɔ'ektɔr vi'dɛɔ]
home movie theater	kino (n) domowe	['kinɔ dɔ'mɔvɛ]
DVD player	odtwarzacz DVD (m)	[ɔtt'vaʒatʃ di vi di]
amplifier	wzmacniacz (m)	['vzmatsɲatʃ]
video game console	konsola (z) do gier	[kɔn'sɔʎa dɔ ger]

video camera	kamera (z) wideo	[ka'mɛra vi'dɛɔ]
camera (photo)	aparat (m) fotograficzny	[a'parat fotogra'fitʃɲi]
digital camera	aparat (m) cyfrowy	[a'parat tsɨf'rɔvi]

vacuum cleaner	odkurzacz (m)	[ɔt'kuʒatʃ]
iron (e.g., steam ~)	żelazko (n)	[ʒɛ'ʎaskɔ]
ironing board	deska (z) do prasowania	['dɛska dɔ prasɔ'vaɲa]
telephone	telefon (m)	[tɛ'lefɔn]
mobile phone	telefon (m) komórkowy	[tɛ'lefɔn kɔmur'kɔvi]

159

| typewriter | maszyna (ż) do pisania | [ma'ʃina dɔ pi'saɲa] |
| sewing machine | maszyna (ż) do szycia | [ma'ʃina dɔ 'ʃit͡ʃa] |

microphone	mikrofon (m)	[mik'rɔfɔn]
headphones	słuchawki (l.mn.)	[swu'hafki]
remote control (TV)	pilot (m)	['pilɜt]

CD, compact disc	płyta CD (ż)	['pwita si'di]
cassette	kaseta (ż)	[ka'sɛta]
vinyl record	płyta (ż)	['pwita]

T&P BOOKS

THE EARTH. WEATHER

74. Outer space
75. The Earth
76. Cardinal directions
77. Sea. Ocean
78. Seas' and Oceans' names
79. Mountains
80. Mountains names
81. Rivers
82. Rivers' names
83. Forest
84. Natural resources
85. Weather
86. Severe weather. Natural disasters

T&P Books Publishing

space	**kosmos** (m)	['kɔsmɔs]
space (as adj)	**kosmiczny**	[kɔs'mitʃni]
outer space	**przestrzeń** (ż) **kosmiczna**	['pʃɛstʃɛɲ kɔs'mitʃna]
world	**świat** (m)	[ɕfʲat]
universe	**wszechświat** (m)	['fʃɛhɕfʲat]
galaxy	**galaktyka** (ż)	[ga'ʎaktika]

star	**gwiazda** (ż)	['gvʲazda]
constellation	**gwiazdozbiór** (m)	[gvʲaz'dɔzbyr]
planet	**planeta** (ż)	[pʎa'nɛta]
satellite	**satelita** (m)	[satɛ'lita]

meteorite	**meteoryt** (m)	[mɛtɛ'ɔrit]
comet	**kometa** (ż)	[kɔ'mɛta]
asteroid	**asteroida** (ż)	[astɛrɔ'ida]

orbit	**orbita** (ż)	[ɔr'bita]
to revolve (~ around the Earth)	**obracać się**	[ɔb'ratsatʃ ɕɛ̃]
atmosphere	**atmosfera** (ż)	[atmɔs'fɛra]

the Sun	**Słońce** (n)	['swɔɲtsɛ]
solar system	**Układ** (m) **Słoneczny**	['ukwad swɔ'nɛtʃni]
solar eclipse	**zaćmienie** (n) **słońca**	[zatʃ'mene 'swɔɲtsa]

the Earth	**Ziemia** (ż)	['ʒemʲa]
the Moon	**Księżyc** (m)	['kɕɛnʒits]

Mars	**Mars** (m)	[mars]
Venus	**Wenus** (ż)	['vɛnus]
Jupiter	**Jowisz** (m)	[ʒviʃ]
Saturn	**Saturn** (m)	['saturn]

Mercury	**Merkury** (m)	[mɛr'kuri]
Uranus	**Uran** (m)	['uran]
Neptune	**Neptun** (m)	['nɛptun]
Pluto	**Pluton** (m)	['plytɔn]

Milky Way	**Droga** (ż) **Mleczna**	['drɔga 'mletʃna]
Great Bear (Ursa Major)	**Wielki Wóz** (m)	['veʎki vus]
North Star	**Gwiazda** (ż) **Polarna**	['gvʲazda pɔ'ʎarna]

Martian	**Marsjanin** (m)	[marsʰ'janin]
extraterrestrial (n)	**kosmita** (m)	[kɔs'mita]

alien	obcy (m)	['ɔbtsi]
flying saucer	talerz (m) latający	['taleʃ ʎataɔ̃tsi]

spaceship	statek (m) kosmiczny	['statɛk kɔs'mitʃni]
space station	stacja (z) kosmiczna	['statsʰja kɔs'mitʃna]
blast-off	start (m)	[start]

engine	silnik (m)	['ɕiʎnik]
nozzle	dysza (z)	['diʃa]
fuel	paliwo (n)	[pa'livɔ]

cockpit, flight deck	kabina (z)	[ka'bina]
antenna	antena (z)	[an'tɛna]
porthole	iluminator (m)	[ilymi'natɔr]
solar panel	bateria (z) słoneczna	[ba'tɛrʰja swɔ'nɛtʃna]
spacesuit	skafander (m)	[ska'fandɛr]

weightlessness	nieważkość (z)	[ne'vaʃkɔçtʃ]
oxygen	tlen (m)	[tlen]

docking (in space)	połączenie (n)	[pɔwɔ̃t'ʃɛne]
to dock (vi, vt)	łączyć się	['wɔ̃tʃitʃ ɕɛ̃]

observatory	obserwatorium (n)	[ɔbsɛrva'tɔrʰjum]
telescope	teleskop (m)	[tɛ'leskɔp]
to observe (vt)	obserwować	[ɔbsɛr'vɔvatʃ]
to explore (vt)	badać	['badatʃ]

75. The Earth

the Earth	Ziemia (z)	['ʒemʲa]
the globe (the Earth)	kula (z) ziemska	['kuʎa 'ʒemska]
planet	planeta (z)	[pʎa'nɛta]

atmosphere	atmosfera (z)	[atmɔs'fɛra]
geography	geografia (z)	[gɛɔg'rafʰja]
nature	przyroda (z)	[pʃi'rɔda]

globe (table ~)	globus (m)	['glɔbus]
map	mapa (z)	['mapa]
atlas	atlas (m)	['atʎas]

Europe	Europa (z)	[ɛu'rɔpa]
Asia	Azja (z)	['azʰja]
Africa	Afryka (z)	['afrika]
Australia	Australia (z)	[aust'raʎja]

America	Ameryka (z)	[a'mɛrika]
North America	Ameryka (z) Północna	[a'mɛrika puw'nɔtsna]
South America	Ameryka (z) Południowa	[a'mɛrika pɔwud'nɔva]

| Antarctica | Antarktyda (ż) | [antark'tɨda] |
| the Arctic | Arktyka (ż) | ['arktɨka] |

76. Cardinal directions

north	północ (ż)	['puwnɔts]
to the north	na północ	[na 'puwnɔts]
in the north	na północy	[na puw'nɔtsɨ]
northern (adj)	północny	[puw'nɔtsnɨ]

south	południe (n)	[pɔ'wudne]
to the south	na południe	[na pɔ'wudne]
in the south	na południu	[na pɔ'wudny]
southern (adj)	południowy	[pɔwud'nɜvɨ]

west	zachód (m)	['zahut]
to the west	na zachód	[na 'zahut]
in the west	na zachodzie	[na za'hɔdʒe]
western (adj)	zachodni	[za'hɔdni]

east	wschód (m)	[fshut]
to the east	na wschód	['na fshut]
in the east	na wschodzie	[na 'fshɔdʒe]
eastern (adj)	wschodni	['fshɔdni]

77. Sea. Ocean

sea	morze (n)	['mɔʒɛ]
ocean	ocean (m)	[ɔ'tsɛan]
gulf (bay)	zatoka (ż)	[za'tɔka]
straits	cieśnina (ż)	[tɕeɕ'nina]

land (solid ground)	ląd (m)	[lɔ̃t]
continent (mainland)	kontynent (m)	[kɔn'tɨnɛnt]
island	wyspa (ż)	['vɨspa]
peninsula	półwysep (m)	[puw'visɛp]
archipelago	archipelag (m)	[arhi'pɛʎak]

bay, cove	zatoka (ż)	[za'tɔka]
harbor	port (m)	[pɔrt]
lagoon	laguna (ż)	[ʎa'guna]
cape	przylądek (m)	[pʃɨlɔ̃dɛk]

atoll	atol (m)	['atɔʎ]
reef	rafa (ż)	['rafa]
coral	koral (m)	['kɔral]
coral reef	rafa (ż) koralowa	['rafa kɔra'lɜva]
deep (adj)	głęboki	[gwɛ̃'bɔki]

depth (deep water)	głębokość (ż)	[gwɛ̃'bɔkɔɕtʃ]
abyss	otchłań (ż)	['ɔthwaɲ]
trench (e.g., Mariana ~)	rów (m)	[ruf]

| current (Ocean ~) | prąd (m) | [prɔ̃t] |
| to surround (bathe) | omywać | [ɔ'mɨvatʃ] |

| shore | brzeg (m) | [bʒɛk] |
| coast | wybrzeże (n) | [vɨb'ʒɛʒe] |

flow (flood tide)	przypływ (m)	['pʃɨpwɨf]
ebb (ebb tide)	odpływ (m)	['ɔtpwɨf]
shoal	mielizna (ż)	[me'lizna]
bottom (~ of the sea)	dno (n)	[dnɔ]

wave	fala (ż)	['faʎa]
crest (~ of a wave)	grzywa (ż) fali	['gʒɨva 'fali]
spume (sea foam)	piana (ż)	['pʲana]

storm (sea storm)	burza (ż)	['buʒa]
hurricane	huragan (m)	[hu'ragan]
tsunami	tsunami (n)	[tsu'nami]
calm (dead ~)	cisza (ż) morska	['tʃiʃa 'mɔrska]
quiet, calm (adj)	spokojny	[spɔ'kɔjnɨ]

| pole | biegun (m) | ['begun] |
| polar (adj) | polarny | [pɔ'ʎarnɨ] |

latitude	szerokość (ż)	[ʃɛ'rɔkɔɕtʃ]
longitude	długość (ż)	['dwugɔɕtʃ]
parallel	równoleżnik (m)	[ruvnɔ'leʒnik]
equator	równik (m)	['ruvnik]

sky	niebo (n)	['nebɔ]
horizon	horyzont (m)	[hɔ'rizɔnt]
air	powietrze (n)	[pɔ'vetʃɛ]

lighthouse	latarnia (ż) morska	[ʎa'tarɲa 'mɔrska]
to dive (vi)	nurkować	[nur'kɔvatʃ]
to sink (ab. boat)	zatonąć	[za'tɔ̃ɔɲtʃ]
treasures	skarby (l.mn.)	['skarbɨ]

78. Seas' and Oceans' names

Atlantic Ocean	Ocean (m) Atlantycki	[ɔ'tsɛan atlan'titski]
Indian Ocean	Ocean (m) Indyjski	[ɔ'tsɛan in'dijski]
Pacific Ocean	Ocean (m) Spokojny	[ɔ'tsɛan spɔ'kɔjnɨ]
Arctic Ocean	Ocean (m) Lodowaty Północny	[ɔ'tsɛan lɔdɔ'vatɨ puw'nɔtsnɨ]
Black Sea	Morze (n) Czarne	['mɔʒɛ 'tʃarnɛ]

Red Sea	Morze (n) Czerwone	['mɔʒɛ tʃɛr'vɔnɛ]
Yellow Sea	Morze (n) Żółte	['mɔʒɛ 'ʒuwtɛ]
White Sea	Morze (n) Białe	['mɔʒɛ 'bʲawɛ]

Caspian Sea	Morze (n) Kaspijskie	['mɔʒɛ kas'pijske]
Dead Sea	Morze (n) Martwe	['mɔʒɛ 'martfɛ]
Mediterranean Sea	Morze (n) Śródziemne	['mɔʒɛ ɕry'dʒemnɛ]

| Aegean Sea | Morze (n) Egejskie | ['mɔʒɛ ɛ'gejske] |
| Adriatic Sea | Morze (n) Adriatyckie | ['mɔʒɛ adrʲja'tiʦke] |

Arabian Sea	Morze (n) Arabskie	['mɔʒɛ a'rabske]
Sea of Japan	Morze (n) Japońskie	['mɔʒɛ ja'pɔɲske]
Bering Sea	Morze (n) Beringa	['mɔʒɛ bɛ'riŋa]
South China Sea	Morze (n) Południowochińskie	['mɔʒɛ powud'nɔvɔ 'hiɲske]

Coral Sea	Morze (n) Koralowe	['mɔʒɛ kɔra'lɔvɛ]
Tasman Sea	Morze (n) Tasmana	['mɔʒɛ tas'mana]
Caribbean Sea	Morze (n) Karaibskie	['mɔʒɛ kara'ipske]

| Barents Sea | Morze (n) Barentsa | ['mɔʒɛ ba'rɛnʦa] |
| Kara Sea | Morze (n) Karskie | ['mɔʒɛ 'karske] |

North Sea	Morze (n) Północne	['mɔʒɛ puw'nɔʦnɛ]
Baltic Sea	Morze (n) Bałtyckie	['mɔʒɛ baw'tiʦke]
Norwegian Sea	Morze (n) Norweskie	['mɔʒɛ nɔr'vɛske]

79. Mountains

mountain	góra (ż)	['gura]
mountain range	łańcuch (m) górski	['waɲʦuh 'gurski]
mountain ridge	grzbiet (m) górski	[gʒbet 'gurski]

summit, top	szczyt (m)	[ʃtʃit]
peak	szczyt (m)	[ʃtʃit]
foot (~ of the mountain)	podnóże (n)	[pɔd'nuʒɛ]
slope (mountainside)	zbocze (n)	['zbɔtʃɛ]

volcano	wulkan (m)	['vuʎkan]
active volcano	czynny (m) wulkan	['tʃiɲi 'vuʎkan]
dormant volcano	wygasły (m) wulkan	[vi'gaswi 'vuʎkan]

eruption	wybuch (m)	['vibuh]
crater	krater (m)	['kratɛr]
magma	magma (ż)	['magma]
lava	lawa (ż)	['ʎava]
molten (~ lava)	rozżarzony	[rɔzʒa'ʒɔni]
canyon	kanion (m)	['kaɲjɔn]
gorge	wąwóz (m)	['vɔ̃vus]

crevice	rozpadlina (m)	[rɔspad'lina]
pass, col	przełęcz (ż)	['pʃɛwɛ̃tʃ]
plateau	płaskowyż (m)	[pwas'kɔviʃ]
cliff	skała (ż)	['skawa]
hill	wzgórze (ż)	['vzguʒɛ]

glacier	lodowiec (m)	[lɜ'dɔveʦ]
waterfall	wodospad (m)	[vɔ'dɔspat]
geyser	gejzer (m)	['gɛjzɛr]
lake	jezioro (m)	[e'ʒɜrɔ]

plain	równina (ż)	[ruv'nina]
landscape	pejzaż (m)	['pɛjzaʃ]
echo	echo (n)	['ɛhɔ]

alpinist	alpinista (m)	[aʎpi'nista]
rock climber	wspinacz (m)	['fspinatʃ]
to conquer (in climbing)	pokonywać	[pɔkɔ'niˑvatʃ]
climb (an easy ~)	wspinaczka (ż)	[fspi'natʃka]

80. Mountains names

The Alps	Alpy (l.mn.)	['aʎpi]
Mont Blanc	Mont Blanc (m)	[mɔn blan]
The Pyrenees	Pireneje (l.mn.)	[pirɛ'nɛe]

The Carpathians	Karpaty (l.mn.)	[kar'pati]
The Ural Mountains	Góry Uralskie (l.mn.)	['gurɨ u'raʎske]
The Caucasus Mountains	Kaukaz (m)	['kaukas]
Mount Elbrus	Elbrus (m)	['ɛʎbrus]

The Altai Mountains	Ałtaj (m)	['awtaj]
The Pamir Mountains	Pamir (m)	['pamir]
The Himalayas	Himalaje (l.mn.)	[hima'lae]
Mount Everest	Mont Everest (m)	[mɔnt ɛ'vɛrɛst]

| The Andes | Andy (l.mn.) | ['andɨ] |
| Mount Kilimanjaro | Kilimandżaro (ż) | [kiliman'dʒarɔ] |

81. Rivers

river	rzeka (m)	['ʒɛka]
spring (natural source)	źródło (n)	['zʲrudwɔ]
riverbed (river channel)	koryto (m)	[kɔ'ritɔ]
basin	dorzecze (n)	[dɔ'ʒɛtʃɛ]
to flow into ...	wpadać	['fpadatʃ]
tributary	dopływ (m)	['dopwɨf]
bank (of river)	brzeg (m)	[bʒɛk]

current (stream)	prąd (m)	[prɔ̃t]
downstream (adv)	z prądem	[s 'prɔ̃dɛm]
upstream (adv)	pod prąd	[pɔt prɔ̃t]

inundation	powódź (ż)	['pɔvutʃ]
flooding	wylew (m) rzeki	['viłef 'ʒɛki]
to overflow (vi)	rozlewać się	[rɔz'levatʃ ɕɛ̃]
to flood (vt)	zatapiać	[za'tapʲatʃ]

| shallow (shoal) | mielizna (ż) | [me'lizna] |
| rapids | próg (m) | [pruk] |

dam	tama (ż)	['tama]
canal	kanał (m)	['kanaw]
reservoir (artificial lake)	zbiornik (m) wodny	['zbɔrnik 'vɔdnʲi]
sluice, lock	śluza (ż)	['ɕlyza]

water body (pond, etc.)	zbiornik (m) wodny	['zbɔrnik 'vɔdnʲi]
swamp (marshland)	bagno (n)	['bagnɔ]
bog, marsh	grzęzawisko (n)	[gʒɛ̃za'viskɔ]
whirlpool	wir (m) wodny	[vir 'vɔdnʲi]

stream (brook)	potok (m)	['pɔtɔk]
drinking (ab. water)	pitny	['pitnʲi]
fresh (~ water)	słodki	['swɔtki]

| ice | lód (m) | [lyt] |
| to freeze over (ab. river, etc.) | zamarznąć | [za'marznɔ̃tʃ] |

82. Rivers' names

| Seine | Sekwana (ż) | [sɛk'fana] |
| Loire | Loara (ż) | [lɔ'ara] |

Thames	Tamiza (ż)	[ta'miza]
Rhine	Ren (m)	[rɛn]
Danube	Dunaj (m)	['dunaj]

Volga	Wołga (ż)	['vɔwga]
Don	Don (m)	[dɔn]
Lena	Lena (ż)	['lena]

Yellow River	Huang He (ż)	[hu'aŋ hɛ]
Yangtze	Jangcy (ż)	['jaŋtsi]
Mekong	Mekong (m)	['mɛkɔŋ]
Ganges	Ganges (m)	['gaŋɛs]

| Nile River | Nil (m) | [niʎ] |
| Congo River | Kongo (ż) | ['kɔŋɔ] |

Okavango River	Okawango (z)	[ɔka'vaŋɔ]
Zambezi River	Zambezi (z)	[zam'bɛzi]
Limpopo River	Limpopo (z)	[lim'pɔpɔ]
Mississippi River	Mississipi (z)	[missis'sipi]

83. Forest

| forest, wood | las (m) | [ʎas] |
| forest (as adj) | leśny | ['leɕɲi] |

thick forest	gąszcz (z)	[gɔ̃ʃʧ]
grove	gaj (m), lasek (ɳ)	[gaj], ['ʎasɛk]
forest clearing	polana (z)	[pɔ'ʎana]

| thicket | zarośla (l.mn.) | [za'rɔɕʎa] |
| scrubland | krzaki (l.mn.) | ['kʃaki] |

| footpath (troddenpath) | ścieżka (z) | ['ɕʧeʃka] |
| gully | wąwóz (m) | ['võvus] |

tree	drzewo (n)	['dʒɛvɔ]
leaf	liść (m)	[liɕʧ]
leaves (foliage)	listowie (n)	[lis'tɔve]

fall of leaves	opadanie (n) liści	[ɔpa'dane 'liɕʧi]
to fall (ab. leaves)	opadać	[ɔ'padaʧ]
top (of the tree)	wierzchołek (m)	[veʃ'hɔwɛk]

branch	gałąź (z)	['gawõɕ]
bough	sęk (m)	[sɛ̃k]
bud (on shrub, tree)	pączek (m)	['põʧɛk]
needle (of pine tree)	igła (z)	['igwa]
pine cone	szyszka (z)	['ʃiʃka]

hollow (in a tree)	dziupla (z)	['dʒypʎa]
nest	gniazdo (n)	['gɲazdɔ]
burrow (animal hole)	nora (z)	['nɔra]

trunk	pień (m)	[peɲ]
root	korzeń (m)	['kɔʒɛɲ]
bark	kora (z)	['kɔra]
moss	mech (m)	[mɛh]

| to uproot (remove trees or tree stumps) | karczować | [kart'ʃɔvaʧ] |

to chop down	ścinać	['ɕʧinaʧ]
to deforest (vt)	wycinać	[vi'ʧinaʧ]
tree stump	pieniek (m)	['penek]
campfire	ognisko (n)	[ɔg'niskɔ]
forest fire	pożar (m)	['pɔʒar]

to extinguish (vt)	gasić	['gaɕitʃ]
forest ranger	leśnik (m)	['leɕnik]
protection	ochrona (ż)	[ɔh'rɔna]
to protect (~ nature)	chronić	['hrɔnitʃ]
poacher	kłusownik (m)	[kwu'sɔvnik]
steel trap	potrzask (m)	['pɔtʃask]

to gather, to pick (vt)	zbierać	['zberatʃ]
to lose one's way	zabłądzić	[zab'wɔdʑitʃ]

84. Natural resources

natural resources	zasoby (l.mn.) naturalne	[za'sɔbɨ natu'raʎnɛ]
minerals	kopaliny (l.mn.) użyteczne	[kɔpa'linɨ uʑɨ'tɛtʃnɛ]
deposits	złoża (l.mn.)	['zwɔʒa]
field (e.g., oilfield)	złoże (n)	['zwɔʒɛ]

to mine (extract)	wydobywać	[vɨdɔ'bɨvatʃ]
mining (extraction)	wydobywanie (n)	[vɨdɔbɨ'vane]
ore	ruda (ż)	['ruda]
mine (e.g., for coal)	kopalnia (ż) rudy	[kɔ'paʎɲa 'rudɨ]
shaft (mine ~)	szyb (m)	[ʃɨb]
miner	górnik (m)	['gurnik]

gas (natural ~)	gaz (m)	[gas]
gas pipeline	gazociąg (m)	[ga'zɔtʃɔ̃k]

oil (petroleum)	ropa (ż) naftowa	['rɔpa naf'tɔva]
oil pipeline	rurociąg (m)	[ru'rɔtʃɔ̃k]
oil well	szyb (m) naftowy	[ʃɨp naf'tɔvɨ]
derrick (tower)	wieża (ż) wiertnicza	['veʒa vert'nitʃa]
tanker	tankowiec (m)	[ta'ŋkɔveʦ]

sand	piasek (m)	['pʲasɛk]
limestone	wapień (m)	['vapeɲ]
gravel	żwir (m)	[ʒvir]
peat	torf (m)	[tɔrf]
clay	glina (ż)	['glina]
coal	węgiel (m)	['vɛŋeʎ]

iron (ore)	żelazo (n)	[ʒɛ'ʎazɔ]
gold	złoto (n)	['zwɔtɔ]
silver	srebro (n)	['srɛbrɔ]
nickel	nikiel (n)	['nikeʎ]
copper	miedź (ż)	[metʃ]

zinc	cynk (m)	[ʦɨŋk]
manganese	mangan (m)	['maŋan]
mercury	rtęć (ż)	[rtɛ̃tʃ]
lead	ołów (m)	['ɔwuf]

mineral	minerał (m)	[mi'nɛraw]
crystal	kryształ (m)	['krɨʃtaw]
marble	marmur (m)	['marmur]
uranium	uran (m)	['uran]

85. Weather

weather	pogoda (ż)	[pɔ'gɔda]
weather forecast	prognoza (ż) pogody	[prɔg'nɔza pɔ'gɔdɨ]
temperature	temperatura (ż)	[tɛmpɛra'tura]
thermometer	termometr (m)	[tɛr'mɔmɛtr]
barometer	barometr (m)	[ba'rɔmɛtr]

humidity	wilgoć (ż)	['vilɡɔtʃ]
heat (extreme ~)	żar (m)	[ʒar]
hot (torrid)	upalny, gorący	[u'paʎnɨ], [gɔ'rɔ̃tsɨ]
it's hot	gorąco	[gɔ'rɔ̃tsɔ]

| it's warm | ciepło | ['tʃepwɔ] |
| warm (moderately hot) | ciepły | ['tʃepwɨ] |

| it's cold | zimno | ['ʒimnɔ] |
| cold (adj) | zimny | ['ʒimnɨ] |

sun	słońce (n)	['swɔɲtsɛ]
to shine (vi)	świecić	['ɕfetʃitʃ]
sunny (day)	słoneczny	[swɔ'nɛtʃnɨ]
to come up (vi)	wzejść	[vzɛjɕtʃ]
to set (vi)	zajść	[zajɕtʃ]

cloud	obłok (m)	['ɔbwɔk]
cloudy (adj)	zachmurzony	[zahmu'ʒɔnɨ]
rain cloud	chmura (ż)	['hmura]
somber (gloomy)	pochmurny	[pɔh'murnɨ]

rain	deszcz (m)	[dɛʃtʃ]
it's raining	pada deszcz	['pada dɛʃtʃ]
rainy (~ day, weather)	deszczowy	[dɛʃt'ʃɔvɨ]
to drizzle (vi)	mżyć	[mʒɨtʃ]

pouring rain	ulewny deszcz (m)	[u'levnɨ dɛʃtʃ]
downpour	ulewa (ż)	[u'leva]
heavy (e.g., ~ rain)	silny	['ɕiʎnɨ]
puddle	kałuża (ż)	[ka'wuʒa]
to get wet (in rain)	moknąć	['mɔknɔ̃tʃ]

fog (mist)	mgła (ż)	[mgwa]
foggy	mglisty	['mglistɨ]
snow	śnieg (m)	[ɕnek]
it's snowing	pada śnieg	['pada ɕnek]

86. Severe weather. Natural disasters

thunderstorm	burza (ż)	['buʒa]
lightning (~ strike)	błyskawica (ż)	[bwiska'vitsa]
to flash (vi)	błyskać	['bwiskatʃ]

thunder	grzmot (m)	[gʒmɔt]
to thunder (vi)	grzmieć	[gʒmetʃ]
it's thundering	grzmi	[gʒmi]

| hail | grad (m) | [grat] |
| it's hailing | pada grad | ['pada grat] |

| to flood (vt) | zatopić | [za'tɔpitʃ] |
| flood, inundation | powódź (ż) | ['pɔvutʃ] |

earthquake	trzęsienie (n) ziemi	[tʃɛ̃'cene 'ʒemi]
tremor, quake	wstrząs (m)	[fstʃɔ̃s]
epicenter	epicentrum (n)	[ɛpi'tsɛntrum]

| eruption | wybuch (m) | ['vibuh] |
| lava | lawa (ż) | ['ʎava] |

twister	trąba (ż) powietrzna	['trɔ̃ba pɔ'vetʃna]
tornado	tornado (n)	[tɔr'nadɔ]
typhoon	tajfun (m)	['tajfun]

hurricane	huragan (m)	[hu'ragan]
storm	burza (ż)	['buʒa]
tsunami	tsunami (n)	[tsu'nami]

cyclone	cyklon (m)	['tsiklɔn]
bad weather	niepogoda (ż)	[nepɔ'gɔda]
fire (accident)	pożar (m)	['pɔʒar]
disaster	katastrofa (ż)	[katast'rɔfa]
meteorite	meteoryt (m)	[mɛtɛ'ɔrit]

avalanche	lawina (ż)	[ʎa'vina]
snowslide	lawina (ż)	[ʎa'vina]
blizzard	zamieć (ż)	['zametʃ]
snowstorm	śnieżyca (ż)	[ɕne'ʒitsa]

FAUNA

87. Mammals. Predators
88. Wild animals
89. Domestic animals
90. Birds
91. Fish. Marine animals
92. Amphibians. Reptiles
93. Insects

T&P Books Publishing

87. Mammals. Predators

predator	**drapieżnik** (m)	[dra'pɛʒnik]
tiger	**tygrys** (m)	['tigris]
lion	**lew** (m)	[lef]
wolf	**wilk** (m)	[viʎk]
fox	**lis** (m)	[lis]
jaguar	**jaguar** (m)	[ja'guar]
leopard	**lampart** (m)	['ʎampart]
cheetah	**gepard** (m)	['gɛpart]
black panther	**pantera** (ż)	[pan'tɛra]
puma	**puma** (ż)	['puma]
snow leopard	**irbis** (m)	['irbis]
lynx	**ryś** (m)	[riɕ]
coyote	**kojot** (m)	['kɔɈt]
jackal	**szakal** (m)	['ʃakaʎ]
hyena	**hiena** (ż)	['hʰena]

88. Wild animals

animal	**zwierzę** (n)	['zveʒɛ̃]
beast (animal)	**dzikie zwierzę** (n)	['dʑike 'zveʒɛ̃]
squirrel	**wiewiórka** (ż)	[ve'vyrka]
hedgehog	**jeż** (m)	[eʃ]
hare	**zając** (m)	['zaɔ̃ts]
rabbit	**królik** (m)	['krulik]
badger	**borsuk** (m)	['bɔrsuk]
raccoon	**szop** (m)	[ʃɔp]
hamster	**chomik** (m)	['hɔmik]
marmot	**świstak** (m)	['ɕfistak]
mole	**kret** (m)	[krɛt]
mouse	**mysz** (ż)	[miʃ]
rat	**szczur** (m)	[ʃtʃur]
bat	**nietoperz** (m)	[ne'tɔpɛʃ]
ermine	**gronostaj** (m)	[grɔ'nɔstaj]
sable	**soból** (m)	['sɔbuʎ]
marten	**kuna** (ż)	['kuna]

| weasel | łasica (ż) | [wa'ɕitsa] |
| mink | norka (ż) | ['nɔrka] |

| beaver | bóbr (m) | [bubr] |
| otter | wydra (ż) | ['vidra] |

horse	koń (m)	[kɔɲ]
moose	łoś (m)	[wɔɕ]
deer	jeleń (m)	['elɛɲ]
camel	wielbłąd (m)	['veʎbwɔ̃t]

bison	bizon (m)	['bizɔn]
aurochs	żubr (m)	[ʒubr]
buffalo	bawół (m)	['bavuw]

zebra	zebra (ż)	['zɛbra]
antelope	antylopa (ż)	[anti'lɔpa]
roe deer	sarna (ż)	['sarna]
fallow deer	łania (ż)	['waɲa]
chamois	kozica (ż)	[kɔ'ʑitsa]
wild boar	dzik (m)	[dʑik]

whale	wieloryb (m)	[ve'lɔrip]
seal	foka (ż)	['fɔka]
walrus	mors (m)	[mɔrs]
fur seal	kot (m) morski	[kɔt 'mɔrski]
dolphin	delfin (m)	['dɛʎfin]

bear	niedźwiedź (m)	['nedʑvetʃ]
polar bear	niedźwiedź (m) polarny	['nedʑvetʃ pɔ'ʎarni]
panda	panda (ż)	['panda]

monkey	małpa (ż)	['mawpa]
chimpanzee	szympans (m)	['ʃimpans]
orangutan	orangutan (m)	[ɔra'ŋutan]
gorilla	goryl (m)	['gɔriʎ]
macaque	makak (m)	['makak]
gibbon	gibon (m)	['gibɔn]

| elephant | słoń (m) | ['swɔɲ] |
| rhinoceros | nosorożec (m) | [nɔsɔ'rɔʒɛts] |

| giraffe | żyrafa (ż) | [ʒi'rafa] |
| hippopotamus | hipopotam (m) | [hipɔ'pɔtam] |

| kangaroo | kangur (m) | ['kaŋur] |
| koala (bear) | koala (ż) | [kɔ'aʎa] |

mongoose	mangusta (ż)	[ma'ŋusta]
chinchilla	szynszyla (ż)	[ʃin'ʃiʎa]
skunk	skunks (m)	[skuŋks]
porcupine	jeżozwierz (m)	[e'ʒɔzveʃ]

89. Domestic animals

cat	kotka (ż)	['kɔtka]
tomcat	kot (m)	[kɔt]
dog	pies (m)	[pes]
horse	koń (m)	[kɔɲ]
stallion	źrebak (m), ogier (m)	['zʲrɛbak], ['ɔgjer]
mare	klacz (ż)	[kʎatʃ]
cow	krowa (ż)	['krɔva]
bull	byk (m)	[bɨk]
ox	wół (m)	[vuw]
sheep (ewe)	owca (ż)	['ɔftsa]
ram	baran (m)	['baran]
goat	koza (ż)	['kɔza]
billy goat, he-goat	kozioł (m)	['kɔʒʒw]
donkey	osioł (m)	['ɔɕʒw]
mule	muł (m)	[muw]
pig, hog	świnia (ż)	['ɕfiɲa]
piglet	prosiak (m)	['prɔɕak]
rabbit	królik (m)	['krulik]
hen (chicken)	kura (ż)	['kura]
rooster	kogut (m)	['kɔgut]
duck	kaczka (ż)	['katʃka]
drake	kaczor (m)	['katʃɔr]
goose	gęś (ż)	[gɛ̃ɕ]
tom turkey, gobbler	indyk (m)	['indɨk]
turkey (hen)	indyczka (ż)	[in'dɨtʃka]
domestic animals	zwierzęta (l.mn.) domowe	[zve'ʒɛnta dɔ'mɔvɛ]
tame (e.g., ~ hamster)	oswojony	[ɔsfɔɔnɨ]
to tame (vt)	oswajać	[ɔs'fajatʃ]
to breed (vt)	hodować	[hɔ'dɔvatʃ]
farm	ferma (ż)	['fɛrma]
poultry	drób (m)	[drup]
cattle	bydło (n)	['bɨdwɔ]
herd (cattle)	stado (n)	['stadɔ]
stable	stajnia (ż)	['stajɲa]
pigsty	chlew (m)	[hlef]
cowshed	obora (ż)	[ɔ'bɔra]
rabbit hutch	klatka (ż) dla królików	['klatka dʎa krɔ'likɔf]
hen house	kurnik (m)	['kurnik]

90. Birds

bird	ptak (m)	[ptak]
pigeon	gołąb (m)	['gɔwõp]
sparrow	wróbel (m)	['vrubɛʎ]
tit	sikorka (ż)	[ɕi'kɔrka]
magpie	sroka (ż)	['srɔka]

raven	kruk (m)	[kruk]
crow	wrona (ż)	['vrɔna]
jackdaw	kawka (ż)	['kafka]
rook	gawron (m)	['gavrɔn]

duck	kaczka (ż)	['katʃka]
goose	gęś (ż)	[gɛ̃ɕ]
pheasant	bażant (m)	['baʒant]

eagle	orzeł (m)	['ɔʒɛw]
hawk	jastrząb (m)	['jastʃɔp]
falcon	sokół (m)	['sɔkuw]
vulture	sęp (m)	[sɛ̃p]
condor (Andean ~)	kondor (m)	['kɔndɔr]

swan	łabędź (m)	['wabɛ̃tʃ]
crane	żuraw (m)	['ʒuraf]
stork	bocian (m)	['bɔtɕan]

parrot	papuga (ż)	[pa'puga]
hummingbird	koliber (m)	[kɔ'libɛr]
peacock	paw (m)	[paf]

ostrich	struś (m)	[struɕ]
heron	czapla (ż)	['tʃapʎa]
flamingo	flaming (m)	['fʎamiŋ]
pelican	pelikan (m)	[pɛ'likan]

nightingale	słowik (m)	['swɔvik]
swallow	jaskółka (ż)	[jas'kuwka]

thrush	drozd (m)	[drɔst]
song thrush	drozd śpiewak (m)	[drɔst 'ɕpevak]
blackbird	kos (m)	[kɔs]

swift	jerzyk (m)	['eʒɨk]
lark	skowronek (m)	[skɔv'rɔnɛk]
quail	przepiórka (ż)	[pʃɛ'pyrka]

woodpecker	dzięcioł (m)	['dʒɛ̃tɕow]
cuckoo	kukułka (ż)	[ku'kuwka]
owl	sowa (ż)	['sɔva]
eagle owl	puchacz (m)	['puhatʃ]

wood grouse	głuszec (m)	['gwuʃɛts]
black grouse	cietrzew (m)	['tɕetʃɛf]
partridge	kuropatwa (ż)	[kurɔ'patfa]

starling	szpak (m)	[ʃpak]
canary	kanarek (m)	[ka'narɛk]
hazel grouse	jarząbek (m)	[ja'ʒɔ̃bɛk]
chaffinch	zięba (ż)	['ʒɛ̃ba]
bullfinch	gil (m)	[giʎ]

seagull	mewa (ż)	['mɛva]
albatross	albatros (m)	[aʎ'batrɔs]
penguin	pingwin (m)	['piŋvin]

91. Fish. Marine animals

bream	leszcz (m)	[leʃtʃ]
carp	karp (m)	[karp]
perch	okoń (m)	['ɔkɔɲ]
catfish	sum (m)	[sum]
pike	szczupak (m)	['ʃtʃupak]

salmon	łosoś (m)	['wɔsɔɕ]
sturgeon	jesiotr (m)	['eɕɔtr]

herring	śledź (m)	[ɕletʃ]
Atlantic salmon	łosoś (m)	['wɔsɔɕ]
mackerel	makrela (ż)	[mak'rɛla]
flatfish	flądra (ż)	[flɔ̃dra]

zander, pike perch	sandacz (m)	['sandatʃ]
cod	dorsz (m)	[dɔrʃ]
tuna	tuńczyk (m)	['tuɲtʃik]
trout	pstrąg (m)	[pstrɔ̃k]

eel	węgorz (m)	['vɛŋɔʃ]
electric ray	drętwa (ż)	['drɛntfa]
moray eel	murena (ż)	[mu'rɛna]
piranha	pirania (ż)	[pi'ranja]

shark	rekin (m)	['rɛkin]
dolphin	delfin (m)	['dɛʎfin]
whale	wieloryb (m)	[ve'lɔrip]

crab	krab (m)	[krap]
jellyfish	meduza (ż)	[mɛ'duza]
octopus	ośmiornica (ż)	[ɔɕmɔr'nitsa]

starfish	rozgwiazda (ż)	[rɔzg'vʲazda]
sea urchin	jeżowiec (m)	[e'ʒɔvets]

seahorse	konik (m) morski	['kɔnik 'mɔrski]
oyster	ostryga (ż)	[ɔst'riga]
shrimp	krewetka (ż)	[krɛ'vɛtka]
lobster	homar (m)	['hɔmar]
spiny lobster	langusta (ż)	[ʎa'ŋusta]

92. Amphibians. Reptiles

| snake | wąż (m) | [võʃ] |
| venomous (snake) | jadowity | [jadɔ'viti] |

viper	żmija (ż)	['ʒmija]
cobra	kobra (ż)	['kɔbra]
python	pyton (m)	['pitɔn]
boa	wąż dusiciel (m)	[võʒ du'ɕiʧeʎ]

grass snake	zaskroniec (m)	[zask'rɔneʦ]
rattle snake	grzechotnik (m)	[gʒɛ'hɔtnik]
anaconda	anakonda (ż)	[ana'kɔnda]

lizard	jaszczurka (ż)	[jaʃt'ʃurka]
iguana	legwan (m)	['legvan]
monitor lizard	waran (m)	['varan]
salamander	salamandra (ż)	[saʎa'mandra]
chameleon	kameleon (m)	[kamɛ'leɔn]
scorpion	skorpion (m)	['skɔrpʰɜn]

turtle	żółw (m)	[ʒuwf]
frog	żaba (ż)	['ʒaba]
toad	ropucha (ż)	[rɔ'puha]
crocodile	krokodyl (m)	[krɔ'kɔdɨʎ]

93. Insects

insect, bug	owad (m)	['ɔvat]
butterfly	motyl (m)	['mɔtiʎ]
ant	mrówka (ż)	['mrufka]
fly	mucha (ż)	['muha]
mosquito	komar (m)	['kɔmar]
beetle	żuk (m), chrząszcz (m)	[ʒuk], [hʃõʃʧ]

wasp	osa (ż)	['ɔsa]
bee	pszczoła (ż)	['pʃʧɔwa]
bumblebee	trzmiel (m)	[tʃmeʎ]
gadfly	giez (m)	[ges]

| spider | pająk (m) | ['paõk] |
| spider's web | pajęczyna (ż) | [paĉt'ʃɨna] |

dragonfly	ważka (ż)	['vaʃka]
grasshopper	konik (m) polny	['kɔnik 'pɔʎni]
moth (night butterfly)	omacnica (ż)	[ɔmats'nitsa]

cockroach	karaluch (m)	[ka'ralyh]
tick	kleszcz (m)	[kleʃtʃ]
flea	pchła (ż)	[phwa]
midge	meszka (ż)	['mɛʃka]

locust	szarańcza (ż)	[ʃa'raɲtʃa]
snail	ślimak (m)	['ɕlimak]
cricket	świerszcz (m)	[ɕferʃtʃ]
lightning bug	robaczek (m) świętojański	[rɔ'batʃɛk ɕfɛ̃tɔ'jaɲski]
ladybug	biedronka (ż)	[bed'rɔŋka]
cockchafer	chrabąszcz (m) majowy	['hrabɔ̃ʃtʃ maɜvi]

leech	pijawka (ż)	[pi'jafka]
caterpillar	gąsienica (ż)	[gɔ̃ɕe'nitsa]
earthworm	robak (m)	['rɔbak]
larva	poczwarka (ż)	[pɔtʃ'farka]

FLORA

94. Trees
95. Shrubs
96. Fruits. Berries
97. Flowers. Plants
98. Cereals, grains

T&P Books Publishing

tree	drzewo (n)	['dʒɛvɔ]
deciduous (adj)	liściaste	[liɕ'tʃastɛ]
coniferous (adj)	iglaste	[igʎastɛ]
evergreen (adj)	wiecznie zielony	[vetʃnɛʒe'lɜnɨ]

apple tree	jabłoń (ż)	['jabwɔɲ]
pear tree	grusza (ż)	['gruʃa]
sweet cherry tree	czereśnia (ż)	[tʃɛ'rɛɕɲa]
sour cherry tree	wiśnia (ż)	['viɕɲa]
plum tree	śliwa (ż)	['ɕliva]

birch	brzoza (ż)	['bʒɔza]
oak	dąb (m)	[dɔ̃p]
linden tree	lipa (ż)	['lipa]
aspen	osika (ż)	[ɔ'ɕika]
maple	klon (m)	['klɜn]

spruce	świerk (m)	['ɕferk]
pine	sosna (ż)	['sɔsna]
larch	modrzew (m)	['mɔdʒɛf]

| fir tree | jodła (ż) | [ɜdwa] |
| cedar | cedr (m) | [tsɛdr] |

| poplar | topola (ż) | [tɔ'pɔʎa] |
| rowan | jarzębina (ż) | [jaʒɛ̃'bina] |

| willow | wierzba iwa (ż) | ['veʒba 'iva] |
| alder | olcha (ż) | ['ɔʎha] |

| beech | buk (m) | [buk] |
| elm | wiąz (m) | [vɔ̃z] |

| ash (tree) | jesion (m) | ['eɕɜn] |
| chestnut | kasztan (m) | ['kaʃtan] |

magnolia	magnolia (ż)	[mag'nɔʎja]
palm tree	palma (ż)	['paʎma]
cypress	cyprys (m)	['tsɨprɨs]

mangrove	drzewo (n) mangrowe	['dʒɛvɔ maɲ'rɔvɛ]
baobab	baobab (m)	[ba'ɔbap]
eucalyptus	eukaliptus (m)	[ɛuka'liptus]
sequoia	sekwoja (ż)	[sɛk'fɔja]

95. Shrubs

bush	krzew (m)	[kʃɛf]
shrub	krzaki (l.mn.)	['kʃaki]
grapevine	winorośl (ż)	[vi'nɔrɔɕʎ]
vineyard	winnica (ż)	[vi'ɲitsa]
raspberry bush	malina (ż)	[ma'lina]
redcurrant bush	porzeczka (ż) czerwona	[pɔ'ʒɛtʃka tʃɛr'vɔna]
gooseberry bush	agrest (m)	['agrɛst]
acacia	akacja (ż)	[a'katsʰja]
barberry	berberys (m)	[bɛr'bɛris]
jasmine	jaśmin (m)	['jaɕmin]
juniper	jałowiec (m)	[ja'wɔvets]
rosebush	róża (ż)	['ruʒa]
dog rose	dzika róża (ż)	['dʒika 'ruʒa]

96. Fruits. Berries

fruit	owoc (m)	['ɔvɔts]
fruits	owoce (l.mn.)	[ɔ'vɔtsɛ]
apple	jabłko (n)	['jabkɔ]
pear	gruszka (ż)	['gruʃka]
plum	śliwka (ż)	['ɕlifka]
strawberry	truskawka (ż)	[trus'kafka]
sour cherry	wiśnia (ż)	['viɕɲa]
sweet cherry	czereśnia (ż)	[tʃɛ'rɛɕɲa]
grape	winogrona (l.mn.)	[vinɔg'rɔna]
raspberry	malina (ż)	[ma'lina]
blackcurrant	czarna porzeczka (ż)	['tʃarna pɔ'ʒɛtʃka]
redcurrant	czerwona porzeczka (ż)	[tʃɛr'vɔna pɔ'ʒɛtʃka]
gooseberry	agrest (m)	['agrɛst]
cranberry	żurawina (ż)	[ʒura'vina]
orange	pomarańcza (ż)	[pɔma'raɲtʃa]
mandarin	mandarynka (ż)	[manda'riŋka]
pineapple	ananas (ż)	[a'nanas]
banana	banan (m)	['banan]
date	daktyl (m)	['daktɨl]
lemon	cytryna (ż)	[tsɨt'rina]
apricot	morela (ż)	[mɔ'rɛʎa]
peach	brzoskwinia (ż)	[bʒɔsk'fiɲa]
kiwi	kiwi (n)	['kivi]

grapefruit	grejpfrut (m)	['grɛjpfrut]
berry	jagoda (ż)	[ja'gɔda]
berries	jagody (l.mn.)	[ja'gɔdi]
cowberry	borówka (ż)	[bɔ'rufka]
field strawberry	poziomka (ż)	[pɔ'ʒɜmka]
bilberry	borówka (ż) czarna	[bɔ'rɔfka 'ʧarna]

97. Flowers. Plants

| flower | kwiat (m) | [kfʲat] |
| bouquet (of flowers) | bukiet (m) | ['buket] |

rose (flower)	róża (ż)	['ruʒa]
tulip	tulipan (m)	[tu'lipan]
carnation	goździk (m)	['gɔʑʲʤik]
gladiolus	mieczyk (m)	['metʃik]

cornflower	bławatek (m)	[bwa'vatɛk]
bluebell	dzwonek (m)	['ʣvɔnɛk]
dandelion	dmuchawiec (m)	[dmu'haveʦ]
camomile	rumianek (m)	[ru'mʲanɛk]

aloe	aloes (m)	[a'lɔɛs]
cactus	kaktus (m)	['kaktus]
rubber plant, ficus	fikus (m)	['fikus]

lily	lilia (ż)	['liʎja]
geranium	pelargonia (ż)	[pɛʎar'gɔɲja]
hyacinth	hiacynt (m)	['hʰjaʦint]

mimosa	mimoza (ż)	[mi'mɔza]
narcissus	narcyz (m)	['narʦis]
nasturtium	nasturcja (ż)	[nas'turʦʰja]

orchid	orchidea (ż)	[ɔrhi'dɛa]
peony	piwonia (ż)	[pi'vɔɲja]
violet	fiołek (m)	[fʰɔwɛk]

pansy	bratek (m)	['bratɛk]
forget-me-not	niezapominajka (ż)	[nezapɔmi'najka]
daisy	stokrotka (ż)	[stɔk'rɔtka]

poppy	mak (m)	[mak]
hemp	konopie (l.mn.)	[kɔ'nɔpje]
mint	mięta (ż)	['menta]

lily of the valley	konwalia (ż)	[kɔn'vaʎja]
snowdrop	przebiśnieg (m)	[pʃɛ'biɕnek]
nettle	pokrzywa (ż)	[pɔk'ʃiva]
sorrel	szczaw (m)	[ʃʧaf]

water lily	lilia wodna (ż)	['liʎja 'vɔdna]
fern	paproć (ż)	['paprɔtʃ]
lichen	porost (m)	['pɔrɔst]

greenhouse (tropical ~)	szklarnia (ż)	['ʃkʎarɲa]
lawn	trawnik (m)	['travnik]
flowerbed	klomb (m)	['klɜmp]

plant	roślina (ż)	[rɔɕ'lina]
grass	trawa (ż)	['trava]
blade of grass	źdźbło (n)	[ʑʲdʒʲbwɔ]

leaf	liść (m)	[liɕtʃ]
petal	płatek (m)	['pwatɛk]
stem	łodyga (ż)	[wɔ'dɨga]
tuber	bulwa (ż)	['buʎva]

| young plant (shoot) | kiełek (m) | ['kewɛk] |
| thorn | kolec (m) | ['kɔlets] |

to blossom (vi)	kwitnąć	['kfitnɔ̃tʃ]
to fade, to wither	więdnąć	['vendnɔ̃tʃ]
smell (odor)	zapach (m)	['zapah]
to cut (flowers)	ściąć	[ɕtʃɔ̃ʲtʃ]
to pick (a flower)	zerwać	['zɛrvatʃ]

98. Cereals, grains

grain	zboże (n)	['zbɔʒɛ]
cereal crops	zboża (l.mn.)	['zbɔʒa]
ear (of barley, etc.)	kłos (m)	[kwɔs]

wheat	pszenica (ż)	[pʃɛ'nitsa]
rye	żyto (n)	['ʒɨtɔ]
oats	owies (m)	['ɔves]
millet	proso (n)	['prɔsɔ]
barley	jęczmień (m)	['entʃmɛ̃]

corn	kukurydza (ż)	[kuku'rɨdza]
rice	ryż (m)	[rɨʃ]
buckwheat	gryka (ż)	['grɨka]

pea plant	groch (m)	[grɔh]
kidney bean	fasola (ż)	[fa'sɔʎa]
soy	soja (ż)	['sɔja]
lentil	soczewica (ż)	[sɔtʃɛ'vitsa]
beans (pulse crops)	bób (m)	[bup]

T&P BOOKS

COUNTRIES OF
THE WORLD

99. Countries. Part 1
100. Countries. Part 2
101. Countries. Part 3

T&P Books Publishing

Afghanistan	**Afganistan** (n)	[avga'nistan]
Albania	**Albania** (ż)	[aʎ'baɲja]
Argentina	**Argentyna** (ż)	[argɛn'tіna]
Armenia	**Armenia** (ż)	[ar'mɛɲja]
Australia	**Australia** (ż)	[aust'raʎja]
Austria	**Austria** (ż)	['austrʰja]
Azerbaijan	**Azerbejdżan** (m)	[azɛr'bɛjdʒan]

The Bahamas	**Wyspy** (l.mn.) **Bahama**	['vіspі ba'hama]
Bangladesh	**Bangladesz** (m)	[baŋʎa'dɛʃ]
Belarus	**Białoruś** (ż)	[bʲa'woruɕ]
Belgium	**Belgia** (ż)	['bɛʎgʰja]
Bolivia	**Boliwia** (ż)	[bɔ'livʰja]
Bosnia and Herzegovina	**Bośnia i Hercegowina** (ż)	['bɔɕɲa i hɛrtsɛgɔ'vina]
Brazil	**Brazylia** (ż)	[bra'zіʎja]
Bulgaria	**Bułgaria** (ż)	[buw'garʰja]

Cambodia	**Kambodża** (ż)	[kam'bɔdʒa]
Canada	**Kanada** (ż)	[ka'nada]
Chile	**Chile** (n)	['tʃіle]
China	**Chiny** (l.mn.)	['hinі]
Colombia	**Kolumbia** (ż)	[kɔ'lymbʰja]
Croatia	**Chorwacja** (ż)	[hɔr'vatsʰja]
Cuba	**Kuba** (ż)	['kuba]
Cyprus	**Cypr** (m)	[tsіpr]
Czech Republic	**Czechy** (l.mn.)	['tʃɛhі]

Denmark	**Dania** (ż)	['daɲja]
Dominican Republic	**Dominikana** (ż)	[dɔmini'kana]
Ecuador	**Ekwador** (m)	[ɛk'fadɔr]
Egypt	**Egipt** (m)	['ɛgipt]
England	**Anglia** (ż)	['aŋʎja]
Estonia	**Estonia** (ż)	[ɛs'tɔɲja]
Finland	**Finlandia** (ż)	[fin'ʎandʰja]
France	**Francja** (ż)	['frantsʰja]
French Polynesia	**Polinezja** (ż) **Francuska**	[pɔli'nɛzʰja fran'tsuska]

Georgia	**Gruzja** (ż)	['gruzʰja]
Germany	**Niemcy** (l.mn.)	['nemtsі]
Ghana	**Ghana** (ż)	['gana]
Great Britain	**Wielka Brytania** (ż)	['veʎka bri'taɲja]
Greece	**Grecja** (ż)	['grɛtsʰja]
Haiti	**Haiti** (n)	[ha'iti]
Hungary	**Węgry** (l.mn.)	['vɛŋrі]

100. Countries. Part 2

Iceland	Islandia (ż)	[isˈʎandʰja]
India	Indie (l.mn.)	[ˈindʰe]
Indonesia	Indonezja (ż)	[indɔˈnɛzʰja]
Iran	Iran (m)	[ˈiran]
Iraq	Irak (m)	[ˈirak]
Ireland	Irlandia (ż)	[irˈʎandʰja]
Israel	Izrael (m)	[izˈraɛʎ]
Italy	Włochy (l.mn.)	[ˈvwɔhɨ]
Jamaica	Jamajka (ż)	[jaˈmajka]
Japan	Japonia (ż)	[jaˈpɔɲja]
Jordan	Jordania (ż)	[ɜrˈdaɲja]
Kazakhstan	Kazachstan (m)	[kaˈzahstan]
Kenya	Kenia (ż)	[ˈkɛɲja]
Kirghizia	Kirgizja (ż), Kirgistan (m)	[kirˈgizʰja], [kirˈgistan]
Kuwait	Kuwejt (m)	[ˈkuvɛjt]
Laos	Laos (m)	[ˈʎaɔs]
Latvia	Łotwa (ż)	[ˈwɔtfa]
Lebanon	Liban (m)	[ˈliban]
Libya	Libia (ż)	[ˈlibʰja]
Liechtenstein	Liechtenstein (m)	[ˈlihtɛnʃtajn]
Lithuania	Litwa (ż)	[ˈlitfa]
Luxembourg	Luksemburg (m)	[ˈlyksɛmburk]

Macedonia (Republic of ~)	Macedonia (ż)	[maʦɛˈdɔɲja]
Madagascar	Madagaskar (m)	[madaˈgaskar]
Malaysia	Malezja (ż)	[maˈlezʰja]
Malta	Malta (ż)	[ˈmaʎta]
Mexico	Meksyk (m)	[ˈmɛksɨk]
Moldova, Moldavia	Mołdawia (ż)	[mɔwˈdavʰja]

Monaco	Monako (n)	[mɔˈnakɔ]
Mongolia	Mongolia (ż)	[mɔˈɲɔʎja]
Montenegro	Czarnogóra (ż)	[tʃarnɔˈgura]
Morocco	Maroko (n)	[maˈrɔkɔ]
Myanmar	Mjanma (ż)	[ˈmjanma]
Namibia	Namibia (ż)	[naˈmibʰja]
Nepal	Nepal (m)	[ˈnɛpaʎ]
Netherlands	Niderlandy (l.mn.)	[nidɛrˈʎandɨ]
New Zealand	Nowa Zelandia (ż)	[ˈnɔva zɛˈʎandʰja]
North Korea	Korea (ż) Północna	[kɔˈrɛa puwˈnɔʦna]
Norway	Norwegia (ż)	[nɔrˈvɛgʰja]

101. Countries. Part 3

Pakistan	Pakistan (m)	[ˈpaˈkistan]
Palestine	Autonomia (ż) Palestyńska	[autɔˈnɔmʰja palesˈtɨɲska]

189

Panama	Panama (ż)	[pa'nama]
Paraguay	Paragwaj (m)	[pa'ragvaj]
Peru	Peru (n)	['pɛru]
Poland	Polska (ż)	['poʎska]
Portugal	Portugalia (ż)	[portu'gaʎja]
Romania	Rumunia (ż)	[ru'muɲja]
Russia	Rosja (ż)	['rɔsʰja]

Saudi Arabia	Arabia (ż) Saudyjska	[a'rabʰja sau'dijska]
Scotland	Szkocja (ż)	['ʃkɔtsʰja]
Senegal	Senegal (m)	[sɛ'nɛgaʎ]
Serbia	Serbia (ż)	['sɛrbʰja]
Slovakia	Słowacja (ż)	[swɔ'vatsʰja]
Slovenia	Słowenia (ż)	[swɔ'vɛɲja]

South Africa	Afryka (ż) Południowa	['afrika pɔwud'nɔva]
South Korea	Korea (ż) Południowa	[kɔ'rɛa pɔwud'nɔva]
Spain	Hiszpania (ż)	[hiʃ'paɲja]
Suriname	Surinam (m)	[su'rinam]
Sweden	Szwecja (ż)	['ʃfɛtsʰja]
Switzerland	Szwajcaria (ż)	[ʃfaj'tsarʰja]
Syria	Syria (ż)	['sirʰja]

Taiwan	Tajwan (m)	['tajvan]
Tajikistan	Tadżykistan (m)	[tadʒi'kistan]
Tanzania	Tanzania (ż)	[tan'zaɲja]
Tasmania	Tasmania (ż)	[tas'maɲja]
Thailand	Tajlandia (ż)	[taj'ʎandʰja]
Tunisia	Tunezja (ż)	[tu'nɛzʰja]
Turkey	Turcja (ż)	['turtsʰja]
Turkmenistan	Turkmenia (ż)	[turk'mɛɲja]

Ukraine	Ukraina (ż)	[ukra'ina]
United Arab Emirates	Zjednoczone Emiraty Arabskie	[zʰednɔt'ʃɔnɛ ɛmi'rati a'rapske]
United States of America	Stany (l.mn.) Zjednoczone Ameryki	['stani zʰednɔt'ʃɔnɛ a'mɛriki]
Uruguay	Urugwaj (m)	[u'rugvaj]
Uzbekistan	Uzbekistan (m)	[uzbɛ'kistan]

Vatican	Watykan (m)	[va'tikan]
Venezuela	Wenezuela (ż)	[vɛnɛzu'ɛʎa]
Vietnam	Wietnam (m)	['vʰetnam]
Zanzibar	Zanzibar (m)	[zan'zibar]

GASTRONOMIC GLOSSARY

This section contains a lot of words and terms associated with food. This dictionary will make it easier for you to understand the menu at a restaurant and choose the right dish

T&P Books Publishing

English-Polish gastronomic glossary

aftertaste	posmak (m)	['pɔsmak]
almond	migdał (m)	['migdaw]
anise	anyż (m)	['aniʃ]
aperitif	aperitif (m)	[apɛri'tif]
appetite	apetyt (m)	[a'pɛtit]
appetizer	przystawka (ż)	[pʃis'tafka]
apple	jabłko (n)	['jabkɔ]
apricot	morela (ż)	[mɔ'rɛʎa]
artichoke	karczoch (m)	['kartʃɔh]
asparagus	szparagi (l.mn.)	[ʃpa'ragi]
Atlantic salmon	łosoś (m)	['wɔsɔɕ]
avocado	awokado (n)	[avɔ'kadɔ]
bacon	boczek (m)	['bɔtʃɛk]
banana	banan (m)	['banan]
barley	jęczmień (m)	['entʃmɛ̃]
bartender	barman (m)	['barman]
basil	bazylia (ż)	[ba'ziʎja]
bay leaf	liść (m) laurowy	[liɕtʃ ʎau'rɔvi]
beans	bób (m)	[bup]
beef	wołowina (ż)	[vɔwɔ'vina]
beer	piwo (n)	['pivɔ]
beetroot	burak (m)	['burak]
bell pepper	słodka papryka (ż)	['swɔdka pap'rika]
berries	jagody (l.mn.)	[ja'gɔdi]
berry	jagoda (ż)	[ja'gɔda]
bilberry	borówka (ż) czarna	[bɔ'rɔfka 'tʃarna]
birch bolete	koźlarz (m)	['kɔʑ/ʎaʃ]
bitter	gorzki	['gɔʃki]
black coffee	czarna kawa (ż)	['tʃarna 'kava]
black pepper	pieprz (m) czarny	[pepʃ 'tʃarni]
black tea	czarna herbata (ż)	['tʃarna hɛr'bata]
blackberry	jeżyna (ż)	[e'ʒina]
blackcurrant	czarna porzeczka (ż)	['tʃarna pɔ'ʒɛtʃka]
boiled	gotowany	[gɔtɔ'vani]
bottle opener	otwieracz (m) do butelek	[ɔt'feratʃ dɛ bu'tɛlek]
bread	chleb (m)	[hlep]
breakfast	śniadanie (n)	[ɕɲa'dane]
bream	leszcz (m)	[leʃtʃ]
broccoli	brokuły (l.mn.)	[brɔ'kuwi]
Brussels sprouts	brukselka (ż)	[bruk'sɛʎka]
buckwheat	gryka (ż)	['grika]
butter	masło (n) śmietankowe	['maswɔ ɕmeta'ŋkɔvɛ]
buttercream	krem (m)	[krɛm]
cabbage	kapusta (ż)	[ka'pusta]

cake	ciastko (n)	['tʃastkɔ]
cake	tort (m)	[tɔrt]
calorie	kaloria (ż)	[ka'lɜrja]
can opener	otwieracz (m) do puszek	[ɔt'feratʃ dɛ 'puʃɛk]
candy	cukierek (m)	[ʦu'kerɛk]
canned food	konserwy (l.mn.)	[kɔn'sɛrvi]
cappuccino	cappuccino (n)	[kapu'tʃinɔ]
caraway	kminek (m)	['kminɛk]
carbohydrates	węglowodany (l.mn.)	[vɛnɛ̃zvɔ'dani]
carbonated	gazowana	[ga'zɔvana]
carp	karp (m)	[karp]
carrot	marchew (ż)	['marhɛf]
catfish	sum (m)	[sum]
cauliflower	kalafior (m)	[ka'ʎafɜr]
caviar	kawior (m)	['kavɜr]
celery	seler (m)	['sɛler]
cep	prawdziwek (m)	[prav'dʒivɛk]
cereal crops	zboża (l.mn.)	['zbɔʒa]
cereal grains	kasza (ż)	['kaʃa]
champagne	szampan (m)	['ʃampan]
chanterelle	kurka (ż)	['kurka]
check	rachunek (m)	[ra'hunɛk]
cheese	ser (m)	[sɛr]
chewing gum	guma (ż) do żucia	['guma dɔ 'ʒutʃa]
chicken	kurczak (m)	['kurtʃak]
chocolate	czekolada (ż)	[tʃɛkɔ'ʎada]
chocolate	czekoladowy	[tʃɛkɔʎa'dɔvi]
cinnamon	cynamon (m)	[ʦi'namɔn]
clear soup	rosół (m)	['rɔsuw]
cloves	goździki (l.mn.)	['gɔzʲdʒiki]
cocktail	koktajl (m)	['kɔktajʎ]
coconut	orzech (m) kokosowy	['ɔʒɛh kɔkɔ'sɔvi]
cod	dorsz (m)	[dɔrʃ]
coffee	kawa (ż)	['kava]
coffee with milk	kawa (ż) z mlekiem	['kava z 'mlekem]
cognac	koniak (m)	['kɔɲjak]
cold	zimny	['ʒimni]
condensed milk	mleko skondensowane	['mlekɔ skɔndɛnsɔ'vanɛ]
condiment	przyprawa (ż)	[pʃip'rava]
confectionery	wyroby (l.mn.) cukiernicze	[vi'rɔbi ʦuker'nitʃɛ]
cookies	herbatniki (l.mn.)	[hɛrbat'niki]
coriander	kolendra (ż)	[kɔ'lendra]
corkscrew	korkociąg (m)	[kɔr'kɔtʃɔ̃k]
corn	kukurydza (ż)	[kuku'ridza]
corn	kukurydza (ż)	[kuku'ridza]
cornflakes	płatki (l.mn.) kukurydziane	['pwatki kukuri'dʒʲanɛ]
course, dish	danie (n)	['dane]
cowberry	borówka (ż)	[bɔ'rufka]
crab	krab (m)	[krap]
cranberry	żurawina (ż)	[ʒura'vina]
cream	śmietanka (ż)	[ɕme'taŋka]
crumb	okruchek (m)	[ɔk'ruhɛk]

cucumber	ogórek (m)	[ɔ'gurɛk]
cuisine	kuchnia (ż)	['kuhɲa]
cup	filiżanka (ż)	[fili'ʒaŋka]
dark beer	piwo (n) ciemne	[pivɔ 'ʧɛmnɛ]
date	daktyl (m)	['daktɨl]
death cap	psi grzyb (m)	[pɕi gʒɨp]
dessert	deser (m)	['dɛsɛr]
diet	dieta (ż)	['dʰeta]
dill	koperek (m)	[kɔ'pɛrɛk]
dinner	kolacja (ż)	[kɔ'ʎatsʰja]
dried	suszony	[su'ʃɔnɨ]
drinking water	woda (ż) pitna	['vɔda 'pitna]
duck	kaczka (ż)	['katʃka]
ear	kłos (m)	[kwɔs]
edible mushroom	grzyb (m) jadalny	[gʒɨp ja'daʎnɨ]
eel	węgorz (m)	['vɛŋɔʃ]
egg	jajko (n)	['jajkɔ]
egg white	białko (n)	['bʲawkɔ]
egg yolk	żółtko (n)	['ʒuwtkɔ]
eggplant	bakłażan (m)	[bak'waʒan]
eggs	jajka (l.mn.)	['jajka]
Enjoy your meal!	Smacznego!	[smatʃ'nɛgɔ]
fats	tłuszcze (l.mn.)	['twuʃʧɛ]
field strawberry	poziomka (ż)	[pɔ'ʒɔmka]
fig	figa (ż)	['figa]
filling	nadzienie (n)	[na'dʑene]
fish	ryba (ż)	['rɨba]
flatfish	flądra (ż)	[flɔ̃dra]
flour	mąka (ż)	['mɔ̃ka]
fly agaric	muchomor (m)	[mu'hɔmɔr]
food	jedzenie (n)	[e'dʑɛne]
fork	widelec (m)	[vi'dɛlɛts]
freshly squeezed juice	sok (m) ze świeżych owoców	[sɔk zɛ 'ɕfeʒɨh ɔ'vɔtsuf]
fried	smażony	[sma'ʒɔnɨ]
fried eggs	jajecznica (ż)	[jaetʃ'nitsa]
fried meatballs	kotlet (m)	['kɔtlɛt]
frozen	mrożony	[mrɔ'ʒɔnɨ]
fruit	owoc (m)	['ɔvɔts]
fruits	owoce (l.mn.)	[ɔ'vɔtsɛ]
game	dziczyzna (ż)	[dʑit'ʃizna]
gammon	szynka (ż)	['ʃiŋka]
garlic	czosnek (m)	['tʃɔsnɛk]
gin	dżin (m), gin (m)	[dʒin]
ginger	imbir (m)	['imbir]
glass	szklanka (ż)	['ʃkʎaŋka]
glass	kielich (m)	['kelih]
goose	gęś (ż)	[gɛ̃ɕ]
gooseberry	agrest (m)	['agrɛst]
grain	zboże (n)	['zbɔʒɛ]
grape	winogrona (l.mn.)	[vinɔg'rɔna]
grapefruit	grejpfrut (m)	['grɛjpfrut]

green tea	zielona herbata (ż)	[ʒeˈlɔna hɛrˈbata]
greens	włoszczyzna (ż)	[vvɔʃtˈʃizna]
halibut	halibut (m)	[haˈlibut]
ham	szynka (ż)	[ˈʃiŋka]
hamburger	farsz (m)	[farʃ]
hamburger	hamburger (m)	[hamˈburgɛr]
hazelnut	orzech (m) laskowy	[ˈɔʒɛh ʎasˈkɔvi]
herring	śledź (m)	[ɕletʃ]
honey	miód (m)	[myt]
horseradish	chrzan (m)	[hʃan]
hot	gorący	[gɔˈrɔ̃tsi]
ice	lód (m)	[lyt]
ice-cream	lody (l.mn.)	[ˈlɔdi]
instant coffee	kawa (ż) rozpuszczalna	[ˈkava rɔspuʃtˈʃaʎna]
jam	dżem (m)	[dʒɛm]
jam	konfitura (ż)	[kɔnfiˈtura]
juice	sok (m)	[sɔk]
kidney bean	fasola (ż)	[faˈsɔʎa]
kiwi	kiwi (n)	[ˈkivi]
knife	nóż (m)	[nuʃ]
lamb	baranina (ż)	[baraˈnina]
lard	smalec (m)	[ˈsmalets]
lemon	cytryna (ż)	[tsitˈrina]
lemonade	lemoniada (ż)	[lemɔˈɲjada]
lentil	soczewica (ż)	[sɔtʃɛˈvitsa]
lettuce	sałata (ż)	[saˈwata]
light beer	piwo (n) jasne	[pivɔ ˈjasnɛ]
liqueur	likier (m)	[ˈliker]
liquors	napoje (l.mn.) alkoholowe	[naˈpɔe aʎkɔhɔˈlɔvɛ]
liver	wątróbka (ż)	[võtˈrupka]
lunch	obiad (m)	[ˈɔbʲat]
mackerel	makrela (ż)	[makˈrɛla]
mandarin	mandarynka (ż)	[mandaˈriŋka]
mango	mango (n)	[ˈmaŋɔ]
margarine	margaryna (ż)	[margaˈrina]
marmalade	marmolada (ż)	[marmɔˈʎada]
mayonnaise	majonez (m)	[maʒnɛs]
meat	mięso (n)	[ˈmensɔ]
melon	melon (m)	[ˈmɛlɔn]
menu	menu (n)	[ˈmenu]
milk	mleko (n)	[ˈmlekɔ]
milkshake	koktajl (m) mleczny	[ˈkɔktajʎ ˈmletʃni]
millet	proso (n)	[ˈprɔsɔ]
mineral water	woda (ż) mineralna	[ˈvɔda minɛˈraʎna]
morel	smardz (m)	[smarts]
mushroom	grzyb (m)	[gʒip]
mustard	musztarda (ż)	[muʃˈtarda]
non-alcoholic	bezalkoholowy	[bɛzaʎkɔhɔˈlɔvi]
noodles	makaron (m)	[maˈkarɔn]
oats	owies (m)	[ˈɔves]
olive oil	olej (m) oliwkowy	[ˈɔlej ɔlifˈkɔvi]
olives	oliwki (ż, l.mn.)	[ɔˈlifki]

omelet	omlet (m)	['ɔmlɛt]
onion	cebula (ż)	[tsɛ'buʎa]
orange	pomarańcza (ż)	[pɔma'rant͡ʃa]
orange juice	sok (m) pomarańczowy	[sɔk pɔmaraɲt'ʃɔvi]
orange-cap boletus	koźlarz (m) czerwony	['kɔzʲʎaʃ t͡ʃɛr'vɔni]
oyster	ostryga (ż)	[ɔst'riga]
pâté	pasztet (m)	['paʃtɛt]
papaya	papaja (ż)	[pa'paja]
paprika	papryka (ż)	[pap'rika]
parsley	pietruszka (ż)	[pet'ruʃka]
pasta	makaron (m)	[ma'karɔn]
pea	groch (m)	[grɔh]
peach	brzoskwinia (ż)	[bʒɔsk'fiɲa]
peanut	orzeszek (l.mn.) ziemny	[ɔ'ʒɛʃɛk 'ʒemnɛ]
pear	gruszka (ż)	['gruʃka]
peel	skórka (ż)	['skurka]
perch	okoń (m)	['ɔkɔɲ]
pickled	marynowany	[marinɔ'vanɪ]
pie	ciasto (n)	['t͡ʃastɔ]
piece	kawałek (m)	[ka'vawɛk]
pike	szczupak (m)	['ʃt͡ʃupak]
pike perch	sandacz (m)	['sandat͡ʃ]
pineapple	ananas (m)	[a'nanas]
pistachios	fistaszki (l.mn.)	[fis'taʃki]
pizza	pizza (ż)	['pitsa]
plate	talerz (m)	['talɛʃ]
plum	śliwka (ż)	['ɕlifka]
poisonous mushroom	grzyb (m) trujący	[gʒɪp truɔ̃tsɪ]
pomegranate	granat (m)	['granat]
pork	wieprzowina (ż)	[vepʃɔ'vina]
porridge	kasza (ż)	['kaʃa]
portion	porcja (ż)	['pɔrtsʰja]
potato	ziemniak (m)	[ʒem'ɲak]
proteins	białka (l.mn.)	['bʲawka]
pub, bar	bar (m)	[bar]
pumpkin	dynia (ż)	['diɲa]
rabbit	królik (m)	['krulik]
radish	rzodkiewka (ż)	[ʒɔt'kefka]
raisin	rodzynek (m)	[rɔ'dzinɛk]
raspberry	malina (ż)	[ma'lina]
recipe	przepis (m)	['pʃɛpis]
red pepper	papryka (ż)	[pap'rika]
red wine	czerwone wino (n)	[t͡ʃɛr'vɔnɛ 'vinɔ]
redcurrant	czerwona porzeczka (ż)	[t͡ʃɛr'vɔna pɔ'ʒɛt͡ʃka]
refreshing drink	napój (m) orzeźwiający	['napuj ɔʒɛzʲvjaɔ̃tsɪ]
rice	ryż (m)	[riʃ]
rum	rum (m)	[rum]
russula	gołąbek (m)	[gɔ'wɔ̃bɛk]
rye	żyto (n)	['ʒitɔ]
saffron	szafran (m)	['ʃafran]
salad	sałatka (ż)	[sa'watka]
salmon	łosoś (m)	['wɔsɔɕ]

salt	sól (ż)	[suʎ]
salty	słony	['swɔnɨ]
sandwich	kanapka (ż)	[ka'napka]
sardine	sardynka (ż)	[sar'dɨŋka]
sauce	sos (m)	[sɔs]
saucer	spodek (m)	['spɔdɛk]
sausage	kiełbasa (ż)	[kew'basa]
seafood	owoce (l.mn.) morza	[ɔ'vɔtsɛ 'mɔʒa]
sesame	sezam (m)	['sɛzam]
shark	rekin (m)	['rɛkin]
shrimp	krewetka (ż)	[krɛ'vɛtka]
side dish	dodatki (l.mn.)	[dɔ'datki]
slice	plasterek (m)	[pʎas'tɛrɛk]
smoked	wędzony	[vɛ̃'dzɔnɨ]
soft drink	napój (m) bezalkoholowy	['napuj bɛzalkɔhɔ'lɔvɨ]
soup	zupa (ż)	['zupa]
soup spoon	łyżka (ż) stołowa	['wɨʃka stɔ'wɔva]
sour cherry	wiśnia (ż)	['viɕɲa]
sour cream	śmietana (ż)	[ɕmʲe'tana]
soy	soja (ż)	['sɔja]
spaghetti	spaghetti (n)	[spa'gɛtti]
sparkling	gazowana	[ga'zɔvana]
spice	przyprawa (ż)	[pʃɨp'rava]
spinach	szpinak (m)	['ʃpinak]
spiny lobster	langusta (ż)	[ʎa'ŋusta]
spoon	łyżka (ż)	['wɨʃka]
squid	kałamarnica (ż)	[kawamar'nitsa]
steak	befsztyk (m)	['bɛfʃtɨk]
stew	pieczeń (ż)	['petʃɛɲ]
still	niegazowana	[nega'zɔvana]
strawberry	truskawka (ż)	[trus'kafka]
sturgeon	mięso (n) jesiotra	['mensɔ e'ɕɔtra]
sugar	cukier (m)	['tsuker]
sunflower oil	olej (m) słonecznikowy	['ɔlej swɔnɛtʃnikɔvɨ]
sweet	słodki	['swɔtki]
sweet cherry	czereśnia (ż)	[tʃɛ'rɛɕɲa]
taste, flavor	smak (m)	[smak]
tasty	smaczny	['smatʃnɨ]
tea	herbata (ż)	[hɛr'bata]
teaspoon	łyżeczka (ż)	[wɨ'ʒɛtʃka]
tip	napiwek (m)	[na'pivɛk]
tomato	pomidor (m)	[pɔ'midɔr]
tomato juice	sok (m) pomidorowy	[sɔk pɔmidɔ'rɔvɨ]
tongue	ozór (m)	['ɔzur]
toothpick	wykałaczka (ż)	[vɨka'watʃka]
trout	pstrąg (m)	[pstrɔ̃k]
tuna	tuńczyk (m)	['tuɲtʃɨk]
turkey	indyk (m)	['indɨk]
turnip	rzepa (ż)	['ʒɛpa]
veal	cielęcina (ż)	[tɕelɛ̃'tɕina]
vegetable oil	olej (m) roślinny	['ɔlej rɔɕliɲɨ]
vegetables	warzywa (l.mn.)	[va'ʒɨva]

vegetarian	**wegetarianin** (m)	[vɛgɛtarʰʲanin]
vegetarian	**wegetariański**	[vɛgɛtarʰʲaɲski]
vermouth	**wermut** (m)	['vɛrmut]
vienna sausage	**parówka** (ż)	[pa'rufka]
vinegar	**ocet** (m)	['ɔtset]
vitamin	**witamina** (ż)	[vita'mina]
vodka	**wódka** (ż)	['vutka]
waffles	**wafle** (l.mn.)	['vaflɛ]
waiter	**kelner** (m)	['kɛʎnɛr]
waitress	**kelnerka** (ż)	[kɛʎ'nɛrka]
walnut	**orzech** (m) **włoski**	['ɔʒɛh 'vwɔski]
water	**woda** (ż)	['vɔda]
watermelon	**arbuz** (m)	['arbus]
wheat	**pszenica** (ż)	[pʃɛ'nitsa]
whisky	**whisky** (ż)	[u'iski]
white wine	**białe wino** (n)	['bʲawɛ 'vinɔ]
wine	**wino** (n)	['vinɔ]
wine list	**karta** (ż) **win**	['karta vin]
with ice	**z lodem**	[z 'lɜdɛm]
yogurt	**jogurt** (m)	[ɜgurt]
zucchini	**kabaczek** (m)	[ka'batʃɛk]

Polish-English gastronomic glossary

łosoś (m)	['wɔsɔɕ]	salmon
łosoś (m)	['wɔsɔɕ]	Atlantic salmon
łyżeczka (ż)	[wi'ʒɛtʃka]	teaspoon
łyżka (ż)	['wiʃka]	spoon
łyżka (ż) stołowa	['wiʃka stɔ'wɔva]	soup spoon
śledź (m)	[ɕlɛtʃ]	herring
śliwka (ż)	['ɕlifka]	plum
śmietana (ż)	[ɕme'tana]	sour cream
śmietanka (ż)	[ɕme'taŋka]	cream
śniadanie (n)	[ɕɲa'dane]	breakfast
żółtko (n)	['ʒuwtkɔ]	egg yolk
żurawina (ż)	[ʒura'vina]	cranberry
żyto (n)	['ʒitɔ]	rye
agrest (m)	['agrɛst]	gooseberry
ananas (m)	[a'nanas]	pineapple
anyż (m)	['aniʃ]	anise
aperitif (m)	[apɛri'tif]	aperitif
apetyt (m)	[a'pɛtit]	appetite
arbuz (m)	['arbus]	watermelon
awokado (n)	[avɔ'kadɔ]	avocado
bób (m)	[bup]	beans
bakłażan (m)	[bak'waʒan]	eggplant
banan (m)	['banan]	banana
bar (m)	[bar]	pub, bar
baranina (ż)	[bara'nina]	lamb
barman (m)	['barman]	bartender
bazylia (ż)	[ba'ziʎja]	basil
befsztyk (m)	['bɛfʃtik]	steak
bezalkoholowy	[bɛzaʎkɔhɔ'lɔvi]	non-alcoholic
białe wino (n)	['bʲawɛ 'vinɔ]	white wine
białka (l.mn.)	['bʲawka]	proteins
białko (n)	['bʲawkɔ]	egg white
boczek (m)	['bɔtʃɛk]	bacon
borówka (ż)	[bɔ'rufka]	cowberry
borówka (ż) czarna	[bɔ'rɔfka 'tʃarna]	bilberry
brokuły (l.mn.)	[brɔ'kuvi]	broccoli
brukselka (ż)	[bruk'sɛʎka]	Brussels sprouts
brzoskwinia (ż)	[bʒɔsk'fiɲa]	peach
burak (m)	['burak]	beetroot
cappuccino (n)	[kapu'tʃinɔ]	cappuccino
cebula (ż)	[tsɛ'buʎa]	onion
chleb (m)	[hlɛp]	bread
chrzan (m)	[hʃan]	horseradish
ciastko (n)	['tʃastkɔ]	cake

ciasto (n)	['tʃastɔ]	pie
cielęcina (ż)	[tʃɛlɛ̃'tʃina]	veal
cukier (m)	['tsuker]	sugar
cukierek (m)	[tsu'kerɛk]	candy
cynamon (m)	[tsɨ'namɔn]	cinnamon
cytryna (ż)	[tsɨt'rɨna]	lemon
czarna herbata (ż)	['tʃarna hɛr'bata]	black tea
czarna kawa (ż)	['tʃarna 'kava]	black coffee
czarna porzeczka (ż)	['tʃarna pɔ'ʒɛtʃka]	blackcurrant
czekolada (ż)	[tʃɛkɔ'ʎada]	chocolate
czekoladowy	[tʃɛkɔʎa'dɔvɨ]	chocolate
czereśnia (ż)	[tʃɛ'rɛɕɲa]	sweet cherry
czerwona porzeczka (ż)	[tʃɛr'vɔna pɔ'ʒɛtʃka]	redcurrant
czerwone wino (n)	[tʃɛr'vɔnɛ 'vinɔ]	red wine
czosnek (m)	['tʃɔsnɛk]	garlic
dżem (m)	[dʒɛm]	jam
dżin (m), gin (m)	[dʒin]	gin
daktyl (m)	['daktɨl]	date
danie (n)	['dane]	course, dish
deser (m)	['dɛsɛr]	dessert
dieta (ż)	['dʰeta]	diet
dodatki (l.mn.)	[dɔ'datki]	side dish
dorsz (m)	[dɔrʃ]	cod
dynia (ż)	['dɨɲa]	pumpkin
dziczyzna (ż)	[dʒit'ʃɨzna]	game
farsz (m)	[farʃ]	hamburger
fasola (ż)	[fa'sɔʎa]	kidney bean
figa (ż)	['figa]	fig
filiżanka (ż)	[fili'ʒaŋka]	cup
fistaszki (l.mn.)	[fis'taʃki]	pistachios
flądra (ż)	[flɔ̃dra]	flatfish
gęś (ż)	[gɛ̃ɕ]	goose
gazowana	[ga'zɔvana]	carbonated
gazowana	[ga'zɔvana]	sparkling
gołąbek (m)	[gɔ'wɔ̃bɛk]	russula
goździki (l.mn.)	['gɔʑdʒiki]	cloves
gorący	[gɔ'rɔ̃tsɨ]	hot
gorzki	['gɔʃki]	bitter
gotowany	[gɔtɔ'vanɨ]	boiled
granat (m)	['granat]	pomegranate
grejpfrut (m)	['grɛjpfrut]	grapefruit
groch (m)	[grɔh]	pea
gruszka (ż)	['gruʃka]	pear
gryka (ż)	['grɨka]	buckwheat
grzyb (m)	[gʒɨp]	mushroom
grzyb (m) jadalny	[gʒɨp ja'daʎnɨ]	edible mushroom
grzyb (m) trujący	[gʒɨp truɔ̃tsɨ]	poisonous mushroom
guma (ż) do żucia	['guma dɔ 'ʒutʃa]	chewing gum
halibut (m)	[ha'libut]	halibut
hamburger (m)	[ham'burgɛr]	hamburger
herbata (ż)	[hɛr'bata]	tea
herbatniki (l.mn.)	[hɛrbat'niki]	cookies

imbir (m)	['imbir]	ginger
indyk (m)	['indɨk]	turkey
jęczmień (m)	['entʃmɛ̃]	barley
jabłko (n)	['jabkɔ]	apple
jagoda (ż)	[ja'gɔda]	berry
jagody (l.mn.)	[ja'gɔdɨ]	berries
jajecznica (ż)	[jaetʃ'nitsa]	fried eggs
jajka (l.mn.)	['jajka]	eggs
jajko (n)	['jajkɔ]	egg
jeżyna (ż)	[e'ʒɨna]	blackberry
jedzenie (n)	[e'dzɛne]	food
jogurt (m)	[ɜgurt]	yogurt
kłos (m)	[kwɔs]	ear
kałamarnica (ż)	[kawamar'nitsa]	squid
kabaczek (m)	[ka'batʃɛk]	zucchini
kaczka (ż)	['katʃka]	duck
kalafior (m)	[ka'ʎafɜr]	cauliflower
kaloria (ż)	[ka'lɜrja]	calorie
kanapka (ż)	[ka'napka]	sandwich
kapusta (ż)	[ka'pusta]	cabbage
karczoch (m)	['kartʃɔh]	artichoke
karp (m)	[karp]	carp
karta (ż) win	['karta vin]	wine list
kasza (ż)	['kaʃa]	cereal grains
kasza (ż)	['kaʃa]	porridge
kawa (ż)	['kava]	coffee
kawa (ż) rozpuszczalna	['kava rɔspuʃt'ʃaʎr.a]	instant coffee
kawa (ż) z mlekiem	['kava z 'mlekem]	coffee with milk
kawałek (m)	[ka'vawɛk]	piece
kawior (m)	['kavɜr]	caviar
kelner (m)	['kɛʎnɛr]	waiter
kelnerka (ż)	[kɛʎ'nɛrka]	waitress
kiełbasa (ż)	[kew'basa]	sausage
kielich (m)	['kelih]	glass
kiwi (n)	['kivi]	kiwi
kminek (m)	['kminɛk]	caraway
koźlarz (m)	['kɔʑʎaʃ]	birch bolete
koźlarz (m) czerwony	['kɔʑʎaʃ tʃɛr'vɔnɨ]	orange-cap boletus
koktajl (m)	['kɔktajʎ]	cocktail
koktajl (m) mleczny	['kɔktajʎ 'mletʃnɨ]	milkshake
kolacja (ż)	[kɔ'ʎatsʰja]	dinner
kolendra (ż)	[kɔ'lendra]	coriander
konfitura (ż)	[kɔnfi'tura]	jam
koniak (m)	['kɔnjak]	cognac
konserwy (l.mn.)	[kɔn'sɛrvɨ]	canned food
koperek (m)	[kɔ'pɛrɛk]	dill
korkociąg (m)	[kɔr'kɔtʃɔ̃k]	corkscrew
kotlet (m)	['kɔtlɛt]	fried meatballs
królik (m)	['krulik]	rabbit
krab (m)	[krap]	crab
krem (m)	[krɛm]	buttercream
krewetka (ż)	[krɛ'vɛtka]	shrimp

kuchnia (ż)	['kuhɲa]	cuisine
kukurydza (ż)	[kuku'riʤa]	corn
kukurydza (ż)	[kuku'riʤa]	corn
kurczak (m)	['kurʧak]	chicken
kurka (ż)	['kurka]	chanterelle
lód (m)	[lyt]	ice
langusta (ż)	[ʎa'ŋusta]	spiny lobster
lemoniada (ż)	[lemɔ'ɲjada]	lemonade
leszcz (m)	[leʃʧ]	bream
liść (m) laurowy	[liʃʧ ʎau'rɔvi]	bay leaf
likier (m)	['liker]	liqueur
lody (l.mn.)	['lɔdi]	ice-cream
mąka (ż)	['mɔka]	flour
majonez (m)	[maʒnɛs]	mayonnaise
makaron (m)	[ma'karɔn]	pasta
makaron (m)	[ma'karɔn]	noodles
makrela (ż)	[mak'rɛla]	mackerel
malina (ż)	[ma'lina]	raspberry
mandarynka (ż)	[manda'riŋka]	mandarin
mango (n)	['maɲɔ]	mango
marchew (ż)	['marhɛf]	carrot
margaryna (ż)	[marga'rina]	margarine
marmolada (ż)	[marmɔ'ʎada]	marmalade
marynowany	[marinɔ'vani]	pickled
masło (n) śmietankowe	['maswɔ ɕmeta'ŋkɔvɛ]	butter
melon (m)	['mɛlɔn]	melon
menu (n)	['menu]	menu
miód (m)	[myt]	honey
mięso (n)	['mensɔ]	meat
mięso (n) jesiotra	['mensɔ e'ɕɔtra]	sturgeon
migdał (m)	['migdaw]	almond
mleko (n)	['mlekɔ]	milk
mleko skondensowane	['mlekɔ skɔndɛnsɔ'vanɛ]	condensed milk
morela (ż)	[mɔ'rɛʎa]	apricot
mrożony	[mrɔ'ʒoni]	frozen
muchomor (m)	[mu'hɔmɔr]	fly agaric
musztarda (ż)	[muʃ'tarda]	mustard
nóż (m)	[nuʃ]	knife
nadzienie (n)	[na'ʤene]	filling
napój (m) bezalkoholowy	['napuj bɛzalkɔhɔ'lɔvi]	soft drink
napój (m) orzeźwiający	['napuj ɔʒɛʑvjaɔ̃tsi]	refreshing drink
napiwek (m)	[na'pivɛk]	tip
napoje (l.mn.) alkoholowe	[na'pɔe aʎkɔhɔ'lɔvɛ]	liquors
niegazowana	[nega'zovana]	still
obiad (m)	['ɔbjat]	lunch
ocet (m)	['ɔʦet]	vinegar
ogórek (m)	[ɔ'gurɛk]	cucumber
okoń (m)	['ɔkɔɲ]	perch
okruchek (m)	[ɔk'ruhɛk]	crumb
olej (m) oliwkowy	['ɔlej ɔlif'kɔvi]	olive oil
olej (m) roślinny	['ɔlej rɔɕliɲi]	vegetable oil
olej (m) słonecznikowy	['ɔlej swɔnɛʧ̑nikɔvi]	sunflower oil

oliwki (ż, l.mn.)	[ɔ'lifki]	olives
omlet (m)	['ɔmlɛt]	omelet
orzech (m) kokosowy	['ɔʒɛh kɔkɔ'sɔvi]	coconut
orzech (m) laskowy	['ɔʒɛh ʎas'kɔvi]	hazelnut
orzech (m) włoski	['ɔʒɛh 'vwɔski]	walnut
orzeszek (l.mn.) ziemny	[ɔ'ʒɛʃɛk 'ʒemnɛ]	peanut
ostryga (ż)	[ɔst'riga]	oyster
otwieracz (m) do butelek	[ɔt'feratʃ dɛ bu'tɛlek]	bottle opener
otwieracz (m) do puszek	[ɔt'feratʃ dɛ 'pɹʃɛk]	can opener
owies (m)	['ɔves]	oats
owoc (m)	['ɔvɔts]	fruit
owoce (l.mn.)	[ɔ'vɔtsɛ]	fruits
owoce (l.mn.) morza	[ɔ'vɔtsɛ 'mɔʒa]	seafood
ozór (m)	['ɔzur]	tongue
płatki (l.mn.) kukurydziane	['pwatki kukuri'dʒʲanɛ]	cornflakes
papaja (ż)	[pa'paja]	papaya
papryka (ż)	[pap'rika]	red pepper
papryka (ż)	[pap'rika]	paprika
parówka (ż)	[pa'rufka]	vienna sausage
pasztet (m)	['paʃtɛt]	pâté
pieczeń (ż)	['petʃɛɲ]	stew
pieprz (m) czarny	[pepʃ 'tʃarni]	black pepper
pietruszka (ż)	[pet'ruʃka]	parsley
piwo (n)	['pivɔ]	beer
piwo (n) ciemne	[pivɔ 'tʃemnɛ]	dark beer
piwo (n) jasne	[pivɔ 'jasnɛ]	light beer
pizza (ż)	['pitsa]	pizza
plasterek (m)	[pʎas'tɛrɛk]	slice
pomarańcza (ż)	[pɔma'raɲtʃa]	orange
pomidor (m)	[pɔ'midɔr]	tomato
porcja (ż)	['pɔrtsʲja]	portion
posmak (m)	['pɔsmak]	aftertaste
poziomka (ż)	[pɔ'ʒɔmka]	field strawberry
prawdziwek (m)	[prav'dʒivɛk]	cep
proso (n)	['prɔsɔ]	millet
przepis (m)	['pʃɛpis]	recipe
przyprawa (ż)	[pʃip'rava]	condiment
przyprawa (ż)	[pʃip'rava]	spice
przystawka (ż)	[pʃis'tafka]	appetizer
psi grzyb (m)	[pɕi gʒip]	death cap
pstrąg (m)	[pstrɔ̃k]	trout
pszenica (ż)	[pʃɛ'nitsa]	wheat
rachunek (m)	[ra'hunɛk]	check
rekin (m)	['rɛkin]	shark
rodzynek (m)	[rɔ'dʑinɛk]	raisin
rosół (m)	['rɔsuw]	clear soup
rum (m)	[rum]	rum
ryż (m)	[riʃ]	rice
ryba (ż)	['riba]	fish
rzepa (ż)	['ʒɛpa]	turnip
rzodkiewka (ż)	[ʒɔt'kefka]	radish
sól (ż)	[suʎ]	salt

słodka papryka (ż)	['swɔdka pap'rika]	bell pepper
słodki	['swɔtki]	sweet
słony	['swɔni]	salty
sałata (ż)	[sa'wata]	lettuce
sałatka (ż)	[sa'watka]	salad
sandacz (m)	['sandatʃ]	pike perch
sardynka (ż)	[sar'diŋka]	sardine
seler (m)	['sɛler]	celery
ser (m)	[sɛr]	cheese
sezam (m)	['sɛzam]	sesame
skórka (ż)	['skurka]	peel
smażony	[sma'ʒɔni]	fried
Smacznego!	[smatʃ'nɛgɔ]	Enjoy your meal!
smaczny	['smatʃni]	tasty
smak (m)	[smak]	taste, flavor
smalec (m)	['smaleʦ]	lard
smardz (m)	[smarʦ]	morel
soczewica (ż)	[sɔtʃɛ'vitsa]	lentil
soja (ż)	['sɔja]	soy
sok (m)	[sɔk]	juice
sok (m) pomarańczowy	[sɔk pɔmaraɲt'ʃɔvi]	orange juice
sok (m) pomidorowy	[sɔk pɔmidɔ'rɔvi]	tomato juice
sok (m) ze świeżych owoców	[sɔk zɛ 'ɕfeʒih ɔ'voʦuʃ]	freshly squeezed juice
sos (m)	[sɔs]	sauce
spaghetti (n)	[spa'gɛtti]	spaghetti
spodek (m)	['spɔdɛk]	saucer
sum (m)	[sum]	catfish
suszony	[su'ʃɔni]	dried
szafran (m)	['ʃafran]	saffron
szampan (m)	['ʃampan]	champagne
szczupak (m)	['ʃtʃupak]	pike
szklanka (ż)	['ʃkʎaŋka]	glass
szparagi (l.mn.)	[ʃpa'ragi]	asparagus
szpinak (m)	['ʃpinak]	spinach
szynka (ż)	['ʃiŋka]	ham
szynka (ż)	['ʃiŋka]	gammon
tłuszcze (l.mn.)	['twuʃtʃɛ]	fats
talerz (m)	['taleʃ]	plate
tort (m)	[tɔrt]	cake
truskawka (ż)	[trus'kafka]	strawberry
tuńczyk (m)	['tuɲtʃik]	tuna
wódka (ż)	['vutka]	vodka
wątróbka (ż)	[võt'rupka]	liver
wędzony	[vɛ̃'dzɔni]	smoked
węglowodany (l.mn.)	[vɛnɛ̃zvɔ'dani]	carbohydrates
węgorz (m)	['vɛŋɔʃ]	eel
włoszczyzna (ż)	[vwɔʃt'ʃizna]	greens
wafle (l.mn.)	['vafle]	waffles
warzywa (l.mn.)	[va'ʒiva]	vegetables
wegetariański	[vɛgɛtarʰ'jaɲski]	vegetarian
wegetarianin (m)	[vɛgɛtarʰ'janin]	vegetarian

wermut (m)	['vɛrmut]	vermouth
whisky (ż)	[u'iski]	whisky
wiśnia (ż)	['viɕɲa]	sour cherry
widelec (m)	[vi'dɛleʦ]	fork
wieprzowina (ż)	[vepʃɔ'vina]	pork
wino (n)	['vinɔ]	wine
winogrona (l.mn.)	[vinɔg'rɔna]	grape
witamina (ż)	[vita'mina]	vitamin
wołowina (ż)	[vɔwɔ'vina]	beef
woda (ż)	['vɔda]	water
woda (ż) **mineralna**	['vɔda minɛ'raʎna]	mineral water
woda (ż) **pitna**	['vɔda 'pitna]	drinking water
wykałaczka (ż)	[vika'watʃka]	toothpick
wyroby (l.mn.) **cukiernicze**	[vi'rɔbi ʦuker'nitʃɛ]	confectionery
z lodem	[z 'lɜdɛm]	with ice
zboża (l.mn.)	['zbɔʒa]	cereal crops
zboże (n)	['zbɔʒɛ]	grain
zielona herbata (ż)	[ʒe'lɜna hɛr'baːa]	green tea
ziemniak (m)	[ʒem'ɲak]	potato
zimny	['ʒimni]	cold
zupa (ż)	['zupa]	soup

www.ingramcontent.com/pod-product-compliance
Lightning Source LLC
LaVergne TN
LVHW051732080426
835511LV00018B/3016